# International Socialism 129

## Winter 2011

# Contributors

**Simon Behrman** is a PhD student at the School of Law, Birkbeck College. He is author of *Shostakovich: Socialism, Stalin and Symphonies*.

**Paul Blackledge** is a regular contributor to *International Socialism*. His most recent book, *Marxism and Ethics*, will be published later this year.

**Adrian Budd** teaches International Politics at London South Bank Univeristy.

**Joseph Choonara** is the author of *Unravelling Capitalism: A Guide to Marxist Political Economy*.

**Gareth Dale** is currently writing a biography of Karl Polanyi.

**Jack Farmer** is an assistant editor of *Socialist Review*.

**Mark Harvey** is a proofreader and socialist activist in London. He completed a doctoral thesis on paradox in the theories of Jacques Lacan.

**Suzanne Jeffery** is a teacher and the Chair of the Campaign against Climate Change Trade Union Group.

**Grace Lally** is a socialist activist based in south London.

**John Newsinger** is the author of *The Blood Never Dried: A People's History of the British Empire* and at the moment is writing books on the IWW and on the US working class in the 1930s.

**Yuri Prasad** is a journalist on *Socialist Worker*.

**John Rose** is the author of *Myths of Zionism*.

**Roddy Slorach** is a socialist activist based in east London.

**Andrew Stone** teaches history and politics in south London and is a workplace representative in the National Union of Teachers.

**Megan Trudell** is currently researching Italy in the wake of the First World War.

**Xanthe Whittaker** is a journalist researching trafficking, migration and sex work.

# The student revolt and the crisis

We enter 2011 in a situation marked by both continuity and—in Britain, at least—dramatic *dis*continuity. The element of continuity is represented, of course, by the global economic and financial crisis. Change comes in the form of the sudden emergence of the first real social movement in Britain for many years, the protests by university and school students against the near-trebling of tuition fees. The night a House of Commons surrounded by students fighting riot police voted for the increase, a visibly shaken Nick Robinson, BBC Political Editor, said: "The government may have won a vote, but they may have lost the argument, and lost control of the streets."

Continuity first: the crisis is now well into its fourth year, but shows no signs of ending. This is not because there is no economic growth. The November survey of purchasing managers suggests manufacturing output is rising in Germany, France, Britain, China, and India. But in its latest *World Economic Outlook*, published in October 2010, the International Monetary Fund (IMF) was gloomy:

> The global recovery remains fragile, because strong policies to foster internal rebalancing of demand from public to private sources and external rebalancing from deficit to surplus economies are not yet in place. Global activity is forecast to expand by 4.8 percent in 2010 and 4.2 percent in 2011, broadly in line with earlier expectations, and downside risks continue to predominate. WEO projections are that output of emerging and developing economies

will expand at rates of 7.1 and 6.4 percent, respectively, in 2010 and 2011. In advanced economies, however, growth is projected at only 2.7 and 2.2 percent, respectively, with some economies slowing noticeably during the second half of 2010 and the first half of 2011, followed by a reacceleration of activity. Slack will remain substantial and unemployment persistently high. Inflation is projected to stay generally low, amid continued excess capacity and high unemployment, with a few exceptions among the emerging economies. Risks to the growth forecasts are mainly to the downside.[1]

In fact the problem is much broader than the famous "imbalances" in the world economy on which the IMF focuses. The recovery is both shaped and undermined by the desperate measures the leading capitalist states took in autumn 2008 to prevent the financial crash producing a global economic depression on the scale of, or perhaps even deeper than, that of the 1930s. The sheer scale of the efforts, particularly by the Federal Reserve Board, the US central bank, is only now becoming clear.

Figures released in early December show that between March 2008 and May 2009 the Fed extended a cumulative total of nearly $9 trillion in short-term loans to 18 financial institutions. These included not just American banking giants such as Citigroup, Merrill Lynch, Goldman Sachs, and Morgan Stanley, but foreign banks with US interests, including Barclays, UBS, and RBS, and issuers of commercial paper associated with non-financial companies like Caterpillar, McDonald's, Harley-Davidson, and Verizon.[2]

These measures prevented total collapse, but not the most severe economic slump since the 1930s in the winter of 2008-9. And the scale of increased public borrowing caused by the crisis and by the state rescue of global capitalism is the first of the major problems to dog the recovery. In 2009 budget deficits grew by five percent of national income in the advanced economies. [3] The financial markets, in alliance with the broader neoliberal coalition pressing for austerity measures to slash budget deficits, have defined the problem as the crisis of sovereign debt.

Since the spring of 2010, this has sent wave after wave of instability through the eurozone as vulnerable states are targeted by the markets and subjected to the tender mercies of "rescues" mounted by the unelected troika of the European Central Bank (ECB), IMF, and European Commission—first Greece, then Ireland, and who next? Portugal? Spain? Italy? Belgium? There

---

1:    IMF, 2010a, pxvi.
2:    For example, Chan and McGinty, 2010, and Tett, 2010.
3:    IMF, 2010a, p17.

are fears that the emergency €440 billion European Financial Stability Facility set up in May may soon be overwhelmed by the demands on it.

"One could be forgiven for thinking the market is a bully who cannot be satiated, as he looks for his next victim," commented Suki Mann, head of credit strategy at Société Générale.[4] Even Germany, Europe's strongest economy, has felt the power of the markets. Chancellor Angela Merkel spooked them in late October when she said that, under the new European Stability Mechanism that is supposed to provide a long-term framework for dealing with financial crises in the eurozone, the holders of European government bonds would have to contribute to future rescues.

The markets reacted by pushing up interest rates on the bonds of the weaker eurozone states. Steve Yardeni, who invented the term "bond vigilante" back in the 1980s, explained: "The bond investors don't want to take a hit and if the politicians make them take a hit they will close the markets down".[5] Merkel told the German parliament: "This is about the primacy of politics, this is about the limits of the markets," but so far the markets seem to be winning.[6]

The sovereign debt crisis then interacts with a second crisis—that of the banks. The dramatic state interventions in autumn 2008 were intended especially to save the major American and European banks from the consequences of the speculative gambles they had made during the financial bubble of the mid-2000s. The IMF Global Financial Stability Report for October 2010 estimates the losses the banks made in 2007-10 at $2.2 trillion. But it argues that about three quarters of these have already been written off, and that the biggest remaining problem lies in the massive borrowing, much of it short-term and raised on wholesale markets, the banks made to finance their failed bets: "over $4 trillion of debt is due to be refinanced in the next 24 months... Wholesale funding (including borrowing from the central bank) represents over 40 percent of total liabilities in the euro area banking systems in aggregate; this contrasts with around 25 percent in the United States, United Kingdom, and Japan".[7] Debt due to be repaid by European banks in 2011 varies from 3.5 percent of Gross Domestic Product in France to 6.4 percent in Spain.[8]

Banks in the eurozone are therefore particularly vulnerable to shifts in

---

4:   *Financial Times*, 23 November 2010 (for some reason this quotation was only carried in the print edition).

5:   Milne, 2010.

6:   Brown, 2010.

7:   IMF, 2010b, p15.

8:   Jenkins and Hughes, 2010.

mood in volatile financial markets. The lead-up to both the Greek and Irish "rescues"—respectively in April-May and November 2010—saw funding dry up for European banks. Ireland is a particularly good example of what the IMF calls "the negative interactions between sovereign and banking risks".[9] What forced the Irish government into the arms of the troika was its decision in October 2008 to take over all the debts of the banks, which swelled the budget deficit to an astonishing 32 percent of national income. The rescued banks in recent months borrowed massively from the ECB simply to keep afloat. Yet they had passed the stress tests organised by the European Union (EU) last summer to prove the health of its banks. This begs the question of how many other unexploded mines may be lurking in the European financial system. This isn't a problem just for the eurozone—the countries whose investors have the biggest exposure in Ireland are Britain ($149bn), Germany ($139bn), and the United States ($69bn).[10]

The eurozone crisis has been marked by serious conflicts between Germany and its EU partners. Their sources have been explored in detail in recent issues of this journal. Crucially, European Economic and Monetary Union (EMU) has widened, not reduced, the divergences among the economies participating in the euro. As Stavros Tombazos shows in a recent paper, German capitalism, through a combination of holding real wages steady and greater labour flexibility, has increased its competitiveness, not simply relative to the weaker, "peripheral" economies of southern Europe, but also by comparison with the other leading continental European state, France. This has allowed Germany to maintain its share of world exports at 9-10 percent, despite the fact that China has overtaken it as the largest exporter of goods. Berlin's insistence that the other eurozone states adopt fiscal discipline amounts to the demand that they too embrace wage repression and labour flexibility.[11]

This hard line has antagonised the rest of the EU. It has also encouraged speculation that Germany may be willing to see the eurozone either contract to a north European rump or collapse altogether. During a row with the Greek prime minister, George Papandreou, at an EU summit dinner in October Merkel is reported to have said: "if this is the sort of club the euro is becoming, perhaps Germany should leave".[12] France would ferociously resist either of these outcomes because it relies on an EMU

---

9:   IMF, 2010b, p3.
10:  http://ftalphaville.ft.com/blog/2010/11/22/412116/irish-exposure-charted/
11:  Tombazos, 2010.
12:  Traynor, 2010.

broad enough to dilute German economic power to underpin its geopolitical position. However the situation evolves, the eurozone crisis highlights a third factor undermining the recovery—the imbalances between creditor and debtor states. Germany's role as an export hub whose capital has kept weaker European economies afloat is replicated globally in the relationship between China and the US. The flows of manufactured goods and capital across the Pacific drove the economic boom of the mid-2000s—and financed the speculative bets by Western banks and shadow banks that precipitated the crash and the slump at the end of the decade.

But, if anything, the tensions resulting from the delicate mix of interdependence and competition between the US and China have grown more serious since the crisis began. The combination of a massive fiscal stimulus and huge loans by state banks to firms pulled the Chinese economy out of a growth recession in 2008-9 and returned it to double-digit growth, reviving in its wake those economies that have increasingly reoriented towards supplying China with manufactured goods and raw materials. Hence the uneven character of the present recovery, where robust growth figures in the "emerging market economies" of the global South contrast with stagnation in much of the advanced capitalist world (with the notable exception of Germany, which now directs a substantial chunk of its exports of high-end manufactures towards China).

There are real questions about how sustainable the "emerging market" growth surge is. The Chinese authorities are now grappling with the consequences of their injection of cheap credit into the economy—a serious inflationary surge and a property bubble. Moreover, depressed consumer markets in the North mean the additional exports built thanks to higher investment in China may find it hard to find buyers. But, more immediately, the uneven recovery has helped intensify both geopolitical and economic frictions between the US and China.

Chronically high unemployment in the American heartland, as Megan Trudell shows elsewhere in this journal, has helped politically to cripple Barack Obama's administration. In November US unemployment rose to 9.8 percent. The *New York Times* commented: "The outlook remains bleak. More than 15 million people are out of work, among them 6.3 million who have been jobless for six months or longer. Many are about to exhaust their unemployment benefits, which have been extended repeatedly by the government because of the severity of the downturn".[13]

The Fed's long-trailed decision announced at the beginning of

---

13: Rich, 2010.

November to go for a new round of "quantitative easing" (QE2)—pumping another $600bn into the financial system by mid-2011—marked effectively a decision to let the dollar fall against other currencies and thereby to cheapen US exports. Devaluation to stimulate a depressed economy has been pursued by successive American administrations since Richard Nixon broke the link between the dollar and gold in August 1971. But the ploy doesn't work so well these days because the Chinese renminbi, the currency of the world's biggest exporter, is pegged against the dollar. Faced with strong American pressure in the lead-up to the G20 summit in Seoul in November, China's rulers refused to budge.

Obama's failure on this front has reinforced perceptions of a US weakened by the crisis. This view is exaggerated: thus the detailed figures of the Fed's loans in 2008-9 show the extent it functions as a global central bank, extending dollar swap lines to ten central banks, including the ECB, the Bank of England, and the Bank of Japan.[14] But undeniably the contrast between Chinese growth and American stagnation has encouraged Beijing to become more assertive—for example, over its various territorial claims in the South China sea, provoking Washington to declare the area a US "strategic interest".

It is against this background of continuing economic crisis and growing frictions among the leading capitalist states that austerity has come to grip public policy in Europe and increasingly the US as well. Given the fragility of the recovery, rapid "fiscal consolidation" makes little economic sense. Even the high priests of neoliberal orthodoxy at the IMF estimate that cutting back on public spending proportionately reduces output and demand in the short term (though they claim it has longer term benefits) and that the effects are likely to be more severe if interest rates are very low and "when many countries adjust at the same time", because it is then harder for exports to make up for the fall in domestic demand: both these conditions prevail in the US and Europe today.[15]

Austerity is driven by politics. It helps to maintain the dominance of the neoliberal coalition that came to power in advanced capitalism in the 1980s. Insisting that the priority lies in deficit cutting effectively takes off the agenda any reconfiguration in the relation between the state and capital, or reduction in the power of the banks. Where government is in the hands of economic liberals, as in the case of the Conservative-Liberal coalition in Britain, austerity has the further advantage of legitimising pressing much

---

14:   China boosterism is criticised from a mainstream perspective in Magnus, 2011.
15:   IMF, 2010a, chapter 3 (quotation from p94).

further with the free-market "reforms" pioneered by Margaret Thatcher and continued by Tony Blair.

In a book on the coalition's formation, David Laws, its short-lived first Chief Secretary to the Treasury, reveals that, even before the general election, senior Lib Dem politicians were inclined towards sharing government with the Tories as the best way to achieve "fiscal consolidation". Thus, as David Runciman observes, "the Lib Dems were already signed up to the Tory position on the economy before negotiations had begun".[16] Laws stresses the ideological affinities binding the coalition together: "The economic liberalism of the Conservative Party and the social liberalism of the Liberal Democrats have been convincingly combined. And the liberals in both parties are now firmly in charge".[17]

The political scientist Anthony King told the *Financial Times*: "This government has moved more radically and rapidly than perhaps any other since 1945. The only comparison is with Margaret Thatcher in 1979, and even then it took her much longer to set out the plans she is remembered for. The jury is out, but the speed of this is quite something."[18] Naomi Klein's "shock doctrine" is a poor explanation of neoliberalism in general, but the radicalism of the coalition's assault on the welfare state certainly fits with Milton Friedman's prediction that "only a crisis—actual or perceived—produces real change... [Then] the politically impossible becomes politically inevitable".[19]

## A new movement

But if, as Ross McKibbin puts it, "the importance of the cuts is not economic but political and ideological", they also have a political downside.[20] This is, quite simply, the mass resistance that they may provoke and that could upend the entire neoliberal applecart. In the course of 2010, general strikes against austerity spread from Greece to France, Spain, and Portugal. The EU-IMF "rescue" of Ireland was rejected by a huge protest march in Dublin. And, of course, the coalition's decision nearly to treble university tuition fees has conjured into existence, since the joint march by the National Union of Students (NUS) and the University and College Union (UCU) on 10 November, a new mass movement in Britain.

This is the first time that Britain has seen significant social protests since

---

16: Runciman, 2010, p21.
17: Laws, 2010, p277.
18: Parker and Timmins, 2010.
19: Friedman, 2002, pxiv. See Klein, 2007, and, for an excellent critique, Davidson, 2009.
20: McKibbin, 2010, p12.

the early 1990s, when the giant movement against the Poll Tax that toppled Thatcher was followed by big marches against pit closures and the introduction of the Criminal Justice Bill. The Blair years were marked by a significant political radicalisation that began with the movement for another globalisation in the late 1990s and then swelled to an unprecedented scale as the Stop the War Coalition was formed after 9/11. But the stubborn loyalty of the trade union bureaucracy to the Labour Party combined with enduring memories among working-class activists of the defeats they had suffered under Thatcher to prevent significant resistance developing from the labour movement to the neoliberal policies forged by Tony Blair and Gordon Brown.

This gap between political radicalisation and economic class struggle probably helps to explain the eventual decline of the anti-war movement, despite the continuing opposition to the wars in Iraq and Afghanistan evident in opinion polls. But the crisis has created a new environment that was reflected in the outburst of strikes and occupations driven by rank and file workers in the early months of 2009. On the whole, however, trade union officialdom was able to contain militancy, to disastrous effect in the biggest national disputes, at Royal Mail in the winter of 2009 and at British Airways more recently.

But the sudden irruption of an insurgent student movement has reshuffled the pack dramatically. Untrammelled by tradition, bureaucratic structures, and the daily routine of wage-labour, students can erupt into revolt very quickly, improvising new tactics as they go along. For once, the tedious media clichés about the Internet have had some validity, as calls to mobilise spread like wildfire via Facebook and the like.

Moreover, the issue that has brought students onto the streets goes to the heart of the Conservative-Liberal coalition's drive to press further the neoliberal transformation of Britain. Under both Tories and New Labour universities have already been restructured along the lines of business enterprises subject to the logic of competition. But the review of student finance by Lord Browne, ex-chief executive of BP, that provides the basis of the government's decision drastically to increase tuition fees, represents a step-change in this process. As Stefan Collini puts it in an excellent critique of the Browne Review,

> essentially, Browne is contending that we should no longer think of higher education as the provision of a public good, articulated through educational judgment and largely financed by public funds (in recent years supplemented by a relatively small fee element). Instead, we should think of it as a lightly regulated market in which consumer demand, in the form of student

choice, is sovereign in determining what is offered by service providers (ie universities).[21]

The students' rebellion thus challenges the marketisation of higher education. Two features of the present insurgency are particularly striking. The first is the role by played by school and sixth-form college students. Britain does not have a tradition of large-scale school-student militancy. In France, for example, from May 1968 to the recent pensions protests, *lycée* (high-school) students have been an important source of militant mobilisation. In Greece, the Communist Party's very strong base among school-students has allowed this ultra-Stalinist organisation to renew itself. In Britain by contrast, while there have been moments of militancy—for example, the school strikes at the start of the war in Iraq in March 2003—they have usually been short-lived. But the street protests that began on Day X (24 November) have been driven by groups of school-students whose anger, impudence, and flair have left the riot police stumbling in their wake.

The second feature of the student movement is the widespread popular support it enjoys. The efforts by the coalition and the tabloids to witch-hunt the students in the wake of the occupation of the Conservative Party headquarters in Millbank Tower on 10 November were a complete flop (though this doesn't mean the government will not seek to revenge itself with savage sentences on the protesters who have been arrested). The students have won widespread support, both formal and informal, from trade unionists.

It's particularly interesting that leading Labour figures tried to position themselves, not in support of the more militant protests, but certainly in sympathy with the students. NUS president Aaron Porter, who initially denounced the Millbank invasion, apologised to the occupation of University College London for NUS having been "perhaps … too cautious and too spineless about being committed to supporting student activism"—a statement confirmed by the subsequent decision by Porter and the NUS executive not to back the 9 December demonstration.[22] Labour's new leader, Ed Miliband, has warned the increase in tuition fees "risk[s] setting back social mobility in Britain for a generation" and called the withdrawal of government funding for humanities degrees "cultural vandalism".[23]

It's easy enough to dismiss such comments as opportunism, as

---

21: Collini, 2010, p23. For a broader analysis of the neoliberal transformation of British universities, see Callinicos, 2006.
22: Kingsley, 2010.
23: Miliband, 2010.

undoubtedly they are. But the point about opportunists is that they respond to the balance of forces as they see it. When Miliband told BBC Radio 4's *Today* programme that he had thought of going out to talk to student protestors in Westminster on Day X, he was sending a very different signal from those Neil Kinnock sent when he sat out the 1984-5 miners' strike in silence, or his deputy, Roy Hattersley, did when he called for "exemplary sentences" for Poll Tax rioters in 1990.

No doubt one reason why Labour has started twisting the knife about tuition fees is because the Liberal Democrats are particularly vulnerable on the issue. And indeed the widespread sense of betrayal at the Lib Dems—who paraded their opposition to tuition fees in successive general elections—is a major source of the anger among the students whose votes they had so assiduously targeted. The twists and turns among Lib Dem cabinet ministers about how they would vote in the crucial 9 December parliamentary division on tuition fees—and especially the shifting, but consistently casuistic self-justifications by Vince Cable, as Business Secretary responsible for the policy—expose the rattrap in which they now find themselves. Having appealed to the social democratic values of Labour voters disgruntled with Blair and Brown, the Liberal Democrats now find themselves partners in a neoliberal assault on those values. They are likely to pay a high price.

But there are deeper reasons why the students won such widespread support. One is their changed structural position. Although access to university still systematically favours those on higher incomes, in 2007-8, 43 percent of English 17 to 30 year olds participated in higher education, 37 percent full-time.[24] University students are not a small, relatively privileged group any more. Both because of their sheer numbers (nearly 2.4 million in 2008-9) and because many are forced to support themselves through wage-labour, often of a particularly precarious nature, they merge into the larger working class population.[25]

At the same time, students still find themselves in a transitional situation, between childhood and complete absorption in the world of work. The uncertainties of this condition can lead to fragmentation, since the individual nature of their assessment sets students against one another. But it can also allow them to move explosively into mass action, as they did in November and December 2010.[26]

The particular militancy of school students is understandable: they

---

24: Department for Innovation, Universities and Skills, 2009.
25: http://www.hesa.ac.uk/index.php?option=com_content&task=view&id=1897&Itemid=239
26: For fuller analysis, see Callinicos and Turner, 1975, and Callinicos, 2006.

are being hit twice over, by the hike in tuition fees and by the abolition of the Education Maintenance Allowance (EMA) introduced under New Labour to help students from poor, working-class households stay on at college after 16. All this underlines the *representative* nature of the student movement. The class injustice students are rebelling against is part and parcel of the class injustice of the coalition's assault on the poor. They are winning support because they have become a symbol of the mass resistance that wide sections of the working class recognise to be necessary.

## Inside the student revolt

The scale of the 10 November national demonstration came as a surprise to many. NUS officials had been expecting 20,000 to join the protest from around the country. On the day, over 50,000 students and lecturers took to the streets of London. The day after, the *Independent* declared that the mass protests a day earlier "ended the high hopes of a new era of consensus politics, promised by David Cameron when he took office exactly six months ago".[27] This opinion is clearly shared by the head of the Metropolitan Police, Sir Paul Stephenson, who announced shortly after the protest that "the game has changed" and "the likelihood is for more disorder on the streets, that is obvious".[28]

Much has been made of the spontaneity of the student revolt—from the occupation of Millbank through to the later "Day X" protests. But it is clear that the impetus for the protests came from the massive mobilisation on 10 November. There had been hints at the strength of feeling among students on the Right to Work demonstration at the Conservative Party conference on 3 October and the subsequent local protests that followed the announcement of the Comprehensive Spending Review on 20 October.

The backing of the NUS meant that student unions all around the country organised transport to London. In many areas the radical left were closely involved in building the demonstration, sometimes working closely with student unions. UCU's support for the demonstration was another factor in the mobilisation, as was the sense of unease amongst even some vice-chancellors at the scale of the attack represented by the Brown Review—Steve Smith, the head of the vice-chancellors' organisation Universities UK, said the £4.2 billion of cuts to higher education spending spelled out in the review "confirm our worst fears".[29]

---

27: *Independent*, 11 November 2010.
28: *Evening Standard*, 25 November 2010.
29: BBC News, 15 October 2010.

This convergence ensured that the demonstration on 10 November was bigger even than the 30,000 strong student protest in December 1984, which took place against the highly politicised backdrop of the Great Miners' Strike. The demonstration was viscerally angry. Many of the protesters had been young children when the Tories were last in power. But the strength of feeling against them and them and their Liberal Democrat coalition partners was tangible. Chants of "Tory scum" and attacks on the Liberals for "turning blue" dominated large sections of the march.

This anger was played out when students deviated from the main route of the march and occupied the courtyard of Millbank Tower. Millbank was a perfect target for the students' anger: it not only accommodates the Conservative Party offices on the seventh floor but is "owned by the Reuben Brothers, prominent Conservative Party donors whose fortune totals some £5 billion".[30] The occupation of Millbank highlighted the importance of organisation alongside the spontaneity. It's unlikely that most students were aware of the link between Millbank and the Tories, but the organised socialists and student radicals who gathered their university delegations behind their banners and marched them into the courtyard certainly were. But this was just the spark. One reason why the media's attempt to witch-hunt those who entered the tower failed was clear from a glance at any photograph of the crowd outside Millbank—it swelled to several thousands of protesters in the space of an hour.

The storming of Millbank altered the dynamic of the movement. Students, many of whom had just six months ago voted for the Lib Dems, were now part of a militant protest, and this militancy created a sense that it was possible to fight back among much wider layers of students than were present on the day. Millbank would not have happened without the official NUS mobilisation but nor would it have happened if activists had been content to simply follow the lead of NUS officials.

In the wake of Millbank, the call for walkouts—independently of NUS—on 24 November spread through the social media and also received heavy coverage in the bourgeois press. In the event, Day X involved huge numbers of protestors around the country. The *Guardian* estimated that up to 130,000 students from schools, colleges and universities had been involved in some form of protest on the day.[31]

The presence of the school and college students on the protests brought a new sense of rage to the streets. They bitterly complained not

---

30: Penny, 2010.
31: Walker, Lewis, Taylor, and Wintour, 2010.

just about the rise in tuition fees and the removal of the EMA but also about their fears for the future—how would they be able to afford education or find jobs in the future?[32]

This class anger merged with bitterness against the police. Many of these youths had experience of police harassment and stop and searches prior to the day. This was exacerbated on the day by the outrageous behaviour of the police. In London on 24 November, protesters as young as 14 found themselves kettled by police until midnight. Outside the kettle, demonstrators on Whitehall faced charges by mounted police. The Metropolitan Police's denials that any horses charged the protesters was quickly disproved by the video evidence on the internet and publicised by the *Guardian*.[33]

By the second day of walkouts on 30 November, students had learned the lessons of the previous week and abandoned the agreed route of the march when it became clear the police intended to kettle them again. Instead, students ran through central London, bringing parts of the city to a standstill. This pattern was repeated on a larger scale on 9 December.

The walkouts of 24 and 30 November also saw massive protests and civil disobedience outside London. Thousands marched in Bristol, Leeds, Liverpool and Manchester. Students have been heavily involved in the "flash" protests against companies like Vodaphone and Topshop, called to draw attention to enormous levels of corporate tax avoidance.

A wave of occupations swept across Britain, from Glasgow to Plymouth. At the time of going to press, there had been over 35 occupations—even the Turner Prize gallery at the Tate was occupied by students from the Slade School of Fine Arts. Some occupations have been small, brief stunts. But others have involved hundreds of students and have seen a high level of ideological debate. Several occupations have held general assemblies that brought together students and workers to discuss the way forward for the movement. Over 300 people attended the assembly at Cambridge University on 5 December .

## What next?

"The threat British students pose—much like the financial crisis bringing them on to the streets—is of contagion," writes Gary Younge. "That their energy, enthusiasm, militancy, rage and raucousness might burn in us all".[34]

---

32: A video filmed for the *Guardian* website gives an excellent insight into the anger of the school students—www.guardian.co.uk/education/video/2010/nov/24/london-student-protests.
33: Gabbatt and Lewis, 2010.
34: Younge, 2010.

The critical question is whether and how the contagion will spread. This issue of *International Socialism* goes to press in the immediate aftermath of the parliamentary vote in favour of raising tuition fees on 9 December. The student revolts of the 1960s show that

> student struggles are extremely volatile. Because of the fragmentation and isolation that is their existence, students can move very quickly between passivity and militancy. When they do rebel they do so with tremendous force, inventiveness and spirit, rapidly generalising and taking the struggle beyond grievances specific to their situation to a rebellion against the capitalist system. At the same time, once the particular struggle they are involved in is on the downturn, they can relapse very quickly into complete apathy.[35]

There is a risk that the present student movement could disappear as a result of demoralisation caused by the coalition pushing the rise in tuition fees into law. But this is highly unlikely. The movement against the Poll Tax only took off *after* it had become law. There is a French slogan: "What Parliament makes, the street can unmake." The protest demonstration by tens of thousands of students in Whitehall on 9 December—once again organised independently of NUS—and the angry clashes with riot police outside Parliament, spreading to Oxford Street and surging around the heir to the throne's Rolls Royce, don't suggest students are about to give up.

The House of Commons vote itself exposed the potential fractures in the coalition. Only a minority of Lib Dem MPs, most of them ministers, voted with the government, while six Tories defied the whips to go into the "No" lobby. The *Financial Times* pointed to the danger it posed of further rebellions by Thatcherite backbenchers disgruntled with David Cameron's leadership and the Lib Dem "soft left": "This is the most rebellious parliament in recent times, according to Philip Cowley and Mark Stuart of Nottingham University, but last night's vote was the first time the Lib Dem left has made common cause with elements of the Tory right".[36]

What happens to the student movement depends critically on its activists are able to continue to build and coordinate mass action in the New Year. The Education Activists Network (EAN), which emerged to coordinate resistance to the cuts and redundancies that were already being pushed through during the dying days of the Brown government, is

---

35: Callinicos and Turner, 1975.
36: Parker and Barker, 2010.

especially important because it brings students together with trade unionists in UCU and other campus unions.

Above all, will the workers' movement follow the example set by the students and mounts serious industrial action against the coalition's policies? The General Council of the Trade Union Congress (TUC) has called a demonstration on 26 March that could become a day of protest on a French scale. A number of public sector unions are discussing coordinated industrial action over pensions. These are potentially important steps in the direction of what the situation requires—a general strike to bring the coalition down.

The rhythm of workers' struggles is generally slower than that of student movements. This reflects the generally higher cost of collective action—lost wages, possibly the sack—for workers. But their collective power is generally much greater because of the economic damage they can inflict on capital by disrupting or paralysing production. The differences in rhythm are reinforced by the role of the trade union bureaucracy, which exists to negotiate with capital the terms of workers' exploitation, and thus to keep the class struggle contained within the limits of capitalism.

We have already noted how the trade union leaders helped to limit discontent with New Labour's neoliberal policies. Their relationship to the coalition is different. Of course, they don't have the same political links to the Tories or the Lib Dems that they still have with Labour. The unions' institutional interests are threatened by some of the measures canvassed by the coalition or by Tory backbenchers—to limit their financial contributions to Labour, for example, and further to tighten up the anti-union laws. Most importantly, the coalition's assault on the public sector poses an existential threat to unions such as the PCS and Unison.

So pressure for a fight is growing inside the trade union movement. A very significant straw in the wind was provided in late November by the outcome of the elections for the Unite general secretaryship. Len McCluskey, the broad left candidate, won with 101,000 votes, followed by his rank and file challenger, Jerry Hicks, with 52,000. Hicks's success shows many trade unionists recognise that they can't rely on the officials, however left wing their rhetoric.

The political differentiation within the trade union bureaucracy is important. It's much better that McCluskey won than his right-wing opponent, Les Bayliss, who ran with the support of the *Daily Mail*. But McCluskey has been responsible for the BA dispute, where the Unite leadership has hardly covered itself in glory. Even the very hard left of the union leadership, which has broken with Labour—unions like the RMT and the Fire Brigade Union, is often stronger on rhetoric than on action, as was shown by the sudden abandonment of the London firefighters' strike in early November. The common function of the trade union bureaucracy in negotiating class compromise is more fundamental than the political divisions within it.

This situation imposes a delicate task on revolutionary socialists, especially when they have won some influence within the trade union machine, as the Socialist Workers Party has in some public sector unions in recent years. Official calls such as that for the 26 March protest can make it easier to mobilise on a large scale. The support (with some hesitations) that UCU has given the student protests is significant. And the trade union leaders need to be held to account. The call for a general strike is, in the first instance, a demand on *them* to use their social power to halt the coalition in their tracks.

But the conservatism of the labour bureaucracy means it cannot be relied on deliver the action required. Historically revolutionaries have sought to build workplace-based organisations of rank and file trade unionists that can fight independently of the officials. The shop stewards organisation that broke the back of Ted Heath's Tory government in 1970-4 represented the high point of rank and file power in this country. The erosion and bureaucratisation of this organisation under the Labour government of 1974-9 were exploited and reinforced by Margaret Thatcher in her assault on the organised working class during the 1980s.[37]

The result was a shift in the balance of power within the unions in favour of the bureaucracy. A vicious circle developed in which the officials' ability to strangle action further weakened and demoralised the rank and file, and thereby increased the bureaucracy's power. Principled activists, among them revolutionaries, have found themselves more and more drawn into holding union organisation together. The respect they have gained, together with discontent at the union leaders' failure to defend their members' interests, has tilted some public sector unions leftwards. But involvement in the union machine can become a trap, in which even the best activists become drawn into giving priority to bargaining at the top.

There is no easy way out of this situation. Ceasing to try to influence the unions, and to fight for leadership within them would be sheer foolishness. The general strikes on the continent have been called by bureaucratic union leaderships, under some pressure from below. At the same time, the fact that the most promising struggles, in France and Greece, have yet to result in victory for the workers' movement underline the dangers of simply operating within the official machine.

---

37: See Callinicos, 1982, for a detailed analysis of the experience of rank and file movements in Britain. Paul Blackledge discusses the role of the reformist bureaucracy in his article below.

The present historical moment offers a real opportunity to renew independent rank and file organisation. The development of the student movement, much more untrammelled by bureaucracy than the unions, and with a demonstrated ability to outflank its official leaders, is very important in this context. The aim must be to build the broadest and most militant struggles from below, whether among students or workers or in the community, while at the same time demanding that the trade unions and the Labour Party give these struggles their support. But the effort to win this support, let alone the demands of union electoral politics, must not be allowed to hold these struggles back.

This is likely to be a time of organisational improvisation. The EAN is an example, a network that has come to play an important role in coordinating the struggle in the universities. A plethora of different coalitions have emerged to resist the cuts, many locally, and nationally the Right to Work Campaign, the National Shop Stewards Network, and the Coalition of Resistance among others. This diversity is inevitable given that we are in the early stages of a new period of social struggles. But the potential that it represents for destructive competition and wasteful duplication makes it vital that a basic degree of coordination is established among all those mobilising against the coalition.

It is also important that this unity in action stretches into the Labour Party, which continues to hold the loyalty of core sections of the working class. Working with Labour is a source of complications. The huge cuts the coalition made in local government expenditure in the Comprehensive Spending Review were no doubt designed to put the Labour councillors who are likely to dominate the cities after the municipal elections in May directly in the firing line. Existing Labour-controlled councils are already implementing cuts in jobs and services. This is an illustration of how Labourism both expresses and contains workers' resistance. But the best way to confront this contradiction is by working with and against Labour politicians and activists *within* the movement against austerity rather than by trying to restrict that movement to the would-be politically enlightened.

To repeat, the most important thing to do now is simply to build the struggle. In a widening and developing movement, the political differences that inevitably exist can be tested against practice, instead of becoming the currency of sectarian backbiting. Suddenly the horizons of revolutionary politics in Britain have widened spectacularly. We need to make sure they stay open.

*AC and JJ*

# References

Brown, John Murray, "Dublin Acts to Save Debt-Laden Economy", *Financial Times* (24 November).

Callinicos, Alex, 1982, "The Rank and file Movement Today", *International Socialism 17* (autumn).

Callinicos, Alex, 2006, *Universities in a Neoliberal World* (Bookmarks).

Callinicos, Alex, and Simon Turner, 1975, "The Student Movement Today", *International Socialism 75* (first series, February), www.marxists.org/history/etol/writers/callinicos/1975/02/students.htm

Chan, Sewell, and Jo Craven McGinty, "Fed Documents Breadth of Emergency Measures", *New York Times* (1 December).

Collini, Stefan, 2010, "Browne's Gamble", *London Review of Books* (4 November).

Davidson, Neil, 2009, "Shock and Awe", *International Socialism 124* (autumn), www.isj.org.uk/?id=587

Department for Innovation, Universities and Skills, 2009, "Participation Rates in Higher Education: Academic Years 1999/2000-2007/2008 (Provisional)" (31 March), www.education.gov.uk/rsgateway/DB/SFR/s000839/SFR02-2009webversion1.pdf

Friedman, Milton, 2002 (1962), *Capitalism and Freedom* (University of Chicago Press).

Gabbatt, Adam, and Paul Lewis, 2010, "Student Protests: Video Shows Mounted Police Charging London Crowd", *Guardian* (26 November), www.guardian.co.uk/uk/2010/nov/26/police-student-protests-horses-charge

IMF, 2010a, *World Economic Outlook: Recovery, Risk, and Rebalancing* (October), www.imf.org/external/pubs/ft/weo/2010/02/pdf/text.pdf

IMF, 2010b, *Global Financial Stability Report: Sovereigns, Funding, and Systemic Liquidity* (October), www.imf.org/external/pubs/ft/gfsr/2010/02/pdf/text.pdf

Jenkins, Patrick, and Jennifer Hughes, 2010, "Banking: Big Gaps to Fill In", *Financial Times* (8 December).

Kingsley, Patrick, "Student Protests: NUS President Apologises for 'Spineless Dithering'", *Guardian* (28 November). www.guardian.co.uk/education/2010/nov/28/student-leader-apologises-over-dithering

Klein, Naomi, 2007, *The Shock Doctrine* (Allen Lane).

Laws, David, 2010, *22 Days in May* (Biteback Publishing).

Magnus, George, 2011, *Uprising: Will Emerging Markets Shape or Shake the World Economy?* (Wiley).

McKibbin, Ross, 2010, "Nothing to Do with the Economy", *London Review of Books* (18 November).

Miliband, Ed, 2010, "These Education Proposals Risk Setting Back Social Mobility for a Generation", *Observer* (5 December). www.guardian.co.uk/commentisfree/2010/dec/04/ed-miliband-tuition-fees1

Milne, Richard, 2010, "Sovereign Debt: In a Monstrous Grasp", *Financial Times* (3 December).

Penny, Laurie, 2010, "The Power of the Broken Pane", *New Statesman* (14 November), www.newstatesman.com/blogs/laurie-penny/2010/11/millbank-property-young-break

Rich, Motoko, 2010, "Few New Jobs as Jobless Rate Rises to 9.8 Percent", *New York Times*, 3 December.

Parker, George, and Alex Barker, "Clegg's Soft Left and Tory Right Unite in Revolt", *Financial Times* (9 December).

Parker, George, and Nicholas Timmins, "Breakneck Coalition", *Financial Times* (29 November).

Runciman, David, 2010, "Look...", *London Review of Books* (16 December).

Tett, Gillian, 2010, "Lessons in a $3,300bn Surprise from the Fed", Financial Times (2 December).

Tombazos, Stavros, 2010, "Centrifugal Tendencies in the Eurozone", paper presented at *Historical Materialism* Conference, London (November).

Traynor, Ian, 2010, "Angela Merkel Warned that Germany Could Abandon the Euro", Guardian (3 December), www.guardian.co.uk/world/2010/dec/03/angela-merkel-germany-abandon-euro

Walker, Peter, Paul Lewis, Matthew Taylor, and Patrick Wintour, 2010, "Student Protests: School's Out Across the UK as Children Take to the Streets", *Guardian* (24 November), www.guardian.co.uk/education/2010/nov/24/student-protests-school-children-streets

Younge, Gary, 2010, "Students' Power is Limited. But Their Anger and Revolt Can Prove Contagious", *Guardian* (5 December), www.guardian.co.uk/commentisfree/2010/dec/05/students-provide-spark-flames-all-us

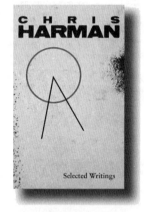

# Mad as hatters?
# The Tea Party movement in the US
*Megan Trudell*

Two years after his election Barack Obama presides over an increasingly divided nation, in both economic and political terms. His failure to deliver on the promise of real change has seen him punished in the midterm elections for Congress and for many state governments, as many whose hopes were raised in 2008 sat out the contest. The result was a serious defeat for the Democrats, with the Republicans securing control of the House of Representatives and coming close to taking the Senate.

The midterm results are an expression of two interconnected developments. First, the Democrats' betrayal of the hopes and aspirations of the tremendous popular movement that delivered Obama's victory—a movement that signalled the potential for a renewal of political engagement on the part of millions of ordinary Americans. Second, the strengthening of conservatism in a Republican Party scarred and divided by the Bush presidency and two deeply unpopular wars, now reinvigorated by the rise of the Tea Party movement.

Underlying both features is the widening gap between the rich in the US, for whom the challenge of the current recession is to fight off any government attempts to increase taxes or damage profitability, and the poor. The impoverishment of greater numbers of people as a result of the recession—fully one quarter of the US population, around 70 million people, rely on government food programmes to some extent, a figure that has trebled since 2006—is piling pressure on the working and middle classes in

US society.[1] The tensions generated by this class polarisation and instability, and the absence of effective government action to alleviate them, go a long way to explaining the contradictory nature of the Tea Party phenomenon.

Predictably, the electoral swing away from the Democrats and the emergence on a national scale of the Tea Party has resurrected the refrain that the US is moving to the right. It's easy to see why this argument has particular resonance in 2010. Tea Party candidates endorsed by Sarah Palin, the Republican vice-presidential hopeful in 2008, included the pro-life, anti-sex, Christine O'Donnell who, in the course of her—fortunately unsuccessful—bid for the Delaware Senate seat, had to defend herself from accusations of witchcraft and, more seriously, stupidity, when she questioned that the Constitution mentioned the separation of church and state.[2] Sharron Angle in Nevada, who also lost her Senate bid, has baselessly accused Canada of letting the 9/11 bombers into the US, and described the city of Dearborn, Michigan, as living under Sharia law and representing a "militant terrorist situation" (Dearborn has seven mosques and 60 churches).

Rand Paul, who successfully won the Kentucky Senate seat, is the son of right wing conservative Republican Ron Paul. Paul Junior is anti-abortion, opposed to gay marriage, and declared in 2002 that "a free society will abide unofficial, private discrimination, even when that means allowing hate-filled groups to exclude people based on the colour of their skin". This year it emerged that he had been part of a college secret society that tied up and blindfolded a female student and made her worship a god called "Aqua Buddha" in a nearby stream.

The argument that the US is moving right is not simply based on the existence of such politicians—not in itself a new phenomenon in US politics—but on the level of support they are receiving. Exit polls for the elections showed that "a sizeable number of voters (40 percent) said that they support the Tea Party political movement (including 21 percent who strongly support it). Fewer (31 percent) said they oppose the movement (23 percent strongly); another 25 percent said they neither support nor oppose it".[3] Among Americans more generally, ie not just those who voted, Tea Party support is in the region of 11 percent of the population—around 34 million people, though this is only half the number who consider themselves to be conservative Christians.

---

1:   As reported by Matt Frei, "Americana", Radio 4, 28 November 2010.
2:   The First Amendment to the Constitution, in the Bill of Rights established in 1789, states: "Congress shall make no law respecting an establishment of religion, or prohibiting the free exercise thereof". Americans are taught about the Bill of Rights in primary school.
3:   Pew Research Center, 2010.

## What are the Tea Parties?

The right wing nature of the Tea Parties' origins is not in question. It was Ron Paul, during his ill-fated bid for the Republican presidential nomination, who organised the first "tea party", his supporters symbolically throwing banners that read "tyranny" and "no taxation without representation" into a box in Boston harbour. Other early protests were ostensibly spontaneous reactions sparked by the conservative bloggers Keli Carender in Seattle and Michelle Malkin in Denver, but were actually organised by an assortment of conservative groups: Young Republicans, Fox News Radio and other right wing radio stations, the conservative youth organisation Young America's Foundation, and the right wing think-tank Americans for Prosperity.[4] The latter is part funded by arch-conservative (and fifth richest person in the US) David Koch, whose father Fred was co-founder of the ultra right wing John Birch Society.

In February 2009 a television business reporter, Rick Santelli, ranted against the Obama government's measures to slow foreclosures and prop up the mortgage companies Freddie Mac and Fanny Mae, calling the bailouts a reward for "bad behaviour" and railing against the funding of so-called "losers' mortgages": "We're thinking of having a Chicago Tea Party in July. All you capitalists that want to show up to Lake Michigan, I'm gonna start organising."[5]

There is ample evidence that the Tea Parties are examples of "astroturfing"—an apparently grassroots movement that is funded and directed by the right of the Republican Party and conservative lobbying organisations. One of those lobbying groups is FreedomWorks, led by Dick Armey, a Republican congressman who co-authored Newt Gingrich's Contract with America during the "Republican Revolution" in 1994 in which Bill Clinton's Democrats lost control of both Congress and the Senate. In 2009, FreedomWorks outlined their "mission":

> For too long, the organised forces of the liberal Left have dominated the grassroots political landscape and delivered huge victories for candidates and policies that grow government and reduce our freedom. We are looking for leaders to help us build our network in all 50 states: a grassroots juggernaut capable of going toe-to-toe with the unions, extreme enviros, and the MoveOn.org's [sic] of the world.[6]

---

4:  Hamsher, 2009.
5:  See www.youtube.com/watch?v=APAD7537RN0&NR=1
6:  www.freedomworks.org/take-action

The Tea Parties have received clear encouragement from sections of the Republican Party machine: Sarah Palin was first provided with her ever-expanding media platform when she was chosen as John McCain's running mate in the presidential race in 2008, and almost all the Tea Party candidates in the midterms stood as Republicans. Fox News has provided the Tea Party movement with blanket and sympathetic coverage, and Palin is rarely off the television screens.

It is difficult to get accurate membership figures of the Tea Party movement as a whole—there are a number of different umbrella organisations claiming to represent hundreds of local groups around the country whose membership numbers range from single figures into the hundreds. As a rough guide, the National Tea Party Federation—to which not all Tea Parties are affiliated—claims 1 million members in 85 organisations. It also cites its affiliates as including Americans for Prosperity and FreedomWorks, among many others.[7] The Tea Party Express, whose leader Mark Williams was expelled from the Federation for racism after writing a letter claiming to be from "the Coloured People" to President Lincoln in praise of slavery, also claims to represent 85 groups.[8]

A New York Times/CBS poll showed that the average Tea Party member is more likely to be an older white male, a Republican voter, a regular church-goer, to own a gun, and to be wealthier than the average US citizen. Some 52 percent of Tea Party supporters believe too much has been made of the problems facing black people—compared with 28 percent of the overall population.[9] However, a deeper look at what "support" for the Tea Party entails is revealing: 78 percent had not donated money or attended any meeting or rally; 47 percent only receive their information about the Tea Party from the television, and most watch Fox News.

Although Tea Party candidates won in some previous Democrat strongholds, notably in Pennsylvania and Ohio, they were mainly successful in areas where conservative Republicanism is strongest—in the South, the Midwest and the Mountain states. Generally, the election results showed that the appeal of Tea Party supporters "stopped at the border of the most densely-populated states and metropolitan areas".[10]

7:  www.thenationalteapartyfederation.com/Membership_List.html
8:  *New York Daily News*, 18 July 2010, www.nydailynews.com/news/politics/2010/07/18/2010-07-18_tea_party_express_leader_mark_williams_expelled_over_colored_people_letter.html#ixzz16OeSMN66.
9:  "National Survey of Tea Party supporters", New York Times/CBS poll, 5-12 April 2010.
10:  Moroney and Dopp, 2010.

## Is the US moving right?

While 40 percent of voters expressed support for the Tea Party, the figure for the population at large is around 28 percent—most Americans do not support the movement. There is good reason, also, to believe that much of the support they do have is more contradictory than a clear indication of a country "moving right".

As much as they expressed the rising prominence of the Tea Party, the midterms told a story of the disillusionment of progressive hopes. The electorate in November 2010 was older, more conservative (41 percent described themselves as such) and wealthier—only 37 percent of voters earned less than $50,000—than was the case two years ago. As often in US elections, the majority was constituted by those who didn't vote at all, and of non-voters in 2010, 54 percent were Democrats, 50 percent approved of the health care legislation, 34 percent were aged between 18-29 and 38 percent between 30-44. Fully 72 percent described their personal financial situation as "only fair" or "poor".[11] For these people, a dashing of their hopes for change has not equated with a move right, but to a disengagement with the political system.

Many young people, who are more likely to lean to the Democrats and less likely to support the Tea Party, stayed away. A survey of young people's political attitudes described the feelings of those they canvassed:

> Suddenly, the generation that in 2008 proudly made the difference as caucus-goers in snowy Iowa for Senator Barack Obama, tell us less than three years later that they are so discouraged with politics that they may sit this one out. A generation marked earlier this decade by their community spirit and optimism, seems on the brink of a despair similar to that of their parents, grandparents and millions of disaffected older voters.[12]

The inadequacy of the stimulus to protect or create jobs, the bank bailouts and the surrender of single-payer health insurance before there was even a fight all worked to demoralise the Democrats' new and enthusiastic base. Obama himself confirmed the squandering of that spirit and optimism when he qualified his famous slogan to Jon Stewart on the Daily Show: "When I say that when we promised during the campaign, 'change you can believe in', it wasn't 'change you can believe in' in 18 months... What I would say is, "Yes, we can", but it is not going to happen overnight".[13]

---

11: Pew Research Center, 2010.
12: Harvard University Institute of Politics, 2010.
13: *Guardian*, 28 October 2010.

The Republicans, therefore, "enjoyed a wide enthusiasm gap" as many natural Democrats did not come out to vote, and it made big gains among political independents: "By 55 percent to 39 percent, more independents voted for the Republican candidate this year; four years ago, independents favoured the Democrats by nearly an identical margin (57 percent to 39 percent). And just two years ago, Barack Obama won the votes of independents (by 52 percent to 44 percent) on his way to the White House".[14]

In reality, most voters weren't very keen on either party. In exit polls both Democrats and Republicans were given unfavourable ratings by 53 percent of those polled.[15] As Pew Research Centre found, "Despite the Republicans' sizeable gains among virtually all demographic groups—with the exceptions of African Americans and young people—voters express a negative view of the party. The outcome of this year's election represented a repudiation of the political status quo, rather than a vote of confidence in the GOP or a statement of support for its policies".[16]

This statement is borne out by the contradictory nature of voters' attitudes to policy. Few voters (19 percent) rated cutting taxes—the Tea Party standard—as the highest priority, while 37 percent favoured job creation and 39 percent prioritised deficit reduction. Voters were also divided over whether to repeal health care reform (48 percent) or to maintain it (16 percent) or even expand it (31 percent). About as many people favoured extending tax-cuts only for families with incomes under $250,000 (37 percent) as favoured extending them for all Americans (39 percent), while 15 percent said they should not be extended for anyone.[17]

The contradictory nature of voters' opinions illustrates the class anxieties felt by a section of the US population. The changes in ordinary Americans' lives over the last three decades have swept away old certainties—a process accelerated dizzyingly by the recession—and much of the Tea Party support is based on a middle class howl of rage and fear at the precariousness and instability of lives that appeared to be privileged and safe.

Over one hundred and fifty years ago Marx described in the Communist Manifesto the impact on the various classes in society of capitalism's continual transformations:

---

14: Pew Research Center, 3 November 2010.
15: CNN, 3 November 2010—http://edition.cnn.com/2010/POLITICS/11/02/election.main/index.html?section=cnn_latest
16: Pew Research Center, 2010.
17: Pew Research Center, 2010.

Constant revolutionising of production, uninterrupted disturbance of all social conditions, everlasting uncertainty and agitation distinguish the bourgeois epoch from all earlier ones. All fixed, fast-frozen relations, with their train of ancient and venerable prejudices and opinions, are swept away, all new-formed ones become antiquated before they can ossify. All that is solid melts into air, all that is holy is profaned, and man is at last compelled to face with sober senses his real conditions of life, and his relations with his kind. [18]

For many Tea Party supporters, and many Americans who don't support them, all that is holy is being profaned. Prosperity for those who work hard, the foundation promise of the American Dream, is in tatters as job security and home ownership are increasingly threatened while the government rescues the rich. In the New York Times/CBS poll, 41 percent of Tea Party supporters felt they were in danger of "falling out of their social class".[19]

What many of the states where Tea Party candidates won (and others where high profile candidates stood but lost) have in common in addition to a tradition of political conservatism, are unemployment rates that are higher than the national average: 10 percent in Ohio, 10.1 percent in Kentucky, 11 percent in South Carolina and 14.4 percent in Nevada.[20] This doesn't mean there is an automatic connection between unemployment and the rise of the Tea Party—the majority of Tea Party supporters are not the most vulnerable to the effects of recession, though 30 percent in the NYT/CBS poll are concerned about losing their jobs—but does contribute to feelings of profound instability and therefore unease in their communities.

As Gary Younge explained, "When Tea Party supporters talk about 'taking our country back', they are—in part—expressing nostalgia. They literally want to take it backwards to a past when people had job security, and a couple on a middle class wage could reasonably expect their children to have a better life than their own".[21]

Not only are their lives as individuals changing beyond anything their grandparents would recognise but, as Ronald Dworkin argues, the Tea Party desire to "take the country back" could also be an attempt to articulate the fact that the slow decline in US economic power and weight, coupled with military failure in Iraq and Afghanistan, is a body

18: Marx and Engels, 1848.
19: "National Survey of Tea Party supporters", New York Times/CBS poll, 5-12 April 2010.
20: Moroney and Dopp, 2010.
21: *Guardian*, 10 October 2010.

blow to people who have believed in the ideology of the American Dream and the superiority of their country; the material basis of their ideological convictions is fracturing. "All their lives they have assumed that their country is the most powerful, most prosperous, most democratic, economically and culturally the most influential—altogether the most envied and wonderful country in the world. They are coming slowly and painfully to realise that that is no longer true; they are angry and they want someone to blame".[22]

Part of the attraction of the Tea Party is that it articulates a feeling that neither party offers an alternative to the havoc being wreaked; the language of a plague on both Democrat and Republican houses, an urge to hold Congress to account, and the demand for limited government all speak to this sense. Although most Tea Party supporters polled believed the US is heading for "socialism", a big majority consider the definition of the term to mean "government control".[23]

The economic situation remains dire and the Democrats are likely to move to the right as a result of the election. Increased pressure from conservative Republicanism and the acceptance of the argument that the US voting population is right wing points to a further watering down of healthcare legislation, cuts to social security, tougher immigration measures and moves to a Clinton-style "triangulation" policy. This suggests that polarisation of social conditions and politics is likely to increase as growing numbers of Americans are alienated from the political system altogether and their concerns remain unaddressed.

These concerns are overwhelmingly economic—most voters in the midterms, 88 percent, rated economic conditions as not good or poor, and 86 percent said they were very worried or somewhat worried about the economy. "Moral" issues such as gay marriage, abortion and immigration, or concern over the wars Iraq and Afghanistan, rate only a handful of percentage points. This is true even among self-described Tea Party supporters, of whom only 2 percent felt that moral values were the most important problem facing the country, 1 percent felt abortion was the key issue, and 1 percent immigration. The economy was cited as the biggest problem by 23 percent, and "jobs" by 22 percent.[24]

The view of Noam Chomsky, among other left wing observers, that the Tea Party represents incipient fascism, risks lumping together

---

22: Dworkin and others, 2010, p56.
23: "National Survey of Tea Party supporters", New York Times/CBS poll, 5-12 April 2010.
24: "National Survey of Tea Party supporters", New York Times/CBS poll, 5-12 April 2010.

the right wing demagogues and bankrollers together with many who are responding to the economic crisis and the lack of political alternatives with an often unfocused anger, and risks demonising the Tea Party movement's working class sympathisers—who are a minority, but who do exist.[25] Although middle class anger and fear at the uncertain climate and the dramatic social changes that US capitalism is presiding over is being pulled to the right, and while conservative Republicanism is in the ascendance in official politics, there is no discernible wider shift rightwards in public opinion and social attitudes.[26]

It is also significant that the likes of Glenn Beck, the religious radio and TV presenter and Tea Party darling, know this. Beck shows an understanding of Tea Party supporters' anxieties and the relatively progressive nature of social attitudes in the US: rather than spout the usual right wing evangelical line, he mines the seams of people's alienation by combining a traditional conservative emphasis on religion and family with opposition to the wars in Iraq and Afghanistan and the influence of Wall Street.

The economic libertarianism of many Tea Party "leaders" is aggressively pro-free market (Rand Paul's father allegedly has a picture of Friedrich Hayek on his wall) and opposed to all government intervention—including taxation and healthcare provision. However damaging such policies would be to their supporters' real lives, the language of these right wing politicians and radio hosts also translates into vocal opposition to the bank and car industry bailouts, expressing and amplifying—in however distorted a fashion—the pent-up anger and frustration of a far greater number of people than would support their moral positions. One telling statistic from the elections is that, while 41 percent of Republican voters blamed Obama for the economic situation and 55 percent of Democrat voters blamed Bush, 32 percent of Democrat voters and 37 percent of Republican voters blamed Wall Street for the country's economic troubles.[27]

It is also noteworthy that many of the more overtly reactionary stances have been quietly dropped. The more astute Tea Party spokespeople recognise that such extremism doesn't chime with many people's experience or views. At Beck's "Restoring Honor" rally in Washington in August this year, he spoke to 87,000 people from the Lincoln Memorial in front of a poster of Frederick Douglass while images from the civil rights movement were projected behind him.

---

25: *The Progressive*, 12 April 2010. www.progressive.org/wx041210.html
26: "National Survey of Tea Party supporters", *New York Times*/CBS poll, 5-12 April 2010.
27: Cited in Dworkin and others, 2010, p58.

Key players in the Tea Party elite are libertarian, rather than conservative, not just on the economy but on moral questions such as gay marriage and some, like Beck and Rand Paul, articulate widespread opposition to war and neo-liberalism, albeit refracted through the prism of isolationism and small government. In other words, as much as it is in the right wing libertarian tradition of US history, the Tea Party movement also has shades of opinion through which it "expresses the disquiet of people unhappy about the more atomised and anarchic world they now find themselves in".[28] And, crucially, it gives them something to do about it. As Jane Slaughter and Mark Brenner put it,

> With the economy a mess and neither Democrats nor Republicans producing a solution, the field is open for folks who says the whole system is broken. The Tea Party taps into many people's very real sense of both insecurity and urgency. The movement dares to say that our problems are enormous, not fixable with Band-aids... Besides, ordinary people know—either intellectually or in their gut—that they don't really count in the political system. It was a bilateral consensus, after all, that bailed out the bankers—and may soon cut Social Security benefits, too. The Tea Party feels like something they can get involved in and have a say.[29]

## Workers and the Tea Party

Henry Olsen, of the Conservative think-tank American Enterprise Institute, said before the midterm elections that it is "no coincidence that a disproportionate number of the Democrats' most vulnerable House seats in the South, the north-east and the Midwest are in districts dominated by blue-collar whites".[30] Democrats did in fact lose Senate seats in Pennsylvania and Wisconsin and the presumptive speaker of the House of Representatives, conservative Republican John Boehner, was elected from Ohio.

Although the Tea Party is not supported by large sections of workers, it is the case that working class Americans have been chronically let down by the Democrats, and the Tea Party seems to offer something different. A recent *Observer* interview illustrates this. The paper spoke with two women who used to work for GM in Dayton, Ohio, at a plant that has been closed down:

---

28:  Lilla, 2010, p18.
29:  Slaughter and Brenner, 2010.
30:  David, 2010.

The women, who worked on the assembly line, are bitter. They've worked hard all their lives and played by the rules...Now they're on the scrapheap through no fault of their own. The older one, just turned 50, doubts she'll ever work again. Both believe their children will have an even worse time than them...The federal bailout of GM failed to save their factory. They face a future struggling to make ends meet doing part-time jobs on the minimum wage. They don't think the government cares about them and have no faith in it. Indeed, they don't want its help any more; they'd rather it just went away...For them, the American dream is over. They've joined the Tea Party.[31]

It is hardly surprising that an active and angry movement that blames government and harks back to earlier certainties would attract working class people with their own fury at the destruction of their lives in the economic maelstrom. Workers in the US are face poverty and the loss of their homes through unemployment or, if they are in work, increasing pressure, harassment and uncertainty—the Obama administration is continuing the process of savaging the Democrats' working class and union base.

The US unemployment rate remains at 9.6 percent, 14.8 million people, and the number of long-term unemployed—those out of work for a year or more—has risen from 645,000 in 2007 to 4.5 million by mid-2010.[32] There were 1,297 mass layoffs in the third quarter of 2010 that resulted in 187,091 workers losing their jobs for at least 31 days.[33]

At the same time, productivity increased at a rate of 2.3 percent during the third quarter of 2010. Output increased 3.7 percent and hours worked increased 1.4 percent. Over the last year, productivity was up 2.5 percent, output rose 4.3 percent and numbers of hours worked increased by 1.7 percent.[34] These statistics translate to a terrible and constant strain on workers and their families. As Kim Moody puts it, "This type of across-the-economy productivity increase at a time when workers are being laid off is certain to produce a long-term increase in work intensity that affects workers of all kinds".[35]

A *Labor Notes* survey in July 2009 found that workplace bullying had risen sharply since the recession began: "It may be that a measurable chunk

31: *Observer*, 31 October 2010.
32: "Issues in Labor Statistics", Bureau of Labor Statistics, October 2010. www.bls.gov/opub/ils/pdf/opbils87.pdf
33: Bureau of Labor Statistics, 12 November 2010. www.bls.gov/news.release/mslo.nr0.htm
34: Bureau of Labor Statistics, 1 December 2010, www.bls.gov/news.release/pdf/prod2.pdf
35: Moody, 2010.

of the unemployed have been harassed out of their jobs, fired rather than laid off. Union members report increases in verbal abuse, discipline including discharge, crackdowns on attendance, surveillance, hassling to work faster, forced overtime, and a concerted effort to get rid of older workers."[36]

Despite the pressure, many US workers feel they have no choice but to stay in work longer than they previously planned. A report from October 2010 found that,

> Today, 40 percent of employees plan to retire later than they did two years ago. Perhaps the most significant action employees are taking is delaying their retirement. Since February 2009, the number of employees who are planning to retire later has grown by six percentage points. This change is consistent across all age groups and plan types, and there is an even larger jump (nine percentage points) among those in poor health.[37]

## Potential and limits

The economic situation has generated vast anger across US society, but there are limits to the Tea Party appeal, certainly in connection with the Republicans. There is certainly little enthusiasm for the Republicans generally, and even less among key sections of the electorate; the party took only about 10 percent of black votes and a third of Hispanics', representing no increase, despite the Democrats presiding over the recession. And, neither is the retention of white working class support a given, according to Olsen:

> West Virginia is the capital of the white working class. Fifty-eight percent of the state's voters were whites without a college degree, 19 points higher than the national average. Ninety-five percent are white and 69 percent say they disapprove of Obama's job performance. Despite this, the Democratic governor, Joe Manchin, swept to an easy 10-point victory over Republican John Raese, a wealthy businessman who owns mansions in Florida and expressed doubts about the minimum wage."[38]

In addition, for the Republican Party the Tea Party-induced revival in their fortunes is a volatile and risky development. Moderate Republicans are concerned about the changing nature of the Republican base and the

---

36: Slaughter, 2009.
37: Watson, 2010.
38: David, 2010.

shift to conservative activism; many are angry that Palin's endorsement of Angle and O'Donnell lost crucial Senate seats and stopped the party short of a second "Republican revolution". What the Tea Party movement can do is push official politics to the right, and maintain the pressure on the Obama government in the run-up to 2012 and the presidential election, but it is dubious whether an ultra-conservative presidential campaign can succeed.

Fears that the right wing populism of the Tea Party movement presages fascism are in part a result of a profound pessimism about the possibility of the revival of working class struggle. At the moment, the understandable fury many Americans feel is being voiced by the right—and by at least some in the Tea Party movement through racism and vigilanteism. However, this does not represent working class opinion, but a middle class movement that can be pulled by a stronger movement from below, should that emerge.

Central to the frustrations of working class people is the vacuum where a fighting leadership should be. Not only have the Democrats repeatedly failed to fight for them, but also the union movement has utterly failed to resist the attacks or to put pressure on Obama. At a time when every fibre should be strained to defending members from the assault of job cuts, harassment and increased pressure, organised labour is in crisis. Declining membership and its complicity in capital's restructuring over the last three decades has left the union leaderships in conflict with each other, as Kim Moody outlines: "When all the efforts and strategies designed to slow down, halt, or even reverse labour's loss of power (the election of John Sweeney in 1995, the many mergers, 'partnerships' with capital, new organising tactics, the split at the top in 2005 [the establishment of the Change to Win Federation]) failed to bring any measurable gains for labour, frustration exploded".[39]

The biggest "organising" union, the Service Employees International Union (SEIU) launched raids on other unions and a campaign of internal repression, and the Change to Win split. It's no wonder that, as Bill Fletcher of the Center for Labor Renewal says, the unions have a "deer in the headlights" reaction to challenges like the Tea Party. "Moreover, not knowing how to respond to the Tea Party is the flip side of not knowing how to push Obama".[40]

Paul Harris and Seamus Milne in the *Guardian* have both written that the Democrats need a Tea Party of their own in order to pursue progressive politics. The faith in "progressive politics" notwithstanding,

---

39: Moody, 2010.
40: Slaughter and Brenner, 2010.

they do touch on a central point.[41] The mobilisation of millions of people desperate for change and for representation by the Obama campaign did show that Americans are not all apathetic and right wing, but can be engaged and powerful when something different appears possible. Where Harris and Milne are likely to be disappointed is in their hopes that the Democratic Party itself will regenerate that enthusiasm—the Obama campaign captured a sense that the interests of working Americans would be prioritised; the Obama government has made clear its inability and unwillingness to challenge the priorities of business and the wealthy.

However, there are other movements that can challenge the status quo. Hundreds of thousands of people marched for immigrant rights again in May this year; 200,000 in Washington—far outstripping any Tea Party gathering—in protest at a recent racist Arizona law that allows the police to question the immigration status of anyone they suspect of entering the US illegally.

Crucially, however, any movement capable of challenging US capitalism in ways that will not simply deliver more savage destruction of welfare and jobs under a different government, must be based on the emergence of rank and file activity within the unions, and grassroots organising among the millions of un-unionised US workers: "These are workers at the centre of the nation's most stressful workplaces: four million call centre workers; the 3-4 million or more unorganised union eligible workers in hospitals; the 1.3 million working at Wal-Mart; the nearly 400,000 in meatpacking without a union; and, of course, the countless millions in the South who have no union representation whether in manufacturing, transportation or services".[42]

The history of labour struggles in the US suggests that at some point that pressure will explode. The AFL's inability and incapacity to represent the interests and battles of newly organising workers at the turn of the century, and its repressive tactics, ultimately resulted in the creation of the CIO as a new force to drive industrial unionism. The bureaucratic cowardice that has led to the warfare that dominates the union leaderships today makes them similarly unfit for directing any combativity in the working class when it arises.

That workers will be forced to fight on a large scale at some point is without doubt—as one writer suggested recently, "It seems possible that the Tea Party crowd who want to nullify health care will provoke an angry

---

41: *Guardian*, 3 and 10 November 2010.
42: Moody, 2010.

crowd of a different sort. After all, there are people who need the things that will be taken away".[43] The proposal from Obama's bipartisan Deficit Commission to take $3.9 trillion out of public spending by 2020 represents a profound threat to many poor Americans' lives. The central question, as ever, is whether any organisations that struggles can give rise to will be able to coalesce wider class forces around themselves.

Significant battles over welfare attacks and the treatment of immigrants can provide an alternative pole of attraction that not only gives confidence to workers but suggests solutions to the crisis and a different future, rather than populist yearnings for the past.

43: Dworkin and others, 2010, p58.

# References

David, Peter, 2010, "Lexington: Trouble With the Humans", *Economist* (21 October), www.economist.com/node/17308059

Dworkin, Ronald, Mark Lilla, David Bromwich and Jonathan Raban, 2010, "The Historic Election: Four Views", *New York Review of Books*, volume LVII, number 19, (December 9-22), http://www.nybooks.com/articles/archives/2010/dec/09/historic-election-four-views/

Hamsher, Jane, 2009, "A Teabagger Timeline", *Huffington Post* (19 April), www.huffingtonpost.com/jane-hamsher/a-teabagger-timeline-koch_b_187312.html

Harvard University Institute of Politics, 2010, *Survey of Young Americans' Attitudes Toward Politics and Public Service: 18th Edition* (21 October), http://www.iop.harvard.edu/var/ezp_site/storage/fckeditor/file/101021_IOP_Fall_10 percent20Report_FINAL.pdf

Lilla, Mark, 2010, "The Beck of Revelation", *New York Review of Books*, volume LVII, number 19, (December 9-22), www.nybooks.com/articles/archives/2010/dec/09/beck-revelation

Marx, Karl, and Frederick Engels, 1848, *Manifesto of the Communist Party*, www.marxists.org/archive/marx/works/1848/communist-manifesto/

Moody, Kim, 2010, "The Crisis and the Potential", *Against the Current*, 145 (March-April), www.solidarity-us.org/current/node/2677

Moroney, Tom, and Terrence Dopp, 2010, *Business Week* (5 November), www.businessweek.com/news/2010-11-05/tea-party-election-results-diluted-in-highly-populated-states.html

Pew Research Center, 2010, "A Clear Rejection of the Status Quo, No Consensus About Future Policies" (3 November), http://pewresearch.org/pubs/1789/2010-midterm-elections-exit-poll-analysis

Slaughter, Jane, 2009, "Harassment: The Recession's Hidden Byproduct", *Labor Notes* (July 17), www.labornotes.org/node/2349

Slaughter, Jane, and Mark Brenner, 2010, "Can Labor Out-Organize the Tea Party?", *Labor Notes* (30 September), www.labornotes.org/2010/09/can-labor-out-organize-tea-party

Watson, Towers, 2010, "Retirement Attitudes", www.towerswatson.com/assets/pdf/2717/TowersWatson_Retirement-Pt2-Attitudes_NA-2010-17683.pdf

# Police killings and the law

*Simon Behrman*

.

Many people, even those of us with little or no illusions in the police, felt a deep sense of shock and outrage when on 22 July 2010 the Crown Prosecution Service (CPS) announced that there would be no prosecution of PC Simon Harwood, who was filmed striking Ian Tomlinson shortly before he died during the G20 protests in April 2009. What made the announcement especially perverse was the date on which it was made, the fifth anniversary of the killing by the Metropolitan Police of Jean Charles de Menezes, a killing that also failed to result in any criminal prosecution of the police officers concerned.[1]

It is therefore unsurprising that the question has arisen as to whether the police are becoming more violent. But this is the wrong question. The history of the police force going right back to its inception in the early 19th century has been one of violence. From the attacks on the Chartists, the murder of Alfred Linnell during a protest in 1887, the Battle of Cable Street in 1936, the killing of Blair Peach in 1979 and the miners' strike of 1984-5 the police have repeatedly deployed extreme violence as a tactic.

1:   Portions of this article originated as part of research carried out for British Irish Rights Watch (BIRW). I would like to thank Caroline Parkes and Christopher Stanley at BIRW for supporting and guiding my work there. Alex Callinicos, Joseph Choonara, Gareth Dale, Jacqui Freeman, Gareth Jenkins, Andy Jones, Gonzalo Pozo and Dave Renton all provided detailed criticism of an earlier draft. While I have adopted many of their suggestions and gratefully incorporated some factual corrections I accept sole responsibility for any remaining errors, factual or conceptual.

This history is very well described in a number of books, the best of which remains Audrey Farrell's *Crime, Class and Corruption: The Politics of the Police*.[2] However, it would be equally wrong to deny that there has been a significant shift in the framework within which, over recent years, police violence has taken place. This change is epitomised in how the law treats deliberate killings by the police, and I will therefore concentrate on this area, although my argument also holds when dealing with police violence in general.

The change in how police violence is perceived and dealt with can be clearly seen when comparing two cases where the police shot suspects dead: the shoot to kill scandal in Northern Ireland in 1982 and the killing of de Menezes in London 23 years later. Both cases involved police officers deliberately targeting and killing unarmed suspects. Yet in the earlier case allegations of a shoot to kill policy were hotly denied by the authorities. The ensuing scandal led to criminal prosecutions for manslaughter of the police officers involved in the shootings. A major investigation led to the Stalker/Sampson Report, which is still considered too sensitive to release publicly.

Fast forward to July 2005 when an elite team from the Special Branch entered Stockwell Tube station chasing a terrorist suspect. They were armed with hollow-point ammunition, colloquially known as "dum-dums", designed to explode on impact, ammunition which is normally not authorised for police use. On confronting de Menezes in the Tube carriage, one officer held him down while two others fired their guns seven times into his head at point blank range. No warning had been given to de Menezes. This was in everything but name an extra-judicial execution, or shoot to kill. Yet this time after a botched and frankly stupid attempt at a cover up, it emerged that the actions of the police that day were in accordance with an official policy drawn up by the Metropolitan Police and signed off by the government.

This policy was named "Kratos". It transpired that following the attacks of 9/11 the Met had been planning and training for this policy. To give you a flavour of what Kratos involved, it specified that the police, when faced by a suspected (this adjective cannot be emphasised enough) suicide bomber, were to fire, without issuing any warning, exploding bullets into their brainstem, thus "immediately incapacitating" or killing the suspect. Kratos, incidentally, was based on research carried out by the Met on tactics used by the Sri Lankan police against the Tamils and by the

---

2:    Farrell, 1992; Hernon, 2006; Reiner, 2010. Former Commissioner of the Metropolitan Police, Sir Robert Mark freely admitted to using an illegal weapon to break a navvy's legs when he was a constable in 1930s Manchester—Reiner, 2010, p211.

Israelis against the Palestinians; neither force is known for being restrained in its use of extreme violence.

This time a shoot to kill policy was acknowledged and declared "fit for purpose" despite leading to the murder of an innocent man.[3] Further, there were no criminal prosecutions against the police officers involved. This represents a significant shift from Northern Ireland in 1982. The level of violence used by the police is in essence no different. What is different is its legitimacy in terms of law. Shoot to kill has become legalised, and in doing so it has become normalised. The scandal over the revelation of Kratos was far less than that over shoot to kill in Northern Ireland.

Throughout the period between shoot to kill and Kratos dozens more people were shot dead by the British police including Cherry Groce in 1985, shot by police in her home as they searched for her son, an act which led directly to the Broadwater Farm riot; Diarmuid O'Neill, an unarmed member of the IRA shot dead by police during a raid on a west London hotel in 1996; Harry Stanley, shot dead by police in Hackney in 1999 as he was walking home from the pub. In the last case police had been alerted by a call from someone in Stanley's local pub. The caller reported that Stanley had an Irish accent and was carrying what looked like a sawn-off shotgun in a bag. Stanley was in fact Scottish and the bag contained a table leg. In 2006, less than a year after the killing of de Menezes, Mohammed Abdulkahar was shot by police during a dawn raid on his home in Forest Gate. Once again neither he nor his family were found to be in any way connected to terrorism. Luckily Abdulkahar survived. Overall, according to figures from Inquest, there were 50 deaths caused by police shootings in England and Wales from 1990 until 2009. During the first half of that period there were 21 deaths and over the last decade that figure has risen to 29, an increase of almost 40 percent.[4]

Ever since the late 1970s some on the left have declared that Britain is either in or on the cusp of a police state.[5] Yet even after the miners' strike, various pieces of draconian anti-terrorist legislation and other attacks on civil liberties, the British state remains very much a capitalist democracy. Nevertheless, during this period the use of firearms has become ever more widespread in the police force. It was little noticed, for example, that during the 1990s police forces up and down the country began regularly deploying

---

3:   Sir Chris Fox, Chairman of ACPO, quoted in "Police defend shooting strategy", BBC News Report, 8 March 2006, http://news.bbc.co.uk/1/hi/england/london/4784688.stm.

4:   http://inquest.gn.apc.org/data_death_by_police_shooting.html

5:   See Sparks, 1984, for a very detailed argument as to why repeated and unfounded claims of a "police state" hinder rather than help the working class confront the state.

Armed Response Vehicles (ARV), equipped with a huge stock of firepower.[6] The impetus for this began when the IRA bombing campaign came to the mainland. Indeed, the weaponry introduced including live firearms, plastic bullets and CS gas were all road-tested first in Northern Ireland. The point is that just as these developments in police practice have outlived the Irish "emergency", so too a state of emergency appears to be becoming a more permanent feature of policing policy which has in turn led to a justification for retaining and expanding the right of the police to use lethal force. Examples where "unprecedented" circumstances have been claimed as justification for the use of police-state tactics are mass detentions of anti-capitalist protesters and the threat of suicide bombers. It is very likely that as social instability caused by the economic crisis develops this too will be claimed as justification for the continued use of "emergency" powers.

Of course, Marx and Engels argued that capitalist democracy was a major advance over feudalism and offered to the working class a far better terrain on which to fight than other, more authoritarian, forms of capitalist rule. Yet throughout his writings, from "On the Jewish Question" in 1843 right through to the *Critique of the Gotha Programme* over 30 years later, Marx highlighted two crucial aspects of capitalist democracy. First, democracy and equality in the political sphere mask the massive inequalities that exist in the economic domain where capital operates a dictatorship over labour. Second, as Lenin put it, capitalist democracy provided "the best possible political shell of capitalism".[7] Because the working class poses such a potentially powerful threat to the dictatorship of capital, relying on rule by consent rather than by violence is always the preferred tactic of bourgeois rule. But, and this is the key point, the monopoly on the use of violence that the dictatorship of capital exercises through its state means that killings by the police, along with other forms of state terror, can be accommodated without violating the norms of capitalist democracy. This is achieved via the rule of law, specifically the legal form that, as the Soviet jurist Evgeny Pashukanis argued, shares the same structure as the commodity form. My argument here is that certain police-state tactics such as extra-judicial killings have become possible without the loss of legitimacy and rule by consent conferred by governing under the rule of law. Instead law itself has become a perfect vehicle for such tactics. In short, police violence must be understood not as a departure from capitalist democracy but as a function of it.

---

6:   Reiner, 2010, p101.
7:   Lenin, 1965, p15.

## From policing by terror to policing by consent

In spite of the shocking nature of recent killings by the police, it is important to recognise that throughout their history the police have frequently used extreme violence against suspects, bystanders, demonstrators and workers on strike. The violence deployed by the modern police is in fact far less than that of their predecessors of the 18th and early 19th centuries. Douglas Hay has described how the British ruling class of that period imposed their authority through state terror.[8] From 1688 until 1820 the death penalty was extended from about 50 offences to over 200, most involving crimes against property.[9] Executions were bloody public spectacles intended to instil fear into the lower classes. An additional element of this strategy involved armed members of the local gentry, the yeomanry and special constables. If those ad hoc forces failed to keep order they were reinforced by the deployment of the military around the country. This became increasingly necessary with the intensification of riots in the countryside as the effects of the birth of modern capitalism began to bite. Following in the wake of this brute force, judges would be sent into the affected areas to dispense summary justice.

The causes of the riots and the need for the ruling class to impose terror on the populace were rooted in a massive transformation of economic relations during the 18th century. This represented a concerted shift from the remnants of feudalism towards capitalism. Brutal methods were necessary for the ruling class during a period that saw a massive theft from the poor in a process described by Marx as the "primitive accumulation of capital".[10] The new bourgeoisie seized common lands through successive Enclosure Acts, thus impoverishing and starving the local peasantry who relied on these to support and feed themselves. Enclosure had two effects—forcing the rural poor to resort to poaching and scavenging on the estates of the rich, and pushing increased numbers of them from the land into the cities to seek work. The uprooting of communities in the countryside and the chaos of expanding cities with a lack of housing and work for the new arrivals led to social instability fed by anger and desperation from those who had been dispossessed.

This period of transition saw the ruling class deploy a combination of forms of rule inherited from the feudal period, and new forms that better suited a capitalist society. An inheritance from feudalism was the use of terror tempered by mercy. The huge increase in crimes punishable by the

8:   Hay and others, 1977.
9:   Hay and others, 1977, p18.
10:  Marx, 1976, chapter 26.

death penalty was in fact accompanied by a comparative reduction in its actual use. More often those sentenced to death were encouraged to seek clemency from either the king or the property owner against whom they had committed the offence. Assuming they demonstrated a suitable amount of humility, they would be shown mercy and their sentence commuted. Note that in this arrangement law and socio-economic relations appear in one and the same guise. The same person who held a higher social position to you could also at their discretion prosecute you. Following conviction they could accept or reduce the punishment. Sometimes the property owner would negotiate with the convict terms for doing work on their land in exchange for dropping the prosecution. In effect, this was not the rule of law but instead naked class power adorned with some of the rituals of law.

In like manner, the application of physical force was not governed by law, but rather by expediency. Once a riot broke out the armed forces of the state were permitted to use whatever force was necessary to restore the king's peace. This worked up to a point when dealing with the rural poor. For the landed gentry, the debilitating injuries and killing of the local peasants did not disturb their lives or livelihoods on their increasingly large estates. Moreover, the only weapon the peasantry could deploy against the force of the state was their own ability to organise and fight. But face to face against a much better armed and organised military force, they were invariably beaten.

With the growth of the working class in the cities the balance of class forces changed. The urban working class living closer together in built up areas were better able to organise and defend themselves. At the 1819 "Peterloo" massacre in Manchester, for example, the crowd numbered possibly up to 150,000, larger than any riot or uprising since the English Revolution almost two centuries earlier. In addition, many of the protesters had been carrying out practice drills for weeks in advance. With just 1,000 troops and 400 constables, the authorities would only be able to break up the protest through the use of extreme violence, and so it was. Men, women and children were stampeded by horses, sabred and whipped relentlessly through the streets of Manchester. The attack that began shortly before 2pm lasted well into the evening, at the end of which at least 11 were dead and about 500 injured.

Peterloo exposed the limits of the strategy of terror deployed against the working class. Such concentrated violence caused a major scandal that shocked even sections of the middle classes and the establishment. Moreover, the violence failed to subdue the emerging movement for political and civil rights. Instead it led to a growing number of demonstrations, riots and strikes culminating in the great Chartist movement for manhood suffrage.

The Chartists were responsible for, among other things, organising in 1842 the first general strike in history. This new form of resistance was not as easy to deal with as a riot. After all one cannot literally beat a mass of workers back to work. Also, if too many are incapacitated by police and military violence, the capitalists will suffer in the immediate term through fewer workers being able to work. Indeed, the level of violence was far less than in previous uprisings such as Peterloo and at Merthyr in previous decades. The sentences handed out to Chartists were minimal compared with earlier reckonings by the ruling class. No one was sentenced to death and most convictions for rioting or other crimes were punished with terms of imprisonment of a few months up to a few years, although the leading agitators were treated more harshly, many of them sentenced to transportation or much longer jail terms.

The fear of the power of the working class also led the government to concede a number of reforms such as the repeal of the Corn Laws in 1846, which led initially to lower food prices, and the Factory Act 1847 limiting working hours. This was in contrast to the pattern during the 18th century where the ruling class was able to steal wealth from the poor at an ever increasing rate. It was also during this period that the military began to be replaced by the police as the primary tool for enforcing public order. The Metropolitan Police Act of 1829 established the force in the capital. In response to the first Chartist agitation, the 1839 County Police Act was enacted allowing the formation of regional police forces. The fear of disorder from demobilised soldiers returning from the Crimean War led to the 1856 County and Borough Act which established police forces across the whole of the country. This period during the mid-19th century represents British capitalism maturing from the more brutalist primitive accumulation of capital into a settled capitalist democracy. Central to this process was the development of the rule of law as the primary method of enforcing order. Legally regulated state violence was replacing naked class terror.

The police force was founded on the principle of "citizens in uniform". In other words, they were bound by the same laws as anyone else. They were also made structurally independent from the control of either politicians or individual members of the ruling class. Thus they were also bound by law in a manner unlike that of the yeomanry or other military forces, whose authority came directly from the Crown and the socio-economic power exercised in localities by the landed gentry and aristocracy. The establishment of the police was part and parcel of a move away from a form of class rule which saw little separation between economic and juridical power. Within decades the state assumed a monopoly on the application of criminal law and, with the police, a monopoly over the use of violence. This accruing of power by the state at first alarmed sections of the ruling class, which is why many of them initially opposed the setting up of a police force. But it quickly became clear that the use of physical force by the capitalist state would not be deployed against property rights, but against labour and the poor.

In his classic work on the birth of the prison, Michel Foucault shows convincingly how the move from the application of the power of the king to the power of law provided a more efficient and less risky form of social control. The messy system in force during the later feudal period could lead to:

> the fear of the uproar, shouting and cheering that the people usually indulge in, the fear that there would be disorder, violence, and outbursts against the parties, or even against the judges... Before the justice of the sovereign, all voices must be still.[11]

The final word uttered by an apparently neutral and rational law was far more effective in silencing the oppressed. The police became legitimised as "embodiments of impersonal, rational authority", as opposed to the naked class power of the yeomanry.[12] What Foucault glosses over is the fact that this change was a direct result of a set of new economic relationships. The feudal order rested on an ideology of a class born to rule; thus their authority and their right to dispense "justice" was unquestionable. The bourgeoisie, on the other hand, rule on the basis of a series of contractual relations. Economic exploitation is rooted in the payment of wages for labour power. This has the effect of normalising exploitative relations such as in the expression: "A fair day's pay for a fair day's work." Equally, the rule of law is predicated on notions of fairness, reasonableness and equivalence. Phrases such a "paying the price" for committing a crime, or "let the punishment fit the crime" illuminate this aspect of law. This is quite distinct from feudalism when punishment was a demonstration of the "majesty" and power of the monarch, the nobility or the church. The contractual nature specific to capitalist exploitation finds its equivalent in legal relations.

Phil Cohen identifies the police as

---

11: Foucault, 1991, p35-6.
12: Reiner, 2010, p99.

the first branch of the British state to develop an ideological as well as a purely repressive function…to protect the institutions of private property, and to enforce statutory norms of public order primarily designed to ensure the free circulation of commodities, including the commodity of labour power.[13]

At first the urban working class had to be disciplined into accepting these norms. Violence between police and local working class communities, defending what they considered as their own territory, was a common feature right up to World War One. But over time there was a "gradual ideological penetration of 'The Law' into the basic conditions of working class life".[14]

Cohen explains this as a result of social changes in the composition of the working class. While there may be some truth in that, referring to the police as "The Law" also illustrates something else. Unlike their predecessors, the police were not just deployed to put down riots and other major disturbances, but also assigned to manage everyday order in the community. Criminologists sometimes describe this as a dual role involving "parking tickets and class repression".[15] As a result the law and "The Law" gradually came to be seen as indispensable to a well-ordered society, irrespective of class, politics or economics. In short, an ideology of "police fetishism" developed.[16] I would argue that this is a direct result of two other fetishes closely linked together—that of law and commodities.

## Pashukanis

In his 1924 book, *Law and Marxism*, Pashukanis developed what has become known as the "commodity form" theory of law. In it he sought to explain the legal form as one inherently tied to the commodity form. He begins his analysis using the same methodology as Marx does in *Capital*: "In as much as the wealth of capitalist society appears as 'an immense collection of commodities', so this society itself appears as an endless chain of legal relations".[17] What these two sets of relationships—commodity exchange and legal relations—have in common is the notion of the autonomous egoistic individual. When commodity owners go to market to engage in trade, they must each recognise in the others their exclusive

---

13: Cohen, 1979, p120.
14: Cohen, 1979, p126.
15: Reiner, 2010, p17.
16: Reiner, 2010, p3.
17: Pashukanis, 1989, p85.

right of ownership over their commodities; otherwise they cannot expect their own rights to be so recognised. Thus the basic principle of commodity exchange, the freedom of every seller freely to dispose of their property, gives rise to the concept of universal and equal rights, which is an ideological misrepresentation of capitalist relations as a whole, but one that accurately reflects the actual material conditions in which subjects under capitalism find themselves. The claim of one commodity owner on all others to recognise his own rights as such creates a subjective, and thus seemingly natural, desire to recognise those same rights in others.

From this starting point Pashukanis is able to make the following analogy with law: "The [legal] subject as representative and addressee of every possible claim, the succession of subjects linked together by claims on each other, is the fundamental legal fabric which corresponds to the economic fabric".[18] Thus just as we have the market in which every buyer and seller comes metaphorically brandishing their commodities to exchange, so the law is a regulated market of legal subjects haggling over their respective bundles of rights. The rule of capital is thus also necessarily the rule of law.

In "On the Jewish Question" Marx argued that the bourgeoisie emancipated the state from economics and religion by placing it (the state) above society, and thus giving it the appearance of being independent and above the classes.[19] As Pashukanis expresses it:

> By appearing as a guarantor, authority becomes social and public, an authority representing the impersonal interest of the system... Thus there arises, besides direct unmediated class rule, indirect reflected rule in the shape of official state power as a distinct authority, detached from society.[20]

This provides a theoretical underpinning for the transition from naked class rule to rule by law that I discussed earlier. Commodities and legal relations did, of course, exist in many pre-capitalist societies. But in the same way that a society where free alienation of property raises the commodity to its highest and most generalised level, where exploitation becomes mediated via the legal contract, ie where the exploited worker "figures as a legal subject disposing of his labour power as a commodity", so also legal relations reach their highest form under conditions of generalised commodity

18: Pashukanis, 1989, p99.
19: Marx, 1975, p218-9 and generally.
20: Pashukanis, 1989, p137-8.

exchange: "The legal form attains universal significance, legal ideology becomes the ideology par excellence, and defending the class interest of the exploiters appears with ever increasing success as the defence of the abstract principle of legal subjectivity".[21]

The crucial import of Pashukanis's analysis is that he is able to reveal how the specific form of social regulation under capitalism, that is rights-based law, is able successfully to transform the subjective needs of the ruling class into an objective set of relationships for society as a whole, by means of which the coercive role of law is then in turn subjectivised (internalised) by the rest of us.

## The dispersal of responsibilities

At first blush it may seem counter-intuitive to apply a theory of law that identifies the logic of equivalence and autonomous egoistic individualism to the application of lethal force by the state against unarmed individuals. However, if we take at look at how the police are able to justify their actions in law, the relevance of Pashukanis will become apparent.

There was no disputing the fact that de Menezes was neither armed when he was shot, nor was he a terrorist. How could this wilful and unnecessary taking of life not result in any legal sanction? Crucially, the failure to bring any individual or group of police officers to justice over the de Menezes killing was a result of the dispersal of responsibilities created by law.[22] This process rests upon the principle of the autonomous egoistic individual who functions as the commodity owner and legal subject par excellence. In much the same way that the market economy appears as an impersonal and naturalistic process involving an endless chain of buyers and sellers, so law functions in a similar way as each individual stands in relation to all others owing certain duties and possessing certain rights.

One of the aspects of the operation which was highlighted in the inquest into de Menezes's death was the police's bronze, silver, gold structure used for firearms, and other emergency operations. This structure was developed by the Metropolitan Police in order to develop clear command, following the, from their point of view, catastrophic failure of organisation

---

21: Pashukanis, 1989, p45. Engels makes a similar point: "Roman law was the consummate law of simple, ie pre-capitalist, commodity production, which however included most of the relations of the capitalist period. Hence precisely what our city burghers needed at the time of their rise and did not find in the local law of custom"—Frederick Engels, letter to Karl Kautsky, 26 June 1884, quoted in Head, 2008, p31.
22: For a detailed exposition of this argument see Veitch, 2007.

during the Broadwater Farm riots in 1985.[23] One aspect of this system highlighted in the de Menezes inquest was that it removed many crucial strategic and tactical decisions from the officers on the ground and placed them instead in the hands of commanding officers situated miles away in a room in New Scotland Yard. This led to several crucial mistakes in the operation that meant that police officers on the ground missed several opportunities safely to stop de Menezes before he entered the Tube. But it also reinforced the dispersal of responsibilities in such a way that none of the commanding officers, nor any of the officers on the ground could be held criminally liable for the decisions made. This is one reason why the Metropolitan Police as a corporate entity could be successfully prosecuted under health and safety legislation, but that no individual officer was answerable in law for the mistakes made and the decisions taken.

A similar conclusion was reached in the Police Ombudsman's report into the 2003 killing of Neil McConville, a teenage joy-rider in Northern Ireland.[24] According to the Ombudsman, the failure to appoint a Bronze Commander in charge on the ground was a critical factor leading to the death of McConville. Thus the officers who carried out the operation were exonerated from blame. On the other hand the senior officers who held the positions of Silver and Gold Commander respectively were merely reprimanded for bad management. Because they were not on the ground and did not fire any shots they were not culpable either.

Several senior police officers testified during the de Menezes inquest that one of the concerns the Metropolitan Police had when developing the Kratos policy was that the armed police officer on the ground would be very hesitant in executing a suspect without warning without legal safeguards to protect themselves. During Kratos training members of the specialist firearms unit SO19, who would be assigned to carry out the executions, expressed fears that they would be held both morally and legally responsible, particularly should anything go wrong. It was for this reason that the role of the Designated Senior Officer (DSO) was created within the Kratos policy.

The idea was that in a situation where police officers found themselves confronted by a suspected suicide bomber, the DSO, situated in New Scotland Yard, would be responsible for giving the order to shoot.

---

23: http://www.met.police.uk/leslp/docs/Major_incident_procedure_manual_7th_ed.pdf In short, the Gold Commander is responsible for setting the strategy for an operation and the Silver Commander then has to interpret this into a set of suitable tactics, which the Bronze Commander is responsible for implementing on the ground.
24: Ombudsman's Report, 2003, p3.

This would take the pressure off the police officers who would actually have to carry out such an extreme and violent act. But surely this then places full legal responsibility on the DSO? Not so, according to the evidence presented to the de Menezes inquest. For the DSO, Commander Cressida Dick, did not give any such order; indeed, her last order to the SO19 officers before they descended into the Tube was ambiguous. The SO19 officers ended up using deliberately lethal force, due to what they claimed was a reasonable judgement based on de Menezes's behaviour, and coupled with the reports they had received from surveillance officers, senior officers and the DSO during their briefings that morning and throughout the tracking of de Menezes. The responsibility for the killing was thus dispersed amongst the dozens of police officers involved in the operation.

Not only does this dispersal of responsibilities create almost insurmountable problems in holding the police accountable, but it also reinforces the logic of capitalism in which bad things result from the market—unemployment, starvation, recessions etc—not because any individual capitalists are responsible but because that is just the way the system involving countless autonomous egoistic individuals operates.

The Metropolitan Police declared eight months after the killing of de Menezes that Kratos remained "fit for purpose"; the Stockwell shooting had merely been a result of some operational errors.[25] Equally, in the case of McConville, the Ombudsman's recommendations stressed the importance of clear policies, training and command for operations involving potentially lethal force.[26] The report reserved its concluding comment for criticising commanding officers for a lack of effective management.[27] In both these cases the issue under consideration was not posed as one of an agent of the state walking up to a member of the public and, without warning, shooting them in the head, or one of a police officer using a semi-automatic rifle to deal with an alleged juvenile delinquent. Rather the issue was considered to be a lack of efficient organisation. It was to this logic of managing barbaric acts through law that Hannah Arendt was referring in her description of the "banality of evil".[28]

25: Sir Chris Fox, Chairman of the Association of Chief Police Officers, quoted in "Police defend shooting strategy", BBC News Report, 8 March 2006, http://news.bbc.co.uk/1/hi/england/london/4784688.stm.
26: Ombudsman's Report, 2003, 17.1.
27: Ombudsman's Report, 2003, 17.13.
28: Arendt, 1994.

## The "reasonableness" of police killings

Ever since the Police and Criminal Evidence Act 1984 (PACE) the police have been recognised in law as possessing certain special powers, which the rest of us do not have, such as the right to stop and search and detain individuals. However, in terms of the use of force, in the eye of the law they remain neither more nor less than "citizens in uniform". In other words legally they are to be held to account for taking another person's life in much the same way as you or me. The law offers us two main defences for killing someone. The first is the common law of self-defence. The second is contained in Section 3 of the Criminal Law Act 1967, which states that "a person may use such force as is reasonable in the circumstances in the prevention of crime, or in effecting or assisting in the lawful arrest of offenders or suspected offenders or of persons unlawfully at large".

This obviously refers mainly to the police, but it also applies to any one of us confronted by someone committing a criminal act, eg a burglar in our home. The key term common to both this statutory provision and the defence of self-defence is "reasonableness". In order to uphold a defence to a charge of murder or manslaughter, one needs to prove two things—that the force used was both necessary and proportionate. If someone attempts to grab my wallet, it will be necessary for me to use physical force to stop them. If someone merely threatens to steal my wallet tomorrow, it would not be necessary for me physically to attack or restrain them. Assuming that I am actually being mugged, the question then arises as to the level of force I can legitimately apply. If in this scenario I push the thief to the ground then that would probably be considered a proportionate degree of force. If I took out a knife and stabbed them in the chest, then that would almost certainly be considered disproportionate. However, if the thief produces a gun when robbing me, the use of a knife might be considered proportionate and legitimate. A key principle evident in the law here is that of balance and rational calculation. I may only do to you something that can be measured as equivalent to the danger posed by you.

In each and every case where the police shoot a suspect dead, they always claim that they feared deadly and imminent danger from the victim. So the police officers who shot de Menezes "honestly believed" that he was an armed suicide bomber, and therefore shooting him in the head was a reasonable and proportionate response. In law, the fact that they were subsequently shown to be mistaken does not vitiate their claim as to what their subjective fear was at the time they shot him.

It was on the same basis that the case against members of the Royal Ulster Constabulary (RUC) charged with one of the shoot to kill incidents in 1982 was dismissed. The judge in that case, Lord Justice Gibson, argued that the police had reacted reasonably given the potential danger they faced from known members of the IRA. Indeed, notoriously, he went a step too far by commending the defendants for bringing the murdered IRA suspects to the "final court of justice". Although, in an unprecedented move, he subsequently had to retract his remarks from the bench, the logic expressed fits perfectly the way in which the devaluation of the lives of suspects allows the police to justify the use of extreme violence against them.

The jurisprudence has tended to judge what is reasonable from the subjective standpoint of the police officer who has applied lethal force.[29] This then places a disproportionate emphasis on the testimony of the police officer concerned. Again Lord Justice Gibson makes the point crystal clear:

> The question whether there was the necessary criminal intention is not to be judged…by the standard of what one thinks one would have done or should have done had one been in that situation.

> The question is: has the Crown proved beyond any reasonable doubt what was the actual state of mind, belief and understanding of the accused [police officers] in the heat and anxiety of the moment, faced, as they understood it, with but a fleeting second to decide and to act…[30]

This justification was repeated in almost exactly the same terms more than two decades later to justify the murder of de Menezes morally and legally. When placed in the context of the potential threat from terrorists the criteria of what might be considered reasonable are widened considerably. Instead of the law acting as a restraint upon the police officer, the yardstick by which to measure the legitimate extent of lethal force applied by the police has instead been judged on the basis of the extent of the *potential* violence committed by the terrorist. The hyperbole that surrounds the "war on terror", a war whose end cannot be envisaged in a world racked by imperialism, is largely responsible for investing in the concept of a reasonable use of force, a pre-emptive dimension based on quasi-apocalyptic expectations of what terrorists are capable of carrying out. An academic writing on the experience in Northern Ireland points out how

---

29: Asmal, 1985, p85.
30: R v Robinson, (1984). Report in author's possession.

the concept of proportionality became so fluid that it facilitated the use of lethal force by law enforcement agents for almost any crime even if it was only a vague notion of a terrorist crime... This has had the profound subsidiary effect that security forces were enabled to engage with supposed terrorists in situations that would enable them the full protection of the law due to the elasticity and elusiveness of the concept of "reasonableness". [31]

It has sometimes been argued that the problem is simply one of English law being out of step with the jurisprudence of the European Court of Human Rights (ECtHR), which applies a more rigorous or objective test in judging the "honest belief" of the police officer.[32] However, in a case from 2001 concerning yet another lethal shooting of an unarmed suspect by the police the same court held that "it is not for the court to substitute its own opinion of the situation for that of a police officer who was required to react in the heat of the moment".[33] As Clair de Than points out, this judgment has the effect of placing even greater emphasis on the subjective testimony of the police officer: "It does not have to be a reasonable mistake, merely an honest one".[34]

The vague concepts of reasonableness and proportionality, which are integral to law, are given detail and weight by reference to the *perceived* enormity of the crime that *may* take place, in order to justify an extra-judicial policy of shoot to kill. In this way the context of what is considered reasonable is shifted towards more brutal policing methods. This paradigm shift, of which Kratos is a part, is born of an increased use of exceptional measures. This leads many to claim that what is needed is a return to a firmer rule of law in order to resist the tendency to resort to states of emergency to fight the "war on terror". But this is a category mistake, for states of emergency are not departures from law, but are rooted within it.

In a footnote, Pashukanis says that when it comes to

times of heightened revolutionary struggle, we can observe how the official machinery of the bourgeois state apparatus retires into the background as compared with the volunteer corps of the fascists and others. This further substantiates the fact that, when the balance of society is upset, it seeks

---

31: McGuirk, 2004, p3 .
32: de Than, 2001, p419.
33: Brady v UK (3 April 2001), quoted in de Than, 2001, p418.
34: de Than, 2001, p419.

salvation not in the creation of a power standing above society, but in the maximal harnessing of all forces of the classes in conflict.[35]

This passage is problematic as it suggests that the ruling class can simply and consciously put aside the law for its own preservation. If this were so, then it would seem to negate his central point about law's roots in the objective relations of capital, relations in which they themselves dominate. Mark Cowling identifies the problem as that of "the idea of equivalence and the idea of class terror [coming into] conflict with one another".[36]

Pashukanis is right that at the most acute phases of class struggle, such as existed in Russia in 1917 or Italy a few years later, the ruling class does act in the way he describes. But in order to understand the ever closer and more permanent relationship between law and the state of exception, we must look beyond Pashukanis. What has become increasingly evident over the last century has been the fact that in most cases the ruling class is able to manage its way through crises not by abandoning law, but rather by extending its reach.

### The "state of exception"

Giorgio Agamben argues that the "state of exception", which has with increasing frequency been used to justify extreme departures from the liberal norms of the rule of law, is in fact a function of law itself.[37] Here Agamben is drawing on the work of two critics of capitalist democracy; from the right Carl Schmitt who argued that the state of exception is the necessary foundation of sovereign power[38] and from the left Walter Benjamin who posited that "'the state of emergency' in which we live is not the exception but the rule".[39] Indeed, as long ago as 1851 Marx identified the apparent anomaly of states of exception being written into law in his critique of the liberal-democratic French Constitution of November 1848.[40]

There are many problems in Agamben's work, particularly his ahistorical attempt to explain the state of exception as a feature of all

---

35: Pashukanis, 1989, p139n.
36: Cowling, 2008, p191,
37: Agamben, 2005.
38: Schmitt, 1985.
39: Benjamin, 1992, Thesis VIII at pp248-249.
40: Marx, 1851: "Observe...throughout that the French constitution guarantees liberty, but always with the proviso of exceptions made by law, or which may still be made! and all the exceptions made by the Emperor Napoleon, by the restoration, and by Louis Philippe, have not only been retained, but, after the June Revolution, immeasurably multiplied."

human civilisations stretching back to antiquity and beyond. Indeed, in this he departs from all his key influences—Schmitt, Benjamin, Arendt, Foucault—by ignoring the specificity of how power is exercised in modernity. Nonetheless, his work offers some very useful insights by developing the relationship between law and the state of exception that is merely hinted at in Benjamin's "Theses on the Philosophy of History". In doing this Agamben provides a necessary corrective to the idealised celebration of the rule of law that exists amongst the liberal left and indeed among a significant portion of the Marxist left.[41]

It has become a feature of modern capitalist democracies to call in aid tactics which violate the norms of the rule of law, yet which are justified on the basis of defending the rule of law against existential threats, real or imagined. After almost a decade of the "war on terror" examples are familiar and numerous—Guantanamo Bay, extraordinary rendition, water-boarding, control orders, etc. This argument has, of course, also been used by the police when they claim that they are facing "unprecedented circumstances" which necessitate the deployment of more brutal tactics. The danger in this approach was recognised more than 30 years ago by the ECtHR, when the court ruled that there were limits to the use of national security in justifying extreme methods, even, or perhaps especially, legal ones:

> The Court, being aware of the danger such a law poses of undermining or even destroying democracy on the ground of defending it, affirms that the Contracting States may not, in the name of the struggle against terrorism, adopt whatever measures they deem appropriate.[42]

And, in words that brought a cheer from every civil libertarian, Lord Hoffman famously declared in a case which struck down New Labour's policy of detention without trial of terrorist suspects that "the real threat to the life of the nation, in the sense of a people living in accordance with its traditional laws and political values, comes not from terrorism but from laws such as these".[43] However, the decision of the House of Lords in that case was not that it was illegal for the government to detain without trial per se, but that the policy was discriminatory, as it did not apply to British citizens,

---

41: See, for example, Thompson, 1977.

42: Klass v Federal Republic of Germany (1978), quoted in Hillyard, 1993, p266.

43: A and others v Secretary of State for the Home Department (2004), UKHL 56, at para 97—www.publications.parliament.uk/pa/ld200405/ldjudgmt/jd041216/a&oth-1.htm

thus breaching the principle of equivalence. The government responded with control orders, which to date stand in law.

In mainstream discussions of the problem of the state of exception, it is presented as a contradiction which exposes the gap between the self-identity of liberal democratic societies and the abuses committed by certain governments or state agencies. For Agamben, on the other hand, the state of exception is in fact a latent yet integral function of sovereignty, embodied as much in capitalist democracy as in fascist and other authoritarian political systems. Agamben argues that the claim by the state of the need to protect itself, and wider society, against perceived threats requires it to regularly impose sanctions which fall outside the rule of law. The contradiction thus emerges in that the rule of law can only be protected by regularly going outside the rule of law. Agamben gives as an example the Nazi state, which throughout its existence did not abolish the liberal Weimar constitution, but merely suspended it at regular intervals.[44] Thus, legally, the "lawlessness" of the Nazis was in fact rooted in the liberal constitutional Weimar Republic. And in a perverse piece of legal formality, just prior to being sent to the death camps German Jews were stripped of their citizenship, precisely so that they would not be covered by the normal legal rights of other citizens.[45]

In a like manner, although at a far lower level of barbarism, in Britian shoot to kill has evolved from an unofficial and ad hoc tactic into a policy of extra-judicial killing in the form of the Kratos policy. The ability of the police to act beyond the bounds of the rule of law has, paradoxically, become written into law. This creates a space around the *suspected* suicide bomber, where the norms of criminal law and police practice are suspended. Yet its status as an official policy, implemented without violating the norms of governmental procedure, grounds this extra-legal policy within the framework of the law. One police officer has attempted to justify Kratos on the basis that it authorises not shoot to kill but the right to take action which, "in order to save life, may have to take life".[46] Echoes here of the infamous comment made by a senior US Army officer during the Vietnam War: "It became necessary to destroy the town in order to save it." This barbaric contradiction in terms recurs throughout the arguments used to justify draconian anti-terrorist measures. The rule of law must be suspended in order to preserve the rule of law.

---

44: Agamben, 1998, p168.
45: Agamben, 1998, p132.
46: Sir Chris Fox, Chairman of ACPO, quoted in "Police defend shooting strategy", BBC News Report, 8 March 2006, http://news.bbc.co.uk/1/hi/england/london/4784688.stm

The situations in which the police adopt lethal force are often described as "unprecedented", with suspects as "dangerous", "desperate", "won't be taken alive", etc. In striking the balance between the reasonable use of force and the perceived danger posed by the suspect, the mean point gets moved to an extremity. A senior member of the security forces explained how the language of necessity was used to justify lethal force in Northern Ireland: "Was it a decision to kill those people? I don't think it would have been phrased like that. Somebody would have said, 'How far do we go to remove this group of terrorists?' and the answer would have been, 'As far as *necessary*'." [47]

Similar arguments were used by the Nazis and other totalitarian regimes in the cause of maintaining stability and the security of the state. Indeed, it was this logic that led Schmitt from a critical defender of the Weimar Republic into a supporter and theorist for the Nazis. In the conflict between human rights and security, the latter must always trump the former, for without security there cannot be a social framework strong enough to support human rights. This is but a concrete expression of Agamben's point that

> It is as if the judicial order contained an essential fracture between the position of the norm and its application, which, in extreme situations, can be filled only by means of the state of exception, that is, by creating a zone in which application is suspended, but the law, as such, remains in force. [48]

Agamben allows us to grasp the interrelationship between law and the state of exception, and thus fill the gap left in Pashukanis's formulation. In attempting to answer the question as to why the evolution of an official shoot to kill policy has met with relatively little outcry compared to the scandal that followed the killings by the RUC in the early 1980s, Agamben's work illuminates the essential role of law in grounding and thus normalising exceptional and brutal police tactics. The retreat of the organised working class and the concomitant decay in politics have left a gap that has been occupied by law. Benjamin's injunction that we confront "states of emergency" with a real state of emergency is a call to reject the confines of the rule of law when faced with state violence. The failure to do so leads

47: "Political Killings in Northern Ireland", Amnesty UK, February 1994, p5 (emphasis added), available at www.amnesty.org/en/library/asset/EUR45/001/1994/en/5d33d0df-c38d-4a61-b7d8-358b1933b66d/eur450011994en.pdf
48: Agamben, 2005, p31.

one into accepting the legal form on which the legitimacy of state violence rests. This is precisely the mistake made by EP Thompson and his followers who argue that the rule of law is a "universal good" which supposedly transcends capitalism.[49]

A crucial aspect missing from Agamben's analysis is an understanding of what grounds law and the state of exception, as well as what makes these concepts evolve over time. Instead he points to a highly obscure figure in early Roman law, *homo sacer* (sacred man), as a recurring figure in Western societies.[50] The *homo sacer* refers to someone who "may be killed, but not sacrificed." In other words, this person has no value—their life may be taken away without legal sanction. Thus, Agamben argues, the *homo sacer* is representative of those targeted by the law under a state of exception as being beyond the protection of the law. But Agamben is not able to explain why certain groups or individuals are capable of becoming *homo sacer* and others not. Indeed, he goes so far at one point as to suggest that today we may all be *homines sacri*.[51]

He appears to argue (Agamben is obscure at the best of times) that anyone who poses a threat to the state, or whom the state merely perceives as a threat is liable to become the *homo sacer*. If this is so it raises the question of why the working class as a whole or even significant sections of it have not been subjected to this process. The reason why this is so is because the always present, if hidden, power of the working class cannot be legislated or terrorised away. Working class organisation can be smashed, but the latent power of the working class is impossible to eliminate. To place any powerful group in society within the category of the *homo sacer* would fundamentally destabilise the rule of capital. Thus Nazi terror on the streets was necessary politically to break the power of the organised left and the trade unions before those sections of the working class could be made the *homo sacer*.

Nonetheless, even under fascism capital cannot escape the logic of the legal form that, as Pashukanis convincingly argues, is the necessary guarantor of commodity exchange. Thus the fetish of legal formalities that pervaded Nazi rule is not the anomaly it at first appears. The racist content of Nazi law was, of course, qualitatively different than that which exists under capitalist democracy, and all the gains achieved by the working class such as collective bargaining rights were abolished. Yet the basic legal form remained because the economic base of capitalism remained. Not only

---

49: Thompson, 1977, pp258-69.
50: Agamben, 1998.
51: Agamben, 1998, p115.

did the Nazis keep to the legal niceties of the constitutional state, but the working class continued to sell their labour power on the basis of a contractual exchange with employers. For this reason when the demand for labour exceeded supply during the late 1930s, particularly in the construction industry, wages went up in some cases by 30 percent.[52]

So while the *homo sacer* is flawed as an analysis of the generalised form of capitalist rule, as a metaphor it does provide a very useful way of understanding how the police, in the example under discussion here, are able to kill without being legally culpable. Indeed, it would seem to reinforce Pashukanis's theory by identifying the extent to which legal rights are co-determinate with the measuring of value. Subjects who are from the point of view of the state expendable or individually dangerous can be made into *homines sacri*, at the mercy of the state's monopoly of violence. This can certainly apply to, for example, refugees, terrorist suspects or other "subversives". The process by which such lives are devalued, and the way in which the law colludes in this is discussed next.

## Suspect Communities

Contrary to the claims made by the Metropolitan Police following the killing of de Menezes that terrorist attacks on the Tube were unprecedented, the very first bombing of the London Underground took place more than a century earlier in 1883. At first the Irish were blamed, although later it transpired that the bomb had been the work of anarchists. As a result, the police and the press began targeting the Jewish community, which was identified as a hotbed of anarchist refugees from Eastern Europe.

The barrister Richard Harvey has drawn the obvious analogy with Harry Stanley, Diarmuid O'Neill, Neil McConville and Jean Charles de Menezes. What all had in common was membership, or *perceived* membership, of communities which had been viewed as and thus targeted as suspect. Once it was Jewish communities who were perceived as a breeding ground for anarchist violence, followed by the Irish community harbouring Republican terrorists; today it is Muslim communities supposedly encompassing Al Qaida sympathisers that fulfil the role of a suspect community.[53] In this demonisation of minority communities lie the origins of the elite police squads tasked with the use of lethal force. The Special Irish Branch was set up to fight the Irish Republican Fenian movement in the 1880s. This has since changed its name to the less offensive sounding, though no less offensive in deed, Special

---

52: Grunberger, 1974, pp241-242.
53: Harvey, 2006, pp3-4.

Branch. It was officers from SO19 of the Special Branch that carried out the killings of O'Neill, Stanley and de Menezes.

Paddy Hillyard coined the term "suspect community" to describe

> a sub-group of the population that is singled out for state attention as being "problematic". Specifically in terms of policing, individuals may be targeted, not necessarily as a result of suspected wrong doing, but simply because of their presumed membership of that sub-group. Race, ethnicity, religion, class, gender, language, accent, dress, political ideology or any combination of these factors may serve to delineate the sub-group.[54]

Muslims, as a suspect community, are often portrayed as anti-Enlightenment and thus anti human rights, threatening a "civilised" way of life.[55] But, as the authors of a recent study at London Metropolitan University argue, it is also symptomatic of a discourse of "anti-rationality" of the suspect community as fanatical and immune to reason or argument.[56]

In the case of Neil McConville, shot dead in April 2003 by the Police Service of Northern Ireland (PSNI), the justification for his death was created after the event, by suggestions fed by the PSNI that he was variously linked to paramilitaries or drug gangs. In the days following the killing of McConville headlines in the press included allegations of involvement in these criminal activities, all of which were completely untrue. The same thing happened with Harry Stanley, when a list of his previous, spent criminal convictions was read out to the inquest into his death despite their complete irrelevance to the circumstances surrounding the shooting. Again, with de Menezes, the police circulated smears in the media about alleged drug use and his immigration status. Of course none of these allegations were intended to justify the police's actions per se; their aim was to associate the victims with certain groups who would be considered of lesser value—criminals, drug dealers/users, illegal immigrants—thus devaluing their claim to a legal right not to be murdered by the state. As Hillyard points out:

> Once dehumanised, people can be viewed with ethical indifference and moral questions are of no concern to [the police] carrying out their tasks.

---

54: Pantazis and Pemberton , 2009, p649.
55: Fitzpatrick, 2001, p207-212.
56: Nickels and others, 2009.

[The police] are only doing their job. As violence has become increasingly concentrated under state control, moral responsibility is replaced by a technical responsibility.[57]

De Menezes was neither Muslim nor from the Middle East. What set off the chain of events which led to his death was the misidentification of him by the police surveillance team as a "North African male". Likewise, Harry Stanley was shot dead by armed police to whom it had been reported that he had an Irish accent when in fact he was Scottish. What these two examples show is the way in which the suspect community is defined by appearances, by superficial attributes.[58] This reverses the normal modus operandi of policing whereby evidence or hard intelligence is the prerequisite for the use of force. Moreover, the fact that in both these cases the victim was misidentified simply points up the extent to which perceived membership of the suspect community is sufficient to give rise to an "honest belief" by police that lethal use of force is necessary and proportionate. Had Stanley not had an "Irish" accent or de Menezes a darkish skin, both would probably still be alive today. And as we saw above, "honest belief" forms the basis for the legal defence of police officers who kill unarmed or innocent suspects. In this insidious manner racist and cultural stereotypes become legal justifications for the taking of life by state agents.

Hillyard has pointed out how the Prevention of Terrorism Act 1974 (PTA) effectively introduced a "dual system of criminal justice", one system operating under the PTA and the other under ordinary criminal law. As a result a dichotomy developed between terrorist suspects and "ordinary decent criminals".[59] Today we face a similar separation between those subjected to recent anti-terrorist legislation as distinct from regular criminal law.[60] This distinction functions within both law and a broader social context, with one reinforcing the other. The threat from terrorists is exaggerated by politicians and media alike. This in turn creates a greater sense

---

57: Hillyard, 1993, p96.
58: The identification of certain aspects of physical appearance as denoting the potential for criminal behaviour has been a feature of criminology and policing since at least the mid-19th century. See, Horn 2003. This paradigm is at work today in such standard police practice as "profiling".
59: Hillyard, 1993, p93.
60: The blurring of the boundaries between these two spheres of law, for example in the extensive use of stop and search powers under Section 44 of the Terrorism Act 2000, has raised serious concerns about the broader threat to civil liberties. This process is the subject of Agamben's work as discussed above.

of fear of violence about the suspect community in general, and that small minority seeking to use violence in particular. This dynamic then provides a platform for the introduction of ever more draconian laws, and brutal police methods. The argument from the police and others is that the threat from Al Qaida is wholly Muslim just as the threat from the IRA was mostly Irish, and thus it is reasonable to target those communities. Yet we must not forget that this "dual system" is not one of completely distinct and hermetically sealed areas of law. The foundational principles of the rule of law do not permit such a thing. Norms, legal tests and police practice are constantly migrating between the two. Think, for example, of how anti-terror legislation has been used to detain protesters or to stop and search individuals suspected of petty crimes. The state of exception and its associated policing strategies become the norm. Hillyard's detailed study on how violence targeted the Irish community comes to this conclusion:

> It is commonplace to counter-pose the rule of law to the abuse of power or acts of violence. Law, from this perspective, is seen as the antithesis of violence... [But] this dichotomy [is] false... Law is...an integral part of the repression and organisation of state violence.[61]

## Conclusion
In hindsight, the period lasting from the later half of the 19th century through to the 1960s saw the proliferation of various mechanisms that in a thousand strands bound the working class ideologically to capitalism. In Gramscian terms, hegemony was manifested in aspects of civil society such as education, culture, community identity, civic projects, etc. The police were successfully woven into this apparatus as a necessary, if not necessarily benign, method of preserving social cohesion. But, as Reiner puts it, "when neoliberalism unravelled this complex of subtle, hidden controls, the thin blue line turned out to be a Maginot line".[62] Thus, on the one hand, the role of the police in maintaining order within capitalist democracy has not altered fundamentally in the last 150 years or so. Yet, on the other hand, the retreat of the organised working class in the face of neoliberalism has revealed the violence that exists at the heart of policing and the rule of law. The problem has been that throughout this period the ideology of the rule of law has become ever stronger, and indeed has been taken up by

---

61: Hillyard, 1993, p262.
62: Reiner, 2010, p31.

sections of the left as the solution to the problem of police violence. My aim here has been to demonstrate, using Pashukanis's commodity-form theory of law, Agamben's work on the state of exception and Hillyard's description of suspect communities, how the law as such (not merely particular laws or legal systems) is complicit in legitimising police violence, even at the extreme end involving the deliberate killing of innocent people.

This is not to argue that we should, in an ultra-leftist manner, simply reject law in all circumstances. Neither should we be indifferent to changes in the law which increase the powers of the police. The rhetoric of capitalist democracy with its claims to freedom and human rights is always in conflict with its actual operation. Just as we demand the right to be wage-slaves while rejecting wage-slavery, so too we must continue to insist on the right to have legal rights, while having no illusions in the legal form. Campaigns to hold the police to account for their violent acts must be accompanied by a vision that seeks to transcend the "narrow horizons of bourgeois right".[63]

---

63: Marx, 1992, p347.

# References

Agamben, Giorgio, 1998, *Homo Sacer: Sovereign Power and Bare Life* (Stanford University).

Agamben, Giorgio, 2005, *State of Exception* (University of Chicago).

Arendt, Hannah, 1994, *Eichmann in Jerusalem: A Report into the Banality of Evil* (Penguin).

Asmal, Kader, 1985, *Shoot to Kill? International Lawyers' Inquiry in to the Lethal Use of Firearms by the Security Forces in Northern Ireland* (Mercier).

Benjamin, Walter, 1992, "Theses on the Philosophy of History", in *Illuminations* (Fontana), www.marxists.org/reference/archive/benjamin/1940/history.htm

Cohen, Phil, 1979, "Policing the Working Class City", in Bob Fine, Richard Kinsey, John Lea, Sol Picciotto and Jock Young (eds), *Capitalism and the Rule of Law: From Deviancy Theory to Marxism* (Hutchinson).

Cowling, Mark, 2008, *Marxism and Criminological Theory: A Critique and a Toolkit* (Palgrave Macmillan).

de Than, Claire, 2001, "Mistaken Belief in Self-Defence May Justify Use of Lethal Force", *Journal of Criminal Law*, 65 (5).

Farrell, Audrey, 1992, *Crime, Class and Corruption: The Politics of the Police* (Bookmarks).

Fitzpatrick, Peter, 2001, *Modernism and the Grounds of Law* (Cambridge University).

Foucault, Michel, 1991, *Discipline and Punish: The Birth of the Prison* (Penguin).

Grunberger, Richard, 1974, *A Social History of the Third Reich* (Penguin).

Harvey, Richard J, 2006, "Shoot to Kill: Address to Conference on 'Fatal Shootings: Law Practice and Policy in Shoot to Kill Era'", transcript in possession of author.

Hay, Douglas, Peter Linebaugh, John G Rule, E P Thompson, and Cal Winslow, 1977, "Property, Authority and the Criminal Law", in *Albion's Fatal Tree* (Peregrine).

Head, Michael, 2008, *Evgeny Pashukanis: A Critical Reappraisal* (Routledge-Cavendish).

Hernon, Ian, 2006, *Riot!: Civil Insurrection from Peterloo to the Present Day* (Pluto).

Hillyard, Paddy, 1993, *Suspect Communities: People's Experiences of the Prevention of Terrorism Acts on Britain* (Pluto).

Horn, David G, 2003, *The Criminal Body: Lombroso and the Anatomy of Deviance* (Routledge).

Lenin, VI, 1965, *The State and Revolution: The Marxist Theory of the State and the Tasks of the Proletariat* (Progress), www.marxists.org/archive/lenin/works/1917/staterev/index.htm

Marx, Karl, 1851, "The Constitution of the French Republic", in the Chartist paper *Notes to the People*, www.marxists.org/archive/marx/works/1851/06/14.htm

Marx, Karl, 1970, "Preface" to *A Contribution to the Critique of Political Economy* (International Publishers), www.marxists.org/archive/marx/works/1859/critique-pol-economy/preface.htm

Marx, Karl, 1975, "On the Jewish Question", in *Early Writings* (Penguin), www.marxists.org/archive/marx/works/1844/jewish-question/

Marx, Karl, 1976, *Capital: volume 1* (Penguin), www.marxists.org/archive/marx/works/1867-c1/

Marx, Karl, 1992, "Critique of the Gotha Programme", in *The First International and After* (Penguin), available at www.marxists.org/archive/marx/works/1875/gotha/index.htm

McGuirk, Noel, 2004, "Justice—Lessons from Northern Ireland?", in Gorazd Mesko, Milan Pagon and Bojan Dobovsek (eds), *Policing in Central and Eastern Europe: Dilemmas of Contemporary Criminal Justice* (University of Maribor), www.ncjrs.gov/pdffiles1/nij/Mesko/208013.pdf

Nickels, Henri C and Lyn Thomas, Mary J Hickman and Sara Silvestri, 2009, "A Comparative Study of the Representations of 'Suspect' Communities in Multi-Ethnic Britain and of Their Impact on Irish Communities and Muslim Communities—Mapping Newspaper Content", www.londonmet.ac.uk/fms/MRSite/Research/iset/WP13%20H%20Nickels%203.pdf

"Ombudsman's Report on the Circumstances of the Death of Mr Neil McConville on 29 April 2003", www.policeombudsman.org/publicationsuploads/NEILL-McCONVILLE.pdf

Pantazis, Christina and Pemberton, Simon, 2009, "From the 'Old' to the 'New' Suspect Community: Examining the Impacts of Recent UK Counter-Terrorist Legislation", *British Journal of Criminology*, 49.

Pashukanis, Evgeny, 1989, *Law and Marxism: A General Theory* (Pluto), www.marxists.org/archive/pashukanis/1924/law/index.htm

Reiner, Robert, 2010, *The Politics of the Police* (Oxford University).

Schmitt, Carl, 1985, *Political Theology: Four Chapters on the Concept of Sovereignty* (MIT).

Sparks, Colin, 1984, "Towards a Police State?", *International Socialism* 25 (autumn).

Thompson, EP, 1977, *Whigs and Hunters: The Origin of the Black Act* (Peregrine).

Veitch, Scott, 2007, *Law and Irresponsibility: On the Legitimation of Human Suffering* (Routledge-Cavendish).

# Labourism and socialism:
# Ralph Miliband's Marxism

*Paul Blackledge*

It is more than a little ironic that the recent race for the leadership of the Labour Party came down to a contest between the Miliband brothers.[1] For their dad, Ralph, was the author of a devastating socialist critique of the Labour Party, *Parliamentary Socialism*. Ralph Miliband (1924-1994) was, alongside Edward Thompson, Eric Hobsbawm and Perry Anderson, one of the best known academic Marxists of his generation, and an important public intellectual: he was a socialist who always looked beyond the walls of the academy to influence wider debates, and in particular debates within the British and international labour and socialist movements. In a positive but critical review of *Divided Societies*—his excellent defence of class politics in a context of the bulk of the academic left's dismissal of this idea as out of date—Duncan Hallas described Miliband as floating "between the best of the academic left and revolutionary left".[2]

Hallas was right. And it is because of this that Miliband's work deserves to be read by a new generation of socialists. Nevertheless, he should be read critically. Books like *Parliamentary Socialism* (1961), *The State in Capitalist Society* (1969), *Marxism and Politics* (1977), *Capitalist Democracy*

1:    This essay is a revised version of Blackledge, 2008. Thanks to the editors of the collection in which that essay was published, and to Colin Barker, Ian Birchall, Alex Callinicos, Christian Høgsbjerg and Jonny Jones for comments on this revised version.
2:    Hallas, 1990.

*in Britain* (1982) and *Divided Societies* (1989) offer a rich source of insight into politics in modern capitalist societies, but as we shall see they are also flawed in important ways.

In *Parliamentary Socialism* Miliband powerfully exposed how the Labour leadership consistently helped maintain the capitalist system by playing a "major role in the management of discontent", and how the Labour left, despite its tendency to mount periodic "revolts" against the leadership, shared a fundamental worldview with the party's right which meant that these "revolts" remained trapped within the politics of "Labourism": "an ideology of social reform, within the framework of capitalism, with no serious ambition of transcending that framework".[3]

Though *Parliamentary Socialism* is arguably Miliband's finest work,[4] he is perhaps best known in academic circles as one of the two key protagonists, alongside Nicos Poulantzas, of an important, if very flawed, debate on state theory.[5] This debate was significant not only because of its enormous influence on the academic left in the 1970s, but also because for both men it was part of a broader attempt to raise theory to the level of practice. Miliband's own commitment to socialist political practice stretched back at least as far as 1940, when as a 16 year old Jewish refugee from fascism he swore at Marx's grave a private oath of allegiance to "the workers' cause". Later he was active in the left wing Bevanite and Victory for Socialism movements in the Labour Party before playing an important role in the British New Left. In the wake of the collapse of the New Left in the early 1960s he founded and co-edited, alongside the Marxist historian John Saville, the *Socialist Register*.[6] Subtitled a "survey of movements and ideas", by the 1970s Miliband was pushing at the limits of this approach, and in its 1976 issue he opened a debate on how the left could "move on" to become a real living force in British politics.[7]

In the wake of the publication of this essay, he attempted both to theorise socialist political practice, and to shape contemporary events through political activity. Alongside the books noted above, Miliband's essay "The New Revisionism in Britain" (1985) should be required reading for anyone interested in fighting for socialism. In the 1980s he wrote as an activist first within the Socialist Society—which he conceived as a project of "socialist

---

3:   Miliband,1972, p376; 1983, p293.
4:   Burnham, 2008, p48.
5:   For criticisms of the positions taken by both Miliband and Poulantzas see Barker, 1977; 1979a; 1979b.
6:   Blackledge, 2005.
7:   Miliband, 1976.

renewal inside the labour movement"—and then as a key member of the Independent Left Corresponding Society—which was conceived as a left wing think tank advising Tony Benn.[8] He also debated with the Socialist Workers Party (SWP) at our annual Marxism events at sessions attended by his young and enthusiastic son Ed.[9]

Evidently neither we nor his father convinced Ed of the power of Marxism. Superficially, that might seem a minor example of familial betrayal, and at one level it is: there is a continuing tradition of Milibandian Marxism embedded in the *Socialist Register* which has continued as an annual beacon of socialist internationalism in the decade and a half since his death. Nevertheless, there is a sense in which Miliband's more or less right wing Labourite sons followed in their father's footsteps.[10] For the author of *Parliamentary Socialism* ended his days believing that the Labour Party was the only viable alternative to the Tories. Thus in his posthumously published last book, *Socialism for a Sceptical Age* (1994), he reluctantly concluded that "the best the left can hope for in the relevant future…is the strengthening of left reformism as a current of thought and policy in social democratic parties".[11]

That he came to this conclusion in the wake of a serious and sustained attempt to build an independent socialist organisation demands serious consideration on these pages. Miliband dropped out of the Labour Party in the mid-1960s and in both the concluding sections of his second book, *The State in Capitalist Society* and the second edition of *Parliamentary Socialism* (1972), he tentatively suggested that the left should move beyond the negative critique of the Labour Party outlined in the first edition of this book, to begin the more positive process of building a socialist alternative to Labour. Undaunted by a situation in which the Labour Party could not be expected to fight for socialism and where he regarded the extra-parliamentary left as too small and too fragmented to mount a serious challenge to the system, Miliband insisted that the "absence of a viable socialist alternative is no reason for resigned acceptance or for the perpetuation of hopes which have no basis in political reality". If the second half of this sentence might have been written to immunise our generation against illusions in his own son, over the next decade and a half he attempted to

---

8:   Newman, 2002, pp271; 299-308; 2008, pp36-44.
9:   After I'd debated Miliband's legacy at a *Historical Materialism* conference a few years ago I was somewhat surprised to find that Ed Miliband was in the audience. He told me that in his youth he enjoyed tagging along with his dad to Marxism to listen to him debate with the SWP!
10:  Newman, 2002, p339.
11:  Miliband, 1994, p148.

follow through on the promise of the first half of the sentence by making a powerful argument for, and effort to build, "such an alternative".[12]

A comprehensive account of Miliband's attempt to build a new socialist organisation would necessarily involve a detailed account of the history both of the Socialist Society and of his later relationship with Benn. Unfortunately, in lieu of the publication of Tony Armstrong's important research on this topic,[13] the core of my essay deals more narrowly with Miliband's theoretical arguments; only highlighting their influence on his practice in my conclusion. If I consequently focus on the weaknesses of his thought this should not be misconstrued as a wholly negative critique. Miliband is worth criticising because he made a serious attempt to contribute to socialist politics, and this essay is intended to contribute to a critical assessment of his legacy.

Concretely, I suggest that Miliband's shift from a project of building a new socialist party to settling for work inside the Labour Party was not a pragmatic response to the events of the last decade or so of his life, but rather illuminated limitations of his earlier attempt to theorise socialist organisation. Two key issues stand out. On the one hand, his analysis of Labourism never matched the power of his description of Labour's failings. Though he provided mountains of evidence of the conservative nature of both the Labour and trade union bureaucracy, because his explanation for this behaviour was superficial—he conceived Labourism primarily as an ideological error—he failed to provide an adequate frame for revolutionary politics. On the other hand he never adequately came to terms with Lenin's contribution to Marxism, and this failing was related to his inadequate attempt to conceptualise Stalinism.[14] Taken together, these gaps in his thought informed an ambiguous relationship with the Labour left and his final unenthusiastic embrace of the Labour Party.

By contrast with these analytical weaknesses, Miliband had, in a number of articles from "The Transition to the Transition" (1958) through to "Reflections on the Crisis of Communist Regimes" (1989), suggested

---

12: Miliband, 1972, pp376-7; 1969, p245.

13: Armstrong, 2010. For an overview of the Socialist Society see Newman, 2002, pp270-278.

14: Despite a sympathetic analysis of Lenin's *The State and Revolution* (Miliband, 1970), Miliband never adequately addressed Lenin's Marxism. The French philosopher of science Gaston Bachelard described situations like this, when there appears to be a "resistance of thought to thought", as "epistemological obstacles" (Lecourt, 1975, p135). Lenin was such an obstacle to Miliband. Unfortunately, this is a typical failing of contemporary leftists. Thanks to Alex Callinicos for pointing me to Bachelard's argument.

an approach to socialist politics through which a more coherent answer to these questions might be conceived. In these essays he argued that a sound theory of socialist political organisation must include both a systematic account of Stalinism, and a socio-economic analysis of the context of social democratic practice. I argue that it is by following through on these suggestions that socialists might realise the strongest aspects of Miliband's attempt to raise theory to the level of practice as suggested in, among other places, "Moving On" (1976) and *Marxism and Politics*. For though Miliband ultimately failed to realise the project outlined in these writings, the questions he asked about socialist politics and the detailed empirical research he carried out continue to offer a rich source of insight that commands serious and critical attention from the left.

## From Parliamentary Socialism to "Moving On"

Miliband had been thinking about the possibility of building an independent socialist organisation since the days of the first New Left in the late 1950s, and though he broached the topic in the second edition of *Parliamentary Socialism*, it was not until the publication of "Moving On" in 1976 that he explicitly argued for the formation of such a party.

In "Moving On" Miliband posed with stark clarity the key problem facing socialists in the Labour Party: "The belief in the effective transformation of the Labour Party into an instrument of socialist policies is the most crippling of all illusions to which socialists in Britain have been prone", and far from activists capturing the Labour Party, the Labour Party tends to capture the activists.[15]

Despite the unambiguous nature of this claim, the analysis of Labourism outlined in *Parliamentary Socialism* was, as David Coates has pointed out, "very much a buried and underdeveloped one".[16] Miliband defined the "Labourism" characteristic of both the left and right of the party, minimally, by its parliamentarianism: the Labour Party is among the most "dogmatic" of workers' parties, "not about socialism, but about the parliamentary system".[17] When originally penned these lines were intended to inform "an eleventh-hour call for the party to be transformed into an agency for the establishment of socialism, rather than a plea to leave the party".[18] Interestingly, although he signalled his break with this

---

15:  Miliband, 1976, pp128, 131.
16:  Coates, 2003, p73; 1975, p134.
17:  Miliband, 1972, p13.
18:  Newman, 2003, p57; see also Miliband and Saville, 1964, p156; Miliband, 1965, p193.

perspective in the second edition of the book, he did not complement this changed perspective with a deepened analysis of the nature of Labourism. In 1972, as in 1961, he explained the limitations of the Labour Party by the ideology of parliamentarianism. To the extent that he provided some implied socio-economic basis for this claim he suggested that a deep-seated commitment to parliamentary democracy was evident not only within the Labour Party but also within the working class more generally. Consequently, the socialist left would have to address this ideology if they were to challenge Labourism for hegemony within the British labour movement.

In as far as it goes, this argument is unobjectionable: reformism runs deep within the British working class, and the Labour Party, partially at least, reflects this situation. However, this doesn't take us very far, and certainly doesn't provide the kind of systematic socio-economic analysis of Labourism that Miliband himself had demanded as early as 1958.[19] This is important because, although Miliband ably *described* the failings of the Labour Party, by focusing on its ideological aspect rather than its social roots his explanation of these failings tended to be weak. A key consequence of this undeveloped conception of Labourism is that, despite the claim that the belief in the possibility of transforming the Labour Party into a socialist organisation was a "crippling illusion", Miliband never completely closed the door to this idea.

Like Miliband, classical Marxists have pointed to the debilitating consequences of the Labour Party's parliamentarianism. However, whereas Miliband explained this weakness as a function of the ideology of Labourism, classical Marxists have argued that this ideology was in turn rooted in the nature of trade unionism in modern liberal democracies. Within capitalist democracies the trade union bureaucracy acts to mediate between capital and labour, and consequently functions as the structural expression of the partial negation of the power of capital within capitalist social relations. The Labour Party is the political expression of this bureaucracy as it attempts to realise its political goals through the state. This is the social basis of Labour's parliamentarianism. However, because the state is structurally interdependent with capital, this political project cannot point beyond capitalism, and this explains why Lenin judged the Labour Party to be a capitalist workers' party. Though its membership, and more so those who vote for it, are largely working class, the party itself is tied through this pivotal role of the trade union bureaucracy to capitalist social relations from which it cannot escape.[20]

---

19: Miliband, 1958.
20: Cliff and Gluckstein, 1996, p2.

The division of labour between the trade union bureaucracy and the Labour leadership means, moreover, that the Labour Party exists one step removed from the day to day struggles of the working class at the point of production. Though its electoral base is within the working class, the Labour Party tends to view class struggles as problems to be overcome from the point of view of the rational organisation of the state. In periods of capitalist expansion the Labour Party can respond to these struggles with reforms. However, in periods of recession and crisis Labour governments act to stabilise capitalism in the only way possible from the point of view of the capitalist state—they attempt to make workers pay for the crisis. By contrast, because the trade union bureaucracy directly mediates these conflicts it has an interest in acting as a barrier to untrammelled capitalist exploitation. Nevertheless, though more directly rooted in these struggles at the point of production, because the bureaucracy's role is to mediate rather than to overcome the relationship between capital and labour it is fundamentally a conservative social layer, and acts to dampen any movement that threatens to become a broader challenge to capitalism. The labour bureaucracy wants to see a healthy capitalist bakery so that workers might get more crumbs from the cake.

This socio-economic analysis suggests that though the Labour Party might talk left to win elections, when in power it will act in what it perceives to be the national interests of capital. The trade union bureaucracy, by contrast, because of its more direct relationship to struggles at the point of production, will tend to play a double-sided game: though essentially conservative it is able to act in a more radical manner depending on the concrete circumstances. Clearly socialist activists must learn to work both with and against the bureaucracy, depending on the context. And for this reason alone (there are others—unevenness of the class struggle, nature of the state etc), socialists need to be organised independently both from the trade union bureaucracy and more so from the Labour leadership.

This is an important part of the social basis for "Leninist" political organisation. Reformism is a general characteristic of the class struggle under capitalism, and reformist bureaucracies will tend to emerge as the mediation between reformist movements and the state. Moreover, wherever reforms become a real possibility these tendencies to bureaucratisation will tend to be strengthened. Socialist strategic orientation towards these bureaucracies is framed by the fact that they represent a partial negation of capitalism on the basis of movements from below which they nonetheless act to police.[21]

---

21: Callinicos, 1995; Cliff and Gluckstein, 1985.

Effectively to abstract the ideology of parliamentarianism from this mediating role, as did Miliband, lends itself to an approach which misunderstands the revolutionary critique of Labourism.[22] Indeed, Miliband caricatured the classical Marxist critique of reformism simply as an impotent ideological inversion of parliamentarianism. This was the basis for his rejection of the existing parties of the far left, when, in "Moving On", he argued for the creation of a new socialist party. In this essay he repeated his rejection of the Labour Party as a viable agency of socialist transformation because of its dogmatic attachment to parliamentarianism and dismissed the Communist Party because of its undemocratic structure. Others who had similarly distanced themselves from Stalinism and social democracy had been drawn into the orbit of the existing revolutionary left. By contrast, Miliband argued that the alternative Trotskyist organisations, because of their commitment to the insurrectionary model of the October Revolution, exhibited an "ultra-left" tendency to replace parliamentary cretinism with a form of "anti-parliamentary cretinism" that had "virtually no appeal to the British working class movement". Indeed, this ideology helped ensure the continued inability of such groups to break out of the political ghetto.[23]

The next issue of the *Socialist Register* carried replies to Miliband's arguments from activists within the Labour Party, the Communist Party and the SWP. For the SWP Duncan Hallas pointed out that Miliband's use of the term ultra-leftism was problematic because of its obvious ambiguity: the SWP was undoubtedly ultra-left in terms of contemporary debates in Britain, but it was not ultra-left in the sense that Lenin used the concept in 1920-1: what, Hallas asked, did Miliband mean when he used this term?[24]

To the extent that Miliband had addressed this issue he equated ultraleftism with the model of socialist transformation suggested by the Bolshevik Revolution: asserting that this model was inadequate for modern Western societies, where "a strategy of advance has to include a real measure of electoral support".[25] Commenting on this argument, Hallas wrote:

> if what is being said is that the Russia of 1917 and the Britain of today are so radically different that it is out of the question for the course of events in Britain to closely follow the pattern of the Russian events of 60 years ago then there is no dispute... If, however, what is being suggested is that

---

22: Cliff and Gluckstein, 1996, p90; Harman, 1998, pp347-354.
23: Miliband, 1976, p139.
24: Hallas, 1977, p8.
25: Miliband, 1976, p139.

there is, after all, some non-revolutionary road to socialism then we have to part company. "Moving On" does not *state* this position but it gives— to me at least—the impression of a certain equivocation. I hope that is a mistaken impression. For this is fundamental. We already have one major and one minor party—Labour Party and Communist Party—committed to the "parliamentary road"... There is no political space for a third.

Concretely, Hallas agreed that a socialist party "must strive for 'a real measure of electoral legitimation'", but insisted that "this necessary activity can never be its main thrust. That *must* be towards rooting the organisation in the workplaces and in the unions and in a wide variety of types of grassroots direct action. Nothing else makes sense unless you entertain the parliamentary illusion".[26]

Hallas argued that Miliband's "equivocation" over the need for revolution reflected a more general weakness characteristic of the majority of leading figures of the New Left generation of 1956: a "failure", and indeed a "refusal", to "take a clear and unequivocal stand against left reformism. It refused to come to grips with the Communist tradition in its original Leninist form and with the Left Opposition tradition that arose from it. It largely ignored the whole historical experience from 1914 to 1956. Significantly, it hardly discussed the Communist International. In short, it failed to develop a clear and consistent theoretical and political foundation".[27]

In his reply to this point, Miliband clarified his use of the term ultra-left as a description of the British revolutionary left. Ultra-leftism, he argued, involved "working towards the formation of a 'vanguard party' based on 'democratic centralism' and preparing for a seizure of power ... The model also includes...the 'smashing' of the bourgeois state and the establishment of the 'dictatorship of the proletariat'". Together, these features were witness to a "self-defeating and dangerous ... deep contempt for the institutions which make up capitalist democracy".[28] It followed from this argument, according to Miliband, that the ghettoisation of the far left was in part self-imposed. It was their politics that excluded them from cultivating popular support. Miliband provided the theoretical underpinnings for this argument in *Marxism and Politics*; a book which *de facto* rose to Hallas's challenge of addressing the historical experience of the Communist movement between 1914 and 1956.

---

26: Hallas, 1977, p10.
27: Hallas, 1977, p7; see Anderson 1980, p153.
28: Miliband, 1977a, p48.

## Marxism and Politics

Miliband opened *Marxism and Politics* with the assertion that Marxist political analyses had not generally been written as systematic treatises, but had been produced as a series of responses to a multiplicity of events, and as such did not exist as an easily summarised unity: they were, in a nutshell, "unsystematic and fragmentary". Moreover, the very term Marxist was a contested category, with no universally accepted criteria by which a Marxist could be defined.[29] Despite these problems, Miliband aimed to "reconstruct" a systematic politics from the various writings of a selection of Marxist theoreticians; and this reconstruction was explicitly made against the authoritarian "line" that had been "a particular quality of Stalinism"—an approach to politics from which the New Left of the 1950s had broken.[30] Miliband therefore located his discussion of Marxism in the context of the anti-Stalinism of the New Left, but rejected, nominally at least, the various left wing characterisations of the Stalinist regimes. He claimed that while "the subject badly requires serious and sustained Marxist political analysis", socialist anti-Stalinist debates on the nature of the Soviet regime had been "paralysed by the invocation of formulas and slogans—'degenerate workers' state' versus 'state capitalist' and so forth".[31]

Unfortunately, Miliband could not so easily disentangle his ideas from the problem of conceptualising Stalinism. As he himself recognised, the very idea of "Marxism-Leninism" was a Stalinist construct. Consequently, to write a study of the Marxist conception of the party entailed some engagement with the problem of the relationship between Stalinism and "Leninism".[32] With regard to this issue, Miliband's suggestion that "the argument turns on the meaning which is given to Stalinism" is obviously true, but only serves to refocus our attention, as we shall see below, on his own refusal to outline a detailed model of the Soviet regime. Negatively, he wrote, Lenin neither held absolute power, nor showed "the slightest sign" of striving for the kind of absolute power that Stalin came to hold; and although Russia did experience some repression under Lenin, the "sheer scale" of the repression experienced under Stalin's rule "distinguishes it most sharply from Leninism".[33] However, he insisted that, whereas the controversy over the nature of the Soviet regime was "obviously of some importance…no conclusive answer to the question

---

29: Miliband, 1977b, p1.
30: Miliband, 1977b, pp3-4.
31: Miliband, 1977b, p14.
32: Miliband, 1977b, p1.
33: Miliband, 1977b, p145; 1983, p199.

has ever been returned, or can be".[34] Why "no conclusive answer" could be made to the question of the nature of the Soviet Union was left in the air. However, despite Miliband's attempt to bypass this problem he obviously worked with some model of Stalinism, explicit or not, and this included the belief that the Stalinist states, despite their bureaucratic distortions, were regimes "of the left".

In *Socialism for a Sceptical Age* Miliband revealed that, while he believed East European "Communism" had "nothing to do with what Marx meant by communism", the disintegration of the Stalinist states in Eastern Europe had had a "deep influence" on his "thinking about socialism".[35] Indeed, he suggested that the collapse of the Soviet Union marked "the end of a particular alternative to capitalism", which was best understood as one of the many "defeats and disappointments which the left has suffered in recent decades".[36] This conclusion implied that the Soviet Union and its satellites were, if not socialist states, then to some sense progressive social formations when compared to Western capitalism. To a degree, therefore, Miliband offered an answer to a question he had posed in 1989: what did "the crisis of the Communist world signify for people who remain committed to the creation of a cooperative, democratic, egalitarian, and ultimately classless society?" He correctly pointed out that an answer to this question "requires first of all a clear perception of what kind of regimes are in crisis". Explicitly, his characterisation of the "Communist" regimes appeared much more critical than his mourning of the collapse of these states would suggest. He argued that the East European states were "oligarchical collectivist regimes", which were the products of revolutions that brought about "fundamental changes in property relations", whether "internally generated" or "imposed by Soviet command from above". However, although their structure could be traced back to the October Revolution on the one hand, and the social transformations wrought by the conquering Red Army in East Europe after the Second World War on the other, the leadership of these regimes was made up of a "large state bourgeoisie and petty bourgeoisie".[37]

Whereas this description of the Eastern Bloc might be read as implying that Miliband absolutely dissociated his model of socialism from that practiced in the Stalinist states, this was not the case. As early as 1963 he insisted, from a perspective greatly influenced by Isaac Deutscher, that the Eastern

---

34: Miliband, 1977b, pp111-112.
35: Miliband, 1994, pp4, 2; see also 1992, p108; 1983, p225.
36: Miliband, 1994, pp43, 69-70.
37: Miliband, 1989a, pp28-31.

Bloc states "approximated to something we think is socialism".[38] Deutscher explicitly showed that viewing the "revolutions from above" experienced in Eastern Europe after the Second World War as being in any way socialist, as he himself did, involved a break with Marx's notion that socialism could only come through the self-emancipation of the working class.[39] For his part, Miliband sought to frame his vision of socialism in terms of Marx's idea of working class self-emancipation while simultaneously following Deutscher to insist that the Russians had brought about a "revolution from above" in Eastern Europe.[40] Thus in 1974 he insisted that, despite their bureaucratic distortions, these states were not a "total repudiation" of socialism. Moreover, he suggested that though history had been unkind to Deutscher's prediction that the development of the productive forces in Russia in the 1960s would unleash radical progressive reforms across the system, such an optimistic perspective could not forever be discounted.[41]

In 1991 he was careful to link the Stalinist and post-Stalinist regimes with Lenin's revolutionary government: "What we are witnessing", he wrote in 1991, "is the termination of the historical experience that was begun in 1917".[42] More generally, he insisted that these states were "regimes of the left", and that Stalin had interwoven "his own rule, and the terror that went with it, with the building of "socialism" in the Soviet Union".[43] Consequently, as Gorbachev's reforms rose to their culmination, Miliband maintained a "slender hope" that the crisis of the Communist states would not lead to "capitalist restoration", but in the direction of "something approximating to the beginnings of socialist democracy".[44]

The failure of the Soviet Union to evolve in this direction in the late 1980s and early 1990s informed Miliband's pessimistic rejection of the possibility of building a new socialist party and his partial rapprochement with social democracy. He read the collapse of the Soviet Union as involving not only the failure of one possible alternative to capitalism, but also, and as a corollary of this, the dissolution both of the Communist parties and of all revolutionary organisational alternatives to social democracy.

---

38: Kozak, 1995, p275.
39: Deutscher, 1963, p514. Deutscher's influence on the Marxist left informed the pessimism which overtook many nominally anti-Stalinist socialists in the wake of the collapse of the Soviet Union (Blackledge, 2004a, pp3-4). On Deutscher more generally see Cliff, 1963.
40: Miliband, 1989b, pp173, 15.
41: Deutscher, 1960, pp21-23; Miliband, 1974, p393; Compare Newman, 2003, p68.
42: Miliband, 1991b, p17.
43: Miliband, 1980, p6; 1974, p386.
44: Miliband, 1991a, pp382, 388; Compare Miliband, 1994, p45.

Therefore, of the "two types" of left wing political parties known to the 20th century—Communist and social democratic—the demise of the Communist parties meant that "to speak of parties of the left nowadays is to speak above all of social democratic parties".[45]

This argument involved two related conflations: first, he conflated the collapse of the Eastern Bloc states with the collapse of the revolutionary socialist alternative to capitalism. Second, he conflated the organisations built by Lenin with those built by Stalin. If the first assumption illuminates the way that his Deutscherite analysis of Stalinism undermined the vision of socialism as working class self-emancipation, the second assumption tends to abstract the rise of Stalinism from its social context. However, as Miliband himself pointed out, in the period between 1917 and the early 1920s "the party itself was crippled by the weakness of the working class".[46] Moreover, in the decade that followed, the changes wrought by Stalin were so dramatic as to warrant an answer to the question did not quantity transform into quality? That is, did the dramatically increased "scale of repression", noted by Miliband, constitute the negation of all that was positive and progressive in the October Revolution? Miliband's negative answer to this question had direct repercussions for the rest of his discussion of Marxist politics.

For instance, in his analysis of the role of intellectuals within the Marxist movement, he claimed that the "Leninist" injunction that intellectuals should "serve the people" was, in one sense, unproblematic. However, he argued that within the Marxist movement after Lenin's death the interpretation of how the people were to be served had been increasingly redefined such that only the party leader, specifically Stalin or Mao, could decide what it actually entailed.[47] The differences between Lenin's party and those of Stalin or Mao were accordingly ones of degree rather than of quality: "Leninism was a political *style* adapted ... to a particular strategy ... Stalinism ... made a frightful caricature of the style, and made of the strategy what it willed".[48]

At the centre of this style, according to Miliband, was the structure of "democratic centralism", which fostered a subservient "attitude of mind to which Marxists have been prone".[49] By prioritising a discussion of the style of "Marxist" parties over the content of their practice, this argument led Miliband to lose sight of the fundamental nature of the break between Lenin's political practice and the ideology of "Leninism". For Lenin's conception of

---

45: Miliband, 1994, pp138, 143.
46: Miliband, 1974, p384.
47: Miliband, 1977b, p62.
48: Miliband, 1977b, p169.
49: Miliband, 1977b, pp64, 83.

organisation, as Marcel Liebman—Miliband's friend and collaborator on *The Socialist Register*—pointed out in his book *Leninism under Lenin* (1975), was subordinate to his model of revolution.[50] Revolutionary parties were necessary because socialism required a revolutionary overthrow of the old state, and democratic centralist organisation aimed at ensuring effective revolutionary action by guaranteeing, in Liebman's paraphrase of Lenin, "freedom of discussion, unity of action".[51] Furthermore, and in contrast to Miliband's comments on the practice of democratic centralism, Rabinowitch pointed out in his 1976 study of Bolshevism that it was the Bolshevik Party's "internally relatively democratic, tolerant, and decentralised structure and method of operation, as well as its essentially open and mass character" that underpinned its successes in 1917.[52] Indeed, in a letter to Bukharin and Zinoviev which the Stalinists tellingly omitted from his *Collected Works*, Lenin commented that demands for obedience within the Comintern would tend to "destroy the party" by driving "away all not particularly amenable, but intelligent, people" while leaving behind only "obedient fools".[53]

Miliband's focus on the issue of political style acted by comparison to centre his analysis of "Leninism" on the question of form at the expense of content. This opened the door to his characterisation of the parties of the Stalinist Third International as Leninist, despite the fact, as he insisted, that "Leninism as a coherent strategy of insurrectionary politics was never seriously pursued" by the Stalinists.[54] Indeed, he pointed out, with the Popular Front of the 1930s the Third International "abandoned" insurrectionary politics, such that from this point onwards the Western Communist parties "have not been 'revolutionary'."[55] Nonetheless, he and Liebman claimed that because the Communist parties had remained committed to a fundamental transformation of Western societies, there was "a weak sense" in which they remained "revolutionary".[56]

This apparent conceptual slippage is explicable if we look at Miliband's analysis of the Comintern's shift towards the Popular Front in the 1930s. He explained this process as a belated, but realistic, recognition within the Communist movement of the importance of defending

---

50: Liebman, 1975, p108.
51: Liebman, 1975, p51.
52: Rabinowitch, 2004, p311.
53: Lenin quoted in Hallas, 1985, p109; see also Carr, 1972, p305, and Cohen, 1980, p294.
54: Miliband, 1977b, p169.
55: Miliband, 1977b, p172; 1987, p487.
56: Miliband and Liebman, 1984, p9.

bourgeois democracy against the threat of fascism.[57] In so doing he effectively ignored the analysis of the evolution of Comintern policy outlined in Fernando Claudin's *The Communist Movement* (1975)—despite citing this book in the bibliography of *Marxism and Politics*. According to Claudin, changes in Communist policy had little to do with the needs of the workers' movement. On the contrary, they emerged as a cynical attempt by Stalin in the run up the Second World War to foster an alliance with the Western powers against the growing threat of Germany.[58]

The truth of this argument is of more than academic interest, for a great deal rides on the characterisation of the Communist parties after Lenin's death. Five points are important. First, the Popular Front emerged as a reaction to the failures not of revolutionary politics but rather of Moscow's previous *wilfully* ultra-left "Third Period" policy (on this, more below). Second, in the wake of Hitler's victory in Germany there did indeed arise within the Communist parties a genuine desire for working class unity to stop fascism. However, third, this desire was quickly channelled by the Moscow based leadership of the Communist parties in an electoralist direction which aimed to pressurise capitalist governments, primarily Britain and France, into an alliance with Russia against Germany. Fourth, this process was made easier because it was done in the context of the defeat of the workers' movement in Germany, which was obviously of international significance, and on the back of a previous process of removing any independent thinkers from leadership positions within the Communist parties. Finally, at a time when Russia seemed the last hope against Hitler, any movement that might threaten Stalin's relations with Britain and France was labelled Trotsky-fascist, and anyone critical of the new perspective was denounced as a "Trotskyist". The difficulties involved in maintaining revolutionary politics in this context were profound.

Unfortunately, Miliband skirted over these difficulties. So, despite recognising that the move to the Popular Front marked a break with revolutionary politics which was "encouraged" by Stalin, he suggested that it was not "really plausible to attribute" to Stalinist manipulation the ease with which this renunciation was effected. Miliband argued that Stalin had found it easy to push through his programme within the Comintern because insurrectionary politics did not "correspond to very powerful and compelling tendencies in the countries concerned". Moreover, the failure of the expected revolution in the West after the First World War

---

57: Miliband, 1977b, p75.
58: Claudin, 1975, pp176, 182-185; Hallas, 1985, pp141, 144.

confirmed that these countries did not fit the model for which "Leninist" political organisation had been constructed. Thus, with or without the help of Stalin, "the politics of Leninism, insurrectionary politics, failed in the countries of advanced capitalism".[59]

Of course this is true, but it doesn't tell us very much. We need a detailed discussion of the defeats both of the early 1920s and those a decade later, and the relationships of these defeats to, amongst other processes, the ongoing degeneration of the Russian system. The first thing that becomes apparent from such a comparative analysis is that politics pursued by the Comintern in the early 1930s, far from being "Leninist" in any meaningful sense, actually amounted to a bureaucratic caricature of the infantile leftism that Lenin had criticised in the strongest possible terms a decade earlier in *Left Wing Communism an Infantile Disorder*. And whereas the defeats in Germany and elsewhere in the early 1920s were an understandable consequence of the lack of experience of these new parties, the defeats experienced a decade later were in large part a consequence of cynical power plays in Moscow: radical verbiage abroad was merely the flip-side of Stalin's attack on Bukharin at home. To posit these defeats, and especially Hitler's victory over the German workers' movement, as defeats of Leninist organisations is profoundly to misunderstand this very important point.[60]

Nevertheless, Miliband did reject "Leninism" on the grounds that "insurrectionary politics" had never offered a realistic solution to the needs of the Western workers' movement. The corollary of this argument was the claim that some type of reformism was the only viable strategy for the left. For instance, in *Capitalist Democracy in Britain* (1982), he argued that given the "conditions of capitalist democracy", no path to socialism was conceivable other than via a democratically elected government "pledged to carry out" radical reforms: in fact the existence of parliamentary democracy "turns the insurrectionary project into a fantasy".[61] In an exploration of the possible actions of a democratically elected radical government, he argued that once it moved to "carry through far-reaching anti-capitalist measures" it would "arouse the fiercest enmity from conservative forces", such that the government's response to this would be "crucial". Miliband suggested that such a government could survive only if it mobilised its popular support; and in so doing it "must lead to a vast extension of democratic participation

---

59: Miliband, 1977b, pp170-171.
60: For an important survey of these various movements, see Hallas, 1985.
61: Miliband, 1982, pp156-157.

in all areas of civic life—amounting to a very considerable transformation of the character of the state and of existing bourgeois democratic forms".[62] He even went so far as to suggest that such a strategy could realise Marx's proposition that "the working class cannot lay hold of the ready-made state machinery, and wield it for its own purpose".[63]

Aside from what Miliband later admitted was the implausibility of this scenario,[64] Colin Barker pointed out that this strategy was innocent of a realistic model of the role of social democratic parties and trade union leaders within the class struggle. "Miliband forgets that such a government would be a government of parties who never intended … [and] have no tradition of mobilising mass movements." Indeed, Barker pointed out that reformism "is the politics of controlling rather than leading rank and file movements".[65] Interestingly, Miliband made much the same point both in *Capitalist Democracy in Britain* and in *Divided Societies*. In these two books, he wrote that trade unions acted not as radical agencies of socialist advance but as "agencies of containment of struggle", while the leadership of the Labour Party played a similar role at a more explicitly political level.[66] Nevertheless, despite acting in this way, Miliband insisted that the divisions between leaders and rank and file members of both social democratic parties and trade unions was not a simple consequence of oligarchic tendencies, but that it had an important ideological component.[67] With reference to trade union leaders, Miliband argued that, alongside a commitment to constitutionalism, it was the ideology of "a fair day's work for a fair day's pay" that limited their radicalism within parameters set by the reproduction of capitalist relations of production.[68]

As with Miliband's account of the parliamentarianism of the leadership of the Labour Party, this model provided him with a valuable point of departure for a rich description of the politics of the leadership of the trade union movement, but did not offer a structural explanation of the consistently conservative role played by this social layer. Rather, as he made clear in a comment on Robert Michels's famous "Iron Law of Oligarchy"—by which Michels had attempted to explain the conservatism of the leadership of the German Social Democratic Party before the First World War—the

---

62: Miliband, 1977b, pp183-188.
63: Miliband, 1977b, p189.
64: Miliband, 1994, p158.
65: Barker, 1977, p28.
66: Miliband, 1982, pp56, 33, 67-76; 1989b, p69.
67: Miliband, 1982, p69.
68: Miliband, 1982, p61.

central division within the labour movement was based not on structural conditions but on "quite concrete ideological grounds".[69]

Miliband was undoubtedly right to reject Michels's arguments—which involve an elitist rejection not merely of the possibility of socialism but also of any form of democratic organisation.[70] He was also right to root the division between leaders and left activists within the unions in the orientation of the union leaders towards parliamentary, statist politics. Unfortunately, as in his discussion of Labourism, this criticism was weakened by a failure to root the trade union leadership's orientation to the state in their mediating role in the class struggle. This meant, as we shall see in his relationship to the Labour Party in the 1980s, that he tended to overstate the importance of divisions between left and right wing trade union officials, in a way that undermined his attempt to build a socialist organisation. By focusing on the—undoubtedly important—ideological divisions within the trade union bureaucracy at the expense of the—more important—essential structural conservatism of this layer, Miliband effectively tied the fortunes of his socialist project to forces that had no intention of leading a radical socialist transformation of British politics.

From this perspective it is instructive to compare his analysis of the nature of reformism with that offered by Lukács in *History and Class Consciousness*: "the most articulate expression on a theoretical level of the world-historical events of 1917".[71] While this appreciation of Lukács's work is shared by many on the revolutionary left, Lukács's name does not appear in the index of *Marxism and Politics* (although *History and Class Consciousness* is listed in the bibliography).

This is an important omission. For in his early Marxist essays Lukács pointed to just the kind of systematic defence of Marxist political theory which Miliband had suggested did not exist in the introduction to *Marxism and Politics*. In "Towards a Methodology of the Problem of Organisation", Lukács argued that reformist organisations were best understood as structures which attempt to represent the working class, or rather the various strata that together make up the working class, as they exist as a partial negation of capitalism, but which remain engulfed within a reified bourgeois worldview. The problem with such organisations, he argued, was that while the class struggle is a dynamic process, and the consciousness of those proletarian strata involved in struggle are

---

69: Miliband, 1989b, p68; Michels, 1962.
70: For a powerful critique of Michels, see Barker, 2001.
71: Jay, 1984, p103.

open to transformation, the reformist bureaucracy itself tended to ossify, thus holding back the development of socialist class consciousness:

> While the organisations of the sects artificially separate "true" class consciousness (if this can survive at all in such abstract isolation) from the life and development of the class, the organisations of the opportunists achieve a compromise between these strata of consciousness on the lowest possible level, or at best, at the level of the average man. It is self-evident that the actions of the class are largely determined by its average members. But as the average is not static and cannot be determined statistically, but is itself the product of the revolutionary process, it is no less self-evident that an organisation that bases itself on an existing average is doomed to hinder development and even to reduce the general level.[72]

A revolutionary party, according to this view, acts as a corollary of the uneven consciousness of the working class in the class struggle; and whereas reformist parties actively hinder the emergence of widespread revolutionary consciousness, revolutionary parties aim to foster this process. The revolutionary party attempts to act in a way informed by lessons generalised from the high points of a century and a half of such struggles. Moreover, as "the process of revolution is—on a historical scale—synonymous with the process of the development of proletarian class consciousness", the struggle by revolutionaries for hegemony against the influence of reformists within the working class can only succeed with the success of the revolution itself.[73]

Superficially, this perspective coheres with Miliband's argument, as outlined in the conclusion to *The State in Capitalist Society*, that "a serious revolutionary party, in the circumstances of advanced capitalism, has to be the kind of 'hegemonic' party of which Gramsci spoke". However, whereas Lukács and Gramsci insisted that the struggle for hegemony was the precursor to a necessary overthrow of the old state and its replacement with a system of workers' councils, in that book Miliband maintained that the reform of the state "is, of course, possible". Furthermore, he argued that the limitations of such a reformist strategy ultimately derived not from the structural constraints placed on the state by capital, but because of the "ideological and political integration of social democratic leaders into the framework of capitalism". Indeed, he suggested that the increasing absorption of social democracy into the capitalist system meant that the historic role

---

72: Lukács, 1971, pp326-327.
73: Lukács, 1971, pp326, 286.

of the "labour and socialist movement" as "the main driving force of the extension of the democratic features of capitalist societies" was lessened.[74] Miliband therefore suggested a model of revolutionary organisation as a militant type of reformist party, which, unlike the Labour Party, was not hamstrung by its ideological attachment to capitalism.

Miliband thus implicitly dismissed Rosa Luxemburg's critique of reformism: "people who pronounce themselves in favour of the method of legislative reform *in place and in contradistinction to* the conquest of political power and social revolution, do not really choose a more tranquil, calmer and slower road to the *same* goal, but a *different* goal".[75] He effectively answered Luxemburg's defence of revolutionary politics by characterising the alternatives to his own position as "insurrectionary" and "constitutionalist"; a move which by focusing on the moment of transition obscured the differing day to day practice of reformist and revolutionary parties. Lukács suggested that reformist parties emerged in periods of relatively low levels of class struggle as the organisational expression of the struggle of labour against capital within an assumed, reified naturalisation of capitalist relations of production, while revolutionary parties emerged as the organisational expression of the break made by sections of the working class, based upon heightened class struggles, with this reified outlook. In contrast to this approach, Miliband tended to reduce the debate between reformists and revolutionaries, or constitutionalism versus insurrectionism, to a technical question narrowly relating to the moment of transition. Consequently, while he described the policing role played by the leadership of social democratic parties and trade unions, he did not integrate this description into a dynamic model of their function within the capital accumulation process.

This weakness in his discussion of reformism complemented similar problems with his analysis of the state. This is an important issue because both the right and left within the Labour Party oriented to winning the state through parliamentary elections, and because Miliband's analysis of the state suggested that socialist advance through the state was a realistic possibility. In an early, and perceptive, review of *The State in Capitalist Society* Isaac Balbus argued that although Miliband offered "ostensibly a class analysis of advanced capitalist systems" in execution his thesis was a "static", if "sophisticated, version of elite-stratification theory".[76] Similarly, Haldun Gulalp criticised Miliband for conceptualising the state's role of "maintaining and

---

74: Miliband, 1969, pp242-245; 1989b, p68.
75: Luxemburg, 1989, p75.
76: Balbus, 1971, pp40-41.

reproducing the relations of domination" in terms of its links with the dominant class, as opposed to through its "relation to capital accumulation".[77] As Colin Barker argued, by thus abstracting both his conception of the state and of reformism from capitalist social relations, Miliband failed to understand that the state was not a mere instrument of the capitalist class, but was itself a capitalist state.[78] This informed both Miliband's rejection of the classical Marxist claim that the state had to be "smashed" and his failure to address the argument that Lenin's goal was not merely to build a party that could organise an insurrection but that he also aimed to win hegemony away from the social democratic leaders of the workers' movement as a necessary precondition for the transition to socialism.[79]

The famous Twenty-One Conditions for entry into the Comintern were aimed, however clumsily, not, as Miliband suggested, "to split all labour movements from top to bottom", but rather to exclude reformist and centrist leaders from entry into the Comintern, where they would be expected to talk left while acting right.[80] For Lenin, the rationale of the Twenty-One Conditions was to exclude these opportunists so as to build real combat organisations of the working class.[81] Miliband's contrary interpretation of this break informed his consistently expressed regret at the split between reformists and revolutionaries. As he put it in 1964, "the split between Social-Democracy and Communism" not only "tore the Labour movements apart", but also helped ensure that "most Labour leaders had acquired a large stake in moderate reform within capitalism, and a deep fear of militant action".[82] Similarly, in *Marxism and Politics*, he argued that "confronted with a Bolshevik and Communist presence" the leaders of the social democratic parties "became even more 'reformist' than they had been".[83]

He therefore explained the strength of social democratic constitutionalism, in part, by the very existence of revolutionary parties. This superficially plausible argument is sound only so long as we ignore the differing day to day activities of these parties. This approach acts to obscure what Miliband's rich descriptions of reformist organisations actually highlighted: the fact that social democratic parties police mass movements,

---

77: Gulalp, 1987, p311; Compare Harman, 1991, p4.
78: Barker, 1979b.
79: Interestingly, this one-sided view of Leninism parallels anarchist claims that Lenin was a Blanquist (Blackledge, 2010, pp148-153).
80: Miliband, 1989b, p 61.
81: Hallas, 1985, pp162-163.
82: Miliband, 1964, p95.
83: Miliband, 1977b, p170.

while revolutionary organisations attempt to fan the flames of revolt. To judge the effectiveness of the split between social democracy and Communism in Miliband's terms involves assuming away these fundamentally different modes of practice, while simultaneously accepting that social democrats and Communists both aim at the same goal, if at different rates and by different paths. Miliband reinforced this perspective with the assumption that the Comintern's embrace of the Popular Front in the mid-1930s was an organic development which reflected its realisation that insurrectionary politics were a non-starter in the West, and that consequently the only viable form of left politics was one or other form of reformism.

However, as we noted above, Miliband asserted but did not argue this interpretation of the Popular Front; or rather his argument was based on the acceptance of a version of Hegel's aphorism that "what is, is Reason": revolutions had failed in the West, and revolutionary parties had been consistently marginalised. Thus in *Divided Societies* he argued that the "insurrectionary bids for power" attempted by the German Communist Party in the early 1920s were "doomed to failure". However, he also suggested that Germany was the only example of "an advanced capitalist country where a revolution might have succeeded".[84] Unfortunately, this revolutionary opportunity was squandered when the Social Democratic Party (SPD) acted as "the bulwark of the existing order" in 1918.[85] Miliband points out that the revolutionary opportunity was spurned by the Social Democrats before the formation of the Communist Party, and argues that henceforth Communist sectarianism, culminating in the rhetoric of the Third Period, ensured that splits in the labour movement meant that a left wing solution to the crisis of the Weimar state was all but impossible.

This assessment of Weimar history is doubly problematic.[86] If the SPD had acted as the bulwark of the old order in 1918 surely it was an imperative that the left organise themselves in opposition to this party— which, contra Miliband, they had already begun to do during the First World War precisely because of the Party's counter-revolutionary role from 1914 onwards. Moreover, his analysis of the ultra-leftism of the Comintern in the late 1920s and early 1930s was undermined by the same error evident in his explanation of the move to the Popular Front. In both occasions he abstracted the policy on the ground from the machinations in Moscow. He did not analyse the move towards "Third Period" ultra-

---

84: Miliband, 1989b, pp63, 74.
85: Miliband, 1989b, p74.
86: For a superb history of the German Revolution, see Harman, 1982.

leftism in the late 1920 in relation to the Stalinist counter-revolution but as the logical culmination of Leninist politics: "The sectarianism which marked those early years reached new heights in the so-called Third Period".[87] In thus abstracting his criticism of "Leninism" from any serious analysis of how, in Claudin's words, Stalin "vulgarly distort[ed] Lenin's policy",[88] Miliband elided Lenin's own criticisms of formally similar arguments in his *Left-Wing Communism an Infantile Disorder* (1920) through to his defence of the united front tactic in 1922.[89]

Ironically, in *Marxism and Politics*, Miliband approvingly quoted Trotsky's criticisms of the ultra-leftism of the Stalinist Third Period.[90] However, he did not explore either how Trotsky's arguments in the early 1930s built on Lenin's perspectives from a decade earlier, or how the leftism of genuine revolutionaries in the early 1920s differed qualitatively from Stalin's cynical reproduction of similar arguments a few years later. Indeed, it was precisely because Stalin knew Lenin's thinking as well as Trotsky did that his embrace of ultra-left rhetoric illuminated the fundamental nature of the break between his "Leninism" and Lenin's actual practice. It was the wilfully criminal nature of Third Period politics that led Trotsky to conclude that revolutionaries must split from the Communist movement in 1933.[91] According to Trotsky, just as the Second International's capitulation to nationalism in 1914 had created the need for a new international socialist movement, the Comintern's criminal acquiescence in Hitler's rise to power demanded the creation of a new revolutionary party in the 1930s.

By contrast with this position, Miliband believed that while the split between Communism and social democracy was understandable, it had the unfortunate consequence of reinforcing the constitutionalism of the reformist leaders, while simultaneously increasing the isolation of socialist militants. Moreover, in conflating the degeneration of the Communist parties with the demise of the revolutionary alternative to social democracy, Miliband assumed away the significance of the break between Trotskyism and Stalinism. Whereas Trotsky defended the creation of independent revolutionary parties, the logic of Miliband's perspective tended in the direction of reuniting the various fragments of the left by papering over the split of 1914. Ironically, therefore, "Moving On" might best be understood as a rather naive and utopian call to move back to the glory days of the Second International.

---

87: Miliband, 1989b, p63.
88: Claudin, 1975, p154.
89: Hallas 1985, pp38-43, 64-69.
90: Miliband, 1977b, p75.
91: Deutscher, 1963, p200 onwards.

## Conclusion

Commenting with the benefit of two decades of hindsight on the collapse of the first New Left in 1962, Miliband suggested that the foundations of a new socialist party might have been laid in the late 1950s and early 1960s:

> As I see it now, and as I only dimly perceived it then, the *New Reasoner* "rebellion" should have been followed by a sustained and systematic attempt to regroup whoever was willing into a socialist association, league or party, of which the journal might have been the voice. But this is no more than hindsight; and there was then no steam behind any such idea.[92]

While this caveat is true, it demands its own explanation. As I have argued elsewhere, it was the left reformism hegemonic within New Left circles that lent itself to over-optimistic hopes for Labour after a motion calling for unilateral nuclear disarmament was passed by the 1960 party conference, and which in turn resulted in extreme pessimism when, a year later, these hopes were crushed as the party machine turned against the left.[93]

It might be thought that the publication of *Parliamentary Socialism* in 1961 would have put paid to the New Left's illusions in the Labour Party. And indeed, two leading members of the International Socialists, the precursor of the SWP, read it in just this way. Tony Cliff built on its arguments in his first substantial analysis of the Labour Party, while Paul Foot credited it with saving him from a life as a Labour MP.[94] By contrast, Miliband himself, as we have noted, originally intended it as a contribution to saving the Labour Party for the left, and the substance of his analysis remained unchanged even when he came to argue for a new socialist organisation in the 1970s. By the early 1980s his hopes for a new socialist formation once again brought him into the orbit of the Labour left, this time in the shape of the movement around Tony Benn which emerged as a reaction to Thatcher's victory over a moribund right wing Labour government in 1979. In 1981-2 Miliband played a key role in launching a new formation which aimed to move the left beyond the limits of existing left organisations: the Socialist Society. He initially conceived this organisation as an embryonic party that would transcend the limits both of Labourism and Leninism. However, in practice he was increasingly drawn into the orbit of the Labour left. This wasn't a consequence of relating to the Labour left, which in the

---

92: Miliband, 1979a, p27.
93: Blackledge, 2004b; 2006.
94: Cliff, 2002; Foot quoted in Newman, 2002, p77.

context was undoubtedly the right thing for a Marxist to do. Rather *how* he related to the Labour left illuminated weaknesses with his analysis of Labourism generally and his critique of the Labour left more specifically.

Writing at the time, Duncan Hallas pointed to two important characteristics of the Bennite movement which would obviously shape how revolutionaries should relate to it. On the one hand, it was "shallow": Bennism reflected a move to the left among an existing layer of Labour and trade union activists at a time when the mass of the working class were suffering from demoralisation born of defeats in the industrial struggle, first under the Labour government's Social Contract and then under Thatcher. On the other hand, many of the new activists who joined the Labour Party after 1979 did so as part of a movement away from the revolutionary left in a direction that took them increasingly into the orbit of reformism. The ideological impact of these two elements of the Bennite constituency in the context of the downturn in the industrial struggle combined to ensure that there was no native revolutionary current within the Labour Party, and short of an about turn in the class struggle this was unlikely to change.

So while there was a large layer of socialists within the Labour Party whose anger at Thatcherism was real and profound, this layer tended to see the solution to these problems in traditional Labourist, that is electoral, terms. The key weakness with this general perspective was that it left the Bennites open to intense pressure from the right and centre of the party to moderate their arguments to the logic of the parliamentary game: the need to win *Daily Mail* reading swing voters in marginal seats. It followed from this analysis that the role of revolutionaries in this situation was to relate positively to the anger of these activists, working with the Labour left while maintaining their independence from them—explaining that reformism offered no real solution to the underlying problems of British society. This is exactly what the SWP aimed to do.[95]

While Miliband was undoubtedly right to see in Labour supporters the main constituency for any new socialist party, the weaknesses of his purely ideological conception of Labourism coupled with his belief that the state could become an instrument of a socialist government fundamentally weakened his critical faculties in the face of Benn and the Bennites. Thus as late as 1983 he suggested that the Bennites could win the Labour Party to socialism. He argued that, while his original critique of the Labour left was in general correct, he had "underestimated how great was the challenge the new activists would be able to pose to their leaders", and suggested that

---

95: Hallas, 1982, pp27-33.

whether or not these activists would be able to push matters further than he had previously thought was now "more open that I had believed".[96]

This argument involved a complete miscalculation of the political context.[97] Benn's defeat in the 1981 deputy leadership election was the high point for the Labour left which from then on in, and with alarming speed after the defeat of the Great Miners' Strike, was in retreat. Not only did the witch-hunt of the Militant Tendency—today's Socialist Party—begin the day after Benn's defeat, but also Benn submitted to the pressure from the right and centre of the party to conform as early as January 1982 when, at the so-called "Peace of Bishops Stortford", he agreed not to challenge for the leadership of the Party. His reason for doing this followed the electoral logic which Benn shared with the right of the party. When the most right wing elements of the party resigned in March 1981 to form the Social Democratic Party (the Dem side of today's Lib Dems) many Labour Party socialists were glad to see the back of them. However, rather than strengthening the left, the departure of the SDP strengthened the right within the Labour Party. This was most evident in the wake of the first by-election after the SDP split from Labour. When, in July 1981, the SDP candidate Roy Jenkins almost won the safe Labour seat of Warrington, the Labour leadership's eminently electoralist response was to move the party to the right.

The author of *Parliamentary Socialism* should have known better than anyone that this trajectory was the most likely scenario through the 1980s: he had detailed similar developments in the party in the 1920s, 1930s and 1950s. But rather than maintain his independence from the Labour left in a way that would have allowed him to act as a voice of realism on the left, Miliband's interpretation of Labourism as a purely ideological phenomenon opened the door to him being drawn into the Bennites' "crippling illusions" in the Labour Party, illusions he had done more than anyone else to highlight in the past! It was this optimism that quickly turned into its opposite once the scale of Benn's isolation within the party became apparent.

If Miliband's one-sided analyses of Labourism and the state opened the door to these unrealistic conclusions, his too dismissive critique of Leninism left him at some distance removed from the one player within the Socialist Society that might have tempered this hyper-optimism with a more realistic assessment of both the balance of class forces in Britain at the time and the possibility of transforming the Labour Party: the SWP. Isolated from the SWP and eventually overwhelmed by a declining Labour

---

96: Miliband, 1983, p303.
97: On Bennism see Cliff and Gluckstein, 1996, pp348-355, 361-366.

Left, far from renewing the left by overcoming divisions between reformists and revolutionaries the Socialist Society ended up, as Miliband and other leading Socialist Society members agreed, "squeezed" between the SWP to its left and the Labour Party to its right.[98]

Although Miliband's eventual political isolation in the late 1980s was in large part a product of the defeats of the working class over the previous decade, it was also a consequence of his failures either adequately to engage with Lenin's contribution to Marxist politics or to provide a socio-economic analysis of Labourism. If these gaps in his theory informed, first, the weaknesses of his original project of party building, and, second, his eventual retreat from this project, coming to terms with them will help us go beyond the limits of Miliband's Marxism so that we may realise his call to build an independent socialist party in Britain.

98: Newman, 2003, p67; 2002, p307; Miliband, 1983, p303.

# References

Anderson, Perry, 1980, *Arguments Within English Marxism* (Verso).

Armstrong, Tony, 2010, "Thought Leadership and Political Contention: An Historical Investigation into the *New Left Review* and the Socialist Society During the 1980s", PhD Thesis, King's College London.

Balbus, Isaac, 1971, "Ruling Elite Theory vs. Marxist Class Analysis", *Monthly Review*, 23 (May).

Barker, Colin, 1977, "Muscular Reformism", *International Socialism 102* (first series, October), www.marxists.org/history/etol/writers/barker-c/1977/10/miliband.htm

Barker, Colin, 1979a, "A New Reformism: A critique of the Political Theory of Nicos Poulantzas", *International Socialism 4* (spring), www.isj.org.uk/?id=294

Barker, Colin, 1979b, "Miliband and the State—A Slightly Different Critique", unpublished paper presented to the Northern Association of Politics and Sociology.

Barker, Colin, 2001, "Robert Michels and the 'Cruel Game'", in Colin Barker and others (eds), *Leadership and Social Movements* (Manchester University Press).

Blackledge, Paul, 2004a, *Perry Anderson, Marxism and the New Left*, (Merlin).

Blackledge, Paul, 2004b, "Learning From Defeat: Reform, Revolution and the Problem of Organisation in the First New Left", *Contemporary Politics*, volume 10.

Blackledge, Paul, 2005, "A Life on the Left", *International Socialism 105* (winter), www.isj.org.uk/?id=66.

Blackledge, Paul, 2006, "The New Left and the Renewal of Marxism", *International Socialism 112* (autumn), www.isj.org.uk/?id=251

Blackledge, Paul, 2008, "On Moving On from 'Moving On': Miliband, Marxism and Politics", in Clyde Barrow, Peter Burnham, Paul Wetherly (eds), *Class, Power and State in Capitalist Society: Essays on Ralph Miliband* (Palgrave).

Blackledge, Paul, 2010, "Marxism and Anarchism", *International Socialism 125* (winter), www.isj.org.uk/?id=616

Burnham, Peter, 2008, "Parliamentary Socialism, Labourism and Beyond", in Clyde Barrow, Peter Burnham and Paul Wetherly (eds), *Class, Power and State in Capitalist Society: Essays on Ralph Miliband* (Palgrave).

Callinicos, Alex, 1995, *Socialists in the Trade Unions* (Bookmarks).

Carr, Edward Hallett, 1972, *Socialism in One Country*, Volume III (Penguin).

Claudin, Fernando, 1975, *The Communist Movement* (Penguin).

Cliff, Tony, [1962] 2002, "The Labour Party in Perspective", in Cliff, Tony, *In the Thick of the Workers' Struggle* (Bookmarks).

Cliff, Tony, 1963, "The End of the Road: Deutscher's Capitulation to Stalinism", *International Socialism 15* (first series, winter) www.marxists.org/archive/cliff/works/1963/xx/deutscher.htm

Cliff, Tony, and Donny Gluckstein, 1985, *Marxism and Trade Union Struggle* (Bookmarks).

Cliff, Tony, and Donny Gluckstein, 1996, *The Labour Party: A Marxist History* (Bookmarks).

Coates, David, 1975, *The Labour Party and the Struggle for Socialism* (Cambridge University Press).

Coates, David, 2003, "Editorial Introduction", in D Coates (ed), *Paving the Third Way* (Merlin).

Cohen, Stephen, 1980, *Bukharin and the Bolshevik Revolution* (Oxford University Press).

Deutscher, Isaac, 1960, *The Great Contest* (Oxford University Press).

Deutscher, Isaac, 1963, *The Prophet Outcast: Trotsky 1929-1940* (Oxford University Press).

Gulalp, Haldun, 1987, "Capital Accumulation, Classes and the Relative Autonomy of the State", *Science and Society*, volume 51.

Hallas, Duncan, 1977, "How Can We Move On?", *Socialist Register 1977* (Merlin).

Hallas, Duncan, 1982, "Revolutionaries and the Labour Party", *International Socialism 16* (spring), www.marxists.org/archive/hallas/works/1982/revlp/index.htm

Hallas, Duncan, 1985, *The Comintern* (Bookmarks).

Hallas, Duncan, 1990, "Partial Vision", *Socialist Worker Review* 127 (January), www.marxists.org/archive/hallas/works/1990/01/miliband.htm

Harman, Chris, 1982, *The Lost Revolution* (Bookmarks).

Harman, Chris, 1991, "The State and Capitalism Today", *International Socialism 51* (summer), www.isj.org.uk/?id=234

Harman, Chris, 1998, *The Fire Last Time: 1968 and After* (Bookmarks).

Jay, Martin, 1984, *Marxism and Totality* (University of California Press).

Kozak, Marion, 1995, "How It All Began: A Footnote to History", *Socialist Register 1995* (Merlin).

Lecourt, Dominique, 1975, *Marxism and Epistemology* (New Left Books).

Liebman, Marcel, 1975, *Leninism under Lenin* (Jonathan Cape).

Lukács, Georg, 1971, *History and Class Consciousness* (Merlin).

Luxemburg, Rosa, 1989, *Reform or Revolution* (Bookmarks).

Michels, Robert, 1962, *Political Parties* (Free Press).

Miliband, Ralph, 1958, "The Transition to the Transition", *New Reasoner*, 6, www.marxists.org/archive/miliband/1958/xx/transition.htm

Miliband, Ralph, 1964, "Socialism and the Myth of the Golden Past", *Socialist Register 1964* (Merlin), www.marxists.org/archive/miliband/1964/xx/goldenpast.htm

Miliband, Ralph, 1965, "What Does the Left Want?", *Socialist Register 1965* (Merlin), www.marxists.org/archive/miliband/1965/01/leftwant.htm

Miliband, Ralph, 1969, *The State in Capitalist Society* (Quartet).

Miliband, Ralph, 1970, "Lenin's *The State and Revolution*", *Socialist Register 1970* (Merlin), www.marxists.org/archive/miliband/1970/xx/staterev.htm

Miliband, Ralph, 1972, *Parliamentary Socialism* (Merlin).

Miliband, Ralph, 1974, "Stalin and After", *Socialist Register 1973* (Merlin), www.marxists.org/archive/miliband/1973/xx/medvedev.htm

Miliband, Ralph, 1976, "Moving On", *Socialist Register 1976* (Merlin), www.marxists.org/archive/miliband/1976/xx/moveon.htm

Miliband, Ralph, 1977a, "The Future of Socialism in England", *Socialist Register 1977* (Merlin).

Miliband, Ralph, 1977b, *Marxism and Politics* (Clarendon).

Miliband, Ralph, 1979a, "John Saville: A Presentation", in D Martin and D Rubinstein (eds), *Ideology and the Labour Movement: Essays Presented to John Saville* (Croom Helm).

Miliband, Ralph, 1979b, "A Commentary on Rudolph Bahro's Alternative", *Socialist Register 1979* (Merlin), www.marxists.org/archive/miliband/1979/07/bahro.htm

Miliband, Ralph, 1980, "Military Intervention and Socialist Internationalism", *Socialist Register 1980* (Merlin), www.marxists.org/archive/miliband/1980/xx/intervention.htm

Miliband, Ralph, 1982, *Capitalist Democracy in Britain* (Oxford University Press).

Miliband, Ralph, 1983, *Class Power and State Power* (Verso).

Miliband, Ralph, 1985, "The New Revisionism in Britain", *New Left Review*, I/150.

Miliband, Ralph, 1987, "Freedom, Democracy and the American Alliance", *Socialist Register 1987* (Merlin).

Miliband, Ralph, 1989a, "Reflections on the Crisis of Communist Regimes", *New Left Review*, I/177

Miliband, Ralph, 1989b, *Divided Societies* (Oxford University Press).

Miliband, Ralph, 1991a, "What Comes After Communist Regimes?", *Socialist Register 1991* (Merlin), www.marxists.org/archive/miliband/1991/xx/comesafter.htm

Miliband, Ralph, 1991b, "Socialism in Question", *Monthly Review*, 43 (March).

Miliband, Ralph, 1992, "Fukuyama and the Socialist Alternative", *New Left Review*, I/193.

Miliband, Ralph, 1994, *Socialism for a Sceptical Age* (Polity).

Miliband, Ralph, and Marcel Liebman, 1984, "Reflections on Anti-Communism", *Socialist Register 1984* (Merlin), www.marxists.org/archive/miliband/1984/xx/anticomm.htm

Miliband, Ralph, and John Saville, 1964, "Labour Policy and the Labour Left", *Socialist Register 1964* (Merlin), www.marxists.org/archive/saville/1964/01/labour.htm

Newman, Michael, 2002, *Ralph Miliband and the Politics of the New Left* (Merlin).

Newman, Michael, 2003, "Ralph Miliband and the Labour Party", in John Callaghan and others (eds), *Interpreting the Labour Party* (Manchester University Press).

Newman, Michael, 2008, "Ralph Miliband and the New Left", in Clyde Barrow, Peter Burnham, Paul Wetherly (eds), *Class, Power and State in Capitalist Society: Essays on Ralph Miliband* (Palgrave).

Rabinowitch, Alexander, 2004, *The Bolsheviks Come to Power* (Haymarket).

# True crime stories:
# some New Labour memoirs

*John Newsinger*

*A review of John Prescott with Hunter Davies,* **Prezza: Pulling No Punches** *(Headline, 2008), £18.99; Peter Mandelson,* **The Third Man: Life At The Heart Of New Labour** *(Harper Press, 2010), £25; Tony Blair,* **A Journey** *(Hutchinson, 2010), £25*

With David Cameron in power and a full-scale Thatcherite assault under way on the welfare state, working class living standards and the public sector unions, it is easy to forget just how right wing New Labour was. Well, fortunately, two of the architects of New Labour, Tony Blair and Peter Mandelson, together with their loyal ally John Prescott, have rushed into print to remind us.

The three memoirs are very different in tone. Prescott is pathetic: his career has culminated with this proudly working class man joining the ermine vermin and becoming a baron. Prescott is not sure whether to be pleased with or ashamed of himself. Mandelson, another baron, leaves the reader knowing as little about who he is, what be believes in and what he has been up to than he or she did before they opened the book. And then with Blair, one confronts full-blown megalomania. No House of Lords for him—he is one of the Masters of the Universe, an honorary member of the American ruling class.

Nevertheless, these memoirs are useful for providing some insight into the state of the Labour Party and the politics of the New Labour governments, into the way in which they developed their own brand of Thatcherism, thereby preparing the way for the coalition. What is also clear from the Blair and Mandelson memoirs is that they are attempting to construct a Blairite narrative whereby Labour lost the 2010 general election because it was not right wing enough, or as they both put it, was no longer really New Labour. This is, of course, a travesty, but one that can potentially weaken the fight against the coalition. It has to be challenged. But there is a delightful irony in the fact that it was almost certainly the publication of the Blair and Mandelson memoirs and the bad memories they revived that cost their anointed heir, David Miliband, the leadership of the Labour Party.

## One at a time with me first

There is an old joke, nearly as old as the Labour Party, about a working class Labour politician who had abandoned all of his principles except his belief in the emancipation of the working class, but only one at a time and with him first. Whoever first coined this gem could have had John Prescott in mind, although to be fair it does not refer to an individual, but to a particular Old Labour type, to the Old Labour traitor. Is this unfair to Prescott? On the one hand, he can declare "an affinity with the underdog, people who had failed or were being put down", but he can also write with every expectation of sympathy about the shock of briefly rejoining the common herd once he had left office.[1] He had to move out of Admiralty House, give up his country retreat at Dorneywood and even use the Tube: "I had to pay cash and was amazed it cost four pounds." It was "quite a shock to the system all round".[2] And, of course, there's the money. Prescott has had to join the lecture circuit "to earn some money for my retirement".[3] Before rushing to hold a collection for him, it is worth remembering that he has a pension of over £60,000 a year!

Prescott famously failed the 11–plus and to his credit became a staunch defender of comprehensive education, although this was not to stop him from serving as deputy prime minister in the government that began dismantling the comprehensive system. He went out to work at 15, working as a steward in the Merchant Navy. In the early 1960s he became involved in a rank and file revolt against the cosy relationship that existed between the National Union of Seamen (now merged into the RMT) and the employers.

---

1: Prescott, 2008, pp27-28.
2: Prescott, 2008, p3.
3: Prescott, 2008, p354.

He was one of the leaders of the National Seamen's Reform Movement that wrote an important page in trade union history.

Prescott came from a respectable Labour background. His father was a Labour Party councillor, a justice of the peace, and a full-time official in the Transport and Salaried Staffs Association. It does seem that by his early 20s he was already thinking of a career as a union official himself. Consequently his attitude towards the National Union of Seamen was that it should be reformed, with men like himself taking over, whereas the rank and file revolt was driven by rage.

In his memoirs Prescott spends more time trying to distance himself from the militants than he does exploring the injustice and oppression they were revolting against. He is clearly rewriting the past from the respectable position he occupies today. He was, he tells us, against wild cat strikes, and: "I have to admit that some of the more militant were trying to bring down the government, hold the country to ransom".[4] Indeed sometimes he gives the impression that the militants were the real problem. On one occasion he actually had to arm himself with "a big piece of timber" to see off a group of them.[5] Certainly, Prescott's potential as a union official was shown when he secured a return to work in Liverpool after putting the resolution to the vote five times before he won it!

In 1963 he went to Ruskin College and from there to Hull University, where he did a degree. Prescott, who likes to present himself as an 11-plus failure, altogether spent five years in full-time higher education on a full grant and without paying fees. While he was a student he continued his involvement with the seamen and with the local Labour Party. He played a part in the great 1966 seamen's strike and put together *Not Wanted On Voyage-The Seamen's Reply*, a devastating response to the Pearson inquiry into the strike. This was his finest moment. He was still thinking in terms of a career as a full-time official, but in November 1968 he was adopted as Labour candidate for Hull East. At this time he occasionally bought *Socialist Worker*.

Becoming an MP was to change everything. He bought a new house that was "once owned by some rich merchant... It was huge with eight bedrooms and lots of turrets".[6] Even his over-sympathetic biographer, Colin Brown, describes it as "every inch a house for the upper middle classes. Buying it showed he had arrived, but it was not without

---

4:   Prescott, 2008, p56.
5:   Prescott, 2008, p60.
6:   Prescott, 2008, p117.

a conflict of conscience".[7] From this point on, Prescott's working class persona was increasingly to become a means of advancing himself within the Labour Party rather than reflecting any real commitment to the actual working class. And, of course, he had to cope with how attractive he was to women. Prescott writes of Thatcher flirting with him in the Commons: she "would half smile at me...even wink on one occasion".[8] She was not alone: "Towards the end of 1995, I woke up one day to find I'd become a sex symbol".[9]

What of New Labour? Prescott had a vital role to play in convincing the Labour Party membership and the trade unions that the changes Blair, Brown & Co were proposing were merely cosmetic, rather than shifting the party decisively to the right. If getting rid of Clause 4 of the Labour Party's constitution, which called for the common ownership of the means of production, was acceptable to someone as working class as John Prescott, then there was no way it could possibly signal an embrace of Thatcherism. He was the Judas goat that led the party membership unsuspectingly along the road to New Labour.

What is clear from his memoirs is the extent to which he personally had moved to the right. He proudly claims to have invented public-private partnerships, a policy that he complains the Conservatives stole.[10] And once in power in 1997 he was very much in favour of the part privatisation of the Royal Mail and played a vital role in the privatisation of Air Traffic Control, something Labour had condemned in opposition ("I didn't see it as an ideological sell-out, I saw it as the best financial deal for the taxpayer").[11]

As for the Iraq War, "our relationship with the US has always been fundamental". For Prescott, it was all about being loyal to Tony and he shows not the slightest concern with the issues raised by the conflict. Even with all that we know today about the horrendous loss of Iraqi lives, he can still proudly announce that "I would still do the same again".[12]

He was still the old John though. Indeed, his happiest times in office were when he had his old mates from his seafaring days down to Dorneywood for Christmas. "I was most relaxed in the company of

7:   Brown, 1997, p73.
8:   Prescott, 2008, pp137-138.
9:   Prescott, 2008, p205.
10:  Prescott, 2008, pp171-172.
11:  Prescott, 2008, p221.
12:  Prescott, 2008, p287.

people I felt completely at ease with", he writes.[13] There were difficulties, however. During the 2002 firefighters' strike: "Tony left it totally to me". Prescott orchestrated their eventual defeat but only after a bitter dispute. Some people can be so unfair though:

> I got attacked personally by someone I considered one of my oldest friends, a Britannic steward I'd been at sea with. His son was a fireman out on strike. His dad told me I was a "fucking sell-out", letting down the workers when I was supposed to be a union man. I'd been all for the workers, he said, when I'd been at sea with him… He hasn't spoken to me since. [14]

This says it all really.

One interesting point worth noticing is the extent to which the changes in the Labour Party that Prescott helped make possible mean that no one like him will ever become an MP again, let alone a minister. The idea that a trade union militant could win adoption for a safe Labour seat is inconceivable today. Indeed, in Gordon Brown's government there were more millionaires (ten who were worth £35 million between them) than there were former manual workers. And Prescott recognises this change himself: "We won't have many politicians…who have come from my sort of background." This, he moans, "will be a loss", but "we can't go back".[15] So much for the working class!

What do the authors of the other two memoirs make of Prescott? For Mandelson, Prescott was Blair's "political foil". He "loved his job and the status that went with it, and was generally careful to avoid doing anything to put it at risk".[16] And despite their mutual dislike, Mandelson does express his gratitude to Prescott for supporting his proposals to privatise the Royal Mail when he returned to the cabinet in 2008: "I had a particularly gratifying ally".[17] What of Blair? Prescott "brought an authenticity, an appeal to the party's traditional wing, especially within the trade union movement". But the highest praise Blair can think of is that if Prescott were a young man today, he would "probably never have gone near a trade union", but instead would have "most likely have taken a job in industry or the public sector as a manager".[18] Praise indeed!

---

13:  Prescott, 2008, p242.
14:  Prescott, 2008, pp258-259.
15:  Prescott, 2008, p363.
16:  Mandelson, 2010, pp177, 197.
17:  Mandelson, 2010, p479.
18:  Blair, 2010, p326.

## Lord Mandelson's watch

When Peter Mandelson joined Gordon Brown's cabinet at the end of 2008, increasingly desperate Labour MPs welcomed him back as a saviour. At the party conference in September 2009 the man who in many ways embodied everything most contemptible about New Labour, and its embrace of the rich, received a standing ovation. In his memoirs he writes that the party "had at long last learned to love Peter Mandelson".[19] What makes the moment particularly symbolic is that when Mandelson waved to the applauding delegates he had on his wrist a Patek watch that cost over £21,000. Nothing better signifies the extent to which New Labour had devoted itself to the service of the rich than Lord Mandelson's watch.

Mandelson had, like Prescott, come from a Labour background. After a brief flirtation with the left he decided that "I wanted a future in the Labour Party" and that the best way to achieve this "was through the trade union movement".[20] He went to work at the TUC economic department where he seems to have been transformed into an enemy of trade unionism, at least once the movement had served his purposes. Much later he was to have no sympathy whatever for the miners' strike and observes that one of Kinnock's great regrets was that he had not opposed the strike from the outset, but then Kinnock was always "too much of a socialist".[21]

As far as Mandelson was concerned the Labour Party "was…on the wrong side" in the 1986 News International lockout. He was the Party's director of communications at the time and was ordered to have nothing to do with the Murdoch press. But he "made it a point privately to continue briefing and talking to the Murdoch journalists". [22] The enormity of this is lost today because we have become so used to Labour prime ministers and ministers courting Murdoch, but at the time it would have been unthinkable for a Labour leader to have consorted with a reactionary union-buster like Murdoch.

What Mandelson, together with Blair and Brown, set out to do was to transform the Labour Party, to have it embrace Thatcherism. Mandelson supported Thatcher's anti trade union legislation and looked forward to the creation of "a US style entrepreneurial culture" in Britain.[23] This was what the New Labour government was all about. And life was so good: "I had a lively and, when I chose, a decidedly A-list social life." New Labour was

19: Mandelson, 2010, p486.
20: Mandelson, 2010, p60.
21: Mandelson, 2010, p104.
22: Mandelson, 2010, p190.
23: Mandelson, 2010, p265.

chic "and people wanted a bit of that chic at their parties and receptions". Such were the days: "Mick [Jagger] was singing, Kate [Moss] was dancing, and I felt an urge to join in".[24]

Of course it all ended in tears, with not one but two resignations. One would, as Oscar Wilde put it, need a heart of stone not to laugh. Mandelson claims to have had serious reservations about the Iraq war and there is no reason to doubt him. On one occasion he writes of an impatient Blair accusing him of spending too much time talking to George Galloway![25] He provides some further material on "the Blair-Brown civil war".[26] He testifies to the "good relationship" that Brown established with Rupert Murdoch, although he never got on with Rebekah Wade because she was always too close to Blair.[27]

At one point Mandelson insists that "my real job was to serve my constituents". Representing the people of Hartlepool was "my real job". [28] One is entitled to be sceptical about this because there were no billionaires resident in Hartlepool. Indeed, a good case can be made that Mandelson's "real job" barely figures in the pages of his memoirs. He was the man who acted as the go-between for New Labour and the ruling class. The circles Mandelson moved in are absent from his pages, except for one occasion when it is impossible not to mention them. He does feel compelled to explain how he came to be staying on the Russian multi-billionaire Oleg Deripaska's £80 million luxury yacht in 2008. We would never have known about this if George Osborne, also present, had not tried to make political capital out of it. The episode has, of course, since been immortalised in John le Carre's novel, *Our Kind of Traitor*. Mandelson gives the impression that he barely knew Deripaska, but in fact he had been introduced to him by Nat Rothschild as early as October 2004.

Mandelson, as one account observes, "had always been open to the blandishments of the wealthy and he struck up a rapport with Russia's richest man". Nat Rothschild, Old Etonian and former member of the Bullingdon Club, a "near billionaire himself", was a good friend of Mandelson's. Indeed, Mandelson had been a family friend going back to the 1990s and "frequented" Nat's Corfu chateau, one of his many homes. According to one friend, Mandelson "likes to use other people's planes and yachts... Peter likes the comfort of flying on a private jet, staying on

---

24: Mandelson, 2010, pp224-225.
25: Mandelson, 2010, p353,
26: Mandelson, 2010, p14.
27: Mandelson, 2010, p488.
28: Mandelson, 2010, p334.

a nice yacht".[29] In August 2008 he was in Corfu to celebrate the fortieth birthday of Elizabeth Murdoch (Rupert was there, of course) and because of a shortage of accommodation he stayed on Deripaska's yacht. This was all perfectly innocent: "I barely saw him, except for an amusing episode in which…I stumbled across a yoga session he and his wife were taking, and I happily joined in".[30]

One can rest assured, however, that while Mandelson was rubbing shoulders with the super-rich he was thinking of the people of Hartlepool. To be fair, it was not just Mandelson but New Labour that embraced the new Russian super-rich, welcoming them to Britain. In 2006 a fifth of all the houses in London sold for over £8 million were sold to Russians and the higher the price went the higher the proportion bought by Russians. Even Ken Livingstone "went out of his way to applaud the Russian influx".[31] There are even stories that Russian influence was crucial in getting "their London" the Olympic Games.

Mandelson obliquely acknowledges how little he is going to reveal in the title of his memoirs, *The Third Man*. There are a whole number of Graham Greene titles he could have chosen (*The Last Word, The End of the Affair, A Burnt-Out Case, The Confidential Agent*, even *The Comedians*), but instead he chose a reference to the mysterious, unscrupulous Harry Lime. As it is, no one better exemplifies New Labour than Peter Mandelson, a man eager to be of service to his friends, the super-rich.

## Confessions of a war criminal

Which brings us to Blair himself. His is very much a memoir intended to establish his place in history as a great man. In fact what he has produced is an exercise in amoral megalomania, characterised by often execrable prose, sometimes revealing more than he intended.

First, the megalomania. A few quotations will be enough to demonstrate this particular pathology:

> I had a strategy for guiding us from opposition into government; I adhered to it, and I knew that if I did so, I wouldn't fail… I was the eternal warrior against complacency.[32]

29:  Hollingsworth and Lansley, 2010, pp330, 332.
30:  Mandelson, 2010, p27.
31:  Hollingsworth and Lansley, 2010, p347.
32:  Blair, 2010, pp1-2.

I had led the Labour Party to victory. I had reshaped it. I had given it a chance to be a true party of government. All this took a degree of political skill and courage.[33]

I was trying to wear what was effectively a kind of psychological armour which the arrows simply bounced off, and to achieve a kind of weightlessness that allowed me, somehow, to float above the daemonic rabble tearing at my limbs... There was courage in it and I look back now at it with pride.[34]

It is unusual to praise one's own courage, but Blair can't afford to leave anything to chance.

Contrary to what some reviewers have said, he does actually reveal why he joined the Labour Party rather than what seems to be his more natural home in the Conservative Party. Given that he was hostile to the trade unions, was always out of sympathy with the politics of Labourism both Old Left and Old Right, this has always been a bit of a puzzle. While Blair wholeheartedly endorsed much of Thatcherism, in particular the "new laissez-faire approach to industry, battles with the unions", nevertheless the Tories "were also conservative with a small 'c'." What he couldn't stomach was "their stuffiness, their pomp, their worship of tradition". They were still "stamped with the hallmark of a bygone age". He objected to their "baggage, airs and graces".[35]

Blair's objection to the Conservative Party was not political, but cultural. Instead he joined Labour. He portrays himself as a sort of Thatcherite entrist, pretending to be Labour (he even joined CND), but really intent on changing Labour into something else. From the very beginning he recognised that the Labour Party was "in the wrong place" and that it would have to be transformed. As he admits, there were occasions when "I couldn't stop the mask slipping".[36]

The result was that the Labour Party ended up with a leader who was every bit as hostile to trade unionism as any Tory. He makes it absolutely clear that Thatcher's attack on the unions was the right thing to do: she was "correct about the excesses of trade union power". Harold Wilson and Ted Heath had tried "an evolutionary attack on trade union privilege" and had both failed.[37] Of course, the idea that Heath's Industrial Relations Act, his

---

33: Blair, 2010, p27.
34: Blair, 2010, p573.
35: Blair, 2010, pp98, 132.
36: Blair, 2010, p43.
37: Blair, 2010, p. 42.

imprisoning of trade unionists and his fighting of two great class battles with the miners was "evolutionary" is complete rubbish.[38]

Blair goes on to argue that after Wilson's and Heath's failure it was clear that "only a revolutionary [approach]…would succeed. And she had the character, leadership and intelligence to make it happen".[39] John Prescott, it is worth remembering, considers this man to be the Labour Party's greatest leader![40] Thatcher's anti trade union legislation was left in place by New Labour as part of their undertaking to big business that they would not interfere with the balance of class forces her victories had established. This really gets to the heart of New Labour politics: their commitment to a society where big business is dominant culturally, politically and economically and the unions have been successfully curbed.

Blair goes on to inevitably embrace the most successful union buster in modern British history, Rupert Murdoch. He came to have "a grudging respect and even liking" for Murdoch who "had balls".[41] While he had no time for trade unionists, Blair is quite happy to acknowledge that when "I was with a group of entrepreneurs, I felt at home".[42]

Blair famously regrets only two policies in his memoirs: the banning of fox hunting and the Freedom of Information Act. On Iraq, he is absolutely unrepentant. Despite the continuing revelations about the horrors that the invasion has inflicted on that country, Blair not only justifies the attack, but regrets that it was not continued as originally planned with Syria and Iran next. He goes out of his way to praise vice-president Dick Cheney. Cheney, he writes admiringly, "would have worked through the whole lot, Iraq, Syria, Iran, dealing with all their surrogates in the course of it—Hezbollah, Hamas, etc" Cheney recognised that "the world had to be made anew" and despite disagreements, Blair believes "there was much to be said for this insight".[43]

As for the difficulties in Iraq, these were not the responsibility of Britain and the US, but were the fault of Iran. Indeed, Iran, he claims,

---

38: Heath was one of those 1970s politicians who found themselves rapidly outflanked on the right, not just by Thatcher but also by Blair. In 2002 Heath was complaining to Tony Benn that Blair "is a Thatcherite". In the same conversation Heath complained that American presidents were not assassinated "frequently enough as far as the present one is concerned". By February 2003, in the run up to the Iraq war, Heath was demanding to know: "How can we get rid of Blair?" See Benn, 2008, pp51, 97.

39: Blair, 2010, p42.

40: Prescott, 2008, p326.

41: Blair, 2010, p98.

42: Blair, 2010, p116.

43: Blair, 2010, p409.

"was both funding and training al-Qaida operatives".[44] This is a neocon-servative fantasy that almost defies belief. It is intended to justify a future attack on Iran. And this from the supposed Middle East Peace Envoy. More generally, Blair insists that "our alliance with the US gave Britain a huge position", and that, as far as he personally was concerned, he thought people "admired the fact I counted, was a big player, was a world and not just a national leader".[45]

Blair bought into the war on terror without reservation. For him it defined the modern world. He believes there is a great battle under way for the soul of Islam, a battle that might last generations and that would have to be fought on many fronts. Winning is not just a matter of "a military strategy", but requires "a whole new geopolitical framework". He goes on:

> It requires a myriad interventions deep into the affairs of other nations. It requires above all a willingness to see the battle as existential and see it through, to take the time, to spend the treasure, to shed the blood, believing that not to do so is only to postpone the day of reckoning...[46]

Well, we already know that he has no problem with military inter-vention and the shedding of blood, but what we are confronted with here is a Manichaean view of the world that owes more to the *Chronicles of Narnia* (Tony Through The Wardrobe, so to speak) than to any realistic geopolit-ical appreciation. The war on terror was always an ideological construct, a way that the US neoconservatives thought they could justify the increasing use of armed force to sustain the position of US imperialism. Blair actu-ally believes it. For him, the war is still being fought out, but fewer and fewer people are taking it seriously as the defining conflict of the age. He is increasingly confined to an embittered neocon ghetto. American imperi-alism under Obama is finding new ideological clothes to wear.

One of New Labour's great successes was that, having involved the country, despite massive opposition, in one catastrophic American war, they nevertheless were able to go on and successfully involve us in another one. The way the renewed Afghan war was served up is one of the great triumphs of modern "information management", a triumph all the greater because it was accomplished without anyone even being aware that it was

---

44: Blair, 2010, p469.
45: Blair, 2010, p410.
46: Blair, 2010, p349.

going on. In March 2006 John Reid, the secretary for defence, committed British troops to a three-year operation in Afghanistan with the remark that he would be happy if at the end of it they "had not fired a shot".[47] At the same time as he was misleading the British people, Reid was telling Blair something very different:

> as John made very clear, it would be a tough and dangerous mission. The Taliban would fight hard to keep hold of the territory that we had never been able to satisfactorily wrest from them. There would be suicide attacks on our forces.[48]

If this prognosis had been made public at the time, especially in the aftermath of Iraq, there would have been a huge upsurge in opposition to the commitment. Instead the war was kept hidden for as long as possible, and then once the intensity of the fighting made continued secrecy impossible, the government very successfully played the "support our boys" card. The result is a war that cannot be won, that has cost the lives of hundreds of British troops, and is killing an increasing number of Afghan civilians. We must not forget New Labour's second American war.

Since his resignation as prime minister, Blair has devoted much of his time to enriching himself. The lecture circuit has proven immensely profitable for him with a speech at a banquet held by a Chinese property company in November 2007 earning him £237,000 and a speech to a conference of entrepreneurs in Barcelona the following year earning him £240,000. According to one account, by 2009 "he was being described as the world's best-paid speaker, able to pull in more than half a million pounds a month, and earning £400,000 for two half-hour speeches in the Phillipines in March of that year". His topic was "The leader as a Nation Builder in a Time of Globalisation". And he has taken a number of lucrative jobs in the financial sector: "In January 2008, he joined one of Wall Street's best-known banks, JP Morgan...reportedly earning around £2 million a year for a part-time role." That same month he took another part-time job with the Swiss insurance firm Zurich, "for at least £500,000 a year". Within two years of leaving office "Blair was said to have earned as much as £15 million".[49] One has to pinch oneself to remember that this man was once leader of the Labour Party!

47: See Newsinger, 2009, p30.
48: Blair, 2010, p610.
49: Theakston, 2010, pp220-221, 222.

# New Labour Lives!

Both Blair and Mandelson are determined to construct a mythic explanation for the 2010 defeat. According to Mandelson, Brown lost because "voters had come to feel that we had moved away from the key New Labour instincts".[50] Blair goes much further, arguing that Brown had, in fact, abandoned New Labour. He seriously argues that in 2010 he could have defeated Cameron: "Labour won when it was New Labour. It lost because it stopped being New Labour".[51] This is a nonsense. Indeed, a good case can be made that the extent to which Brown warned against Tory cuts actually prevented a complete Labour rout.

What lost Labour the election was the extent to which it was still New Labour. It was New Labour that had seen a collapse in party membership. It was New Labour that had seen inequality increase to levels not seen since before the Second World War. It was New Labour that had turned Britain into a paradise for the rich and super-rich. It was New Labour that left the British economy so vulnerable to financial crisis. And, moreover, Blair goes on to endorse the Cameron-Clegg response to that crisis.[52]

He is not alone in this. Privately, a majority of Labour MPs support the Con Dem regime of cuts. The fact that 111 MPs voted for David Miliband in the first round of the Labour leadership elections and only seven for Diane Abbott shows this. By the fourth ballot David Miliband had the support of 140 MPs. These people might have reservations about the timing of the cuts or the manner in which they are being implemented, they might object to some of the detail, but for most Labour MPs the real objection is that they are not the ones in office carrying them out. New Labour Britain, for example, was already a world leader in "outsourcing", a polite word for the privatisation of public services, and, indeed, boasted of this in business circles.

Labour MPs, with some commendable exceptions, are not spoiling for a fight with the coalition. They have no intention of taking to the streets or standing on picket lines. This reflects the balance of class forces, the balance of class forces that made New Labour possible in the first place. What we are moving into now, however, is a different era. A weak coalition government of inexperienced but remarkably overconfident public school class warriors (the first rule of class warfare for any serious ruling class militant is do not alienate the police, and these people have broken it already) is launching an unprecedented attack on the poor,

---

50: Mandelson, 2010, p561.
51: Blair, 2010, p679.
52: Blair, 2010, pp682-683.

students, public sector workers and, it has to be insisted, on the living standards of millions of white collar workers.

Defeating their assault will change the balance of class forces decisively. Once the cuts begin to bite, Labour MPs will find it increasingly difficult to remain apart from the struggle. Only the hardcore Blairites will continue to stand aside, and without any doubt some of these will actually defect to the Tories. This will provide us with an opportunity to destroy New Labour once and for all.

## References

Benn, Tony, 2008, *More Time For Politics: Diaries 2001-2007* (Arrow Books).

Brown, Colin, 1997, *Fighting Talk: The Biography of John Prescott* (Simon and Schuster).

Hollingsworth, Mark, and Stewart Lansley, 2010, *Londongrad* (Fourth Estate).

Newsinger, John, 2009, *America Right or Wrong: New Labour and Uncle Sam's Wars* (Bookmarks).

Theakston, Kevin, 2010, *After No 10: Former Prime Ministers In British Politics* (Palgrave Macmillan).

# Marxism and disability

*Roddy Slorach*

Many young women full of devotion and good-will have been engaged in superficial charities. They have tried to feed the hungry without knowing the causes of poverty. They have tried to minister to the sick without understanding the cause of disease. They have tried to raise up fallen sisters without understanding the brutal arm of necessity that struck them down... We attempt social reforms where we need social transformations.[1]

Evidence shows the recession in the UK has already hit disabled people hard.[2] The new government's huge public spending cuts include further attacks on meagre but vital disability benefits.[3] Their aim is to roll-back hard-won

---

1: Keller, 1913, quoted in Crow, 2000. An iconic figure in the disability movement, Helen Keller is better known for her deafblindness and disability activism than for her revolutionary politics—see Davis, 2003. Thanks for help and comments are due to Iain Ferguson, John Parrington, Julie Devaney, Keir McKechnie, Nicola Owen, Paul Brown, Richard Moth, Rob Murthwaite, Simon Behrman and, in particular, Gareth Jenkins, Joseph Choonara and Pat Stack. I did not always follow their advice, and responsibility for content lies solely, of course, with me. Special thanks to Daniela for her patience and encouragement. This article is dedicated to the memory of Elaine White and Gary Kelly.

2: *Independent*, 28 December 2009. The report, by Leonard Cheshire Disability, shows disabled people as particularly vulnerable to cuts in public services, both as employees (one in three disabled workers are in the public sector) and as service users. See www.lcdisability. org/?lid=11293

3: A study by the Institute for Fiscal Studies estimates that benefits reforms will cost 20 percent of current DLA recipients their entitlement. See www.ifs.org.uk/publications/5246

'social reforms' affecting all sections of the working class.. Understanding the nature of disability discrimination can therefore play a part in defending these reforms and uniting resistance to the attacks which lie ahead.

This article aims to articulate a Marxist approach to the issues of disability and impairment and to begin a debate which is perhaps overdue. Is the discrimination faced by disabled people a form of oppression like that suffered by other minorities under capitalism? What happened to the disability movement and the social model of disability which inspired it? Is it possible—and desirable—to achieve a society free of disability?

## The nature and extent of impairment

Disability is a widely misused and misunderstood concept, as illustrated by the World Health Organisation (WHO) definition:

> Disabilities is an umbrella term, covering impairments, activity limitations, and participation restrictions. An impairment is a problem in body function or structure; an activity limitation is a difficulty encountered by an individual in executing a task or action; while a participation restriction is a problem experienced by an individual in involvement in life situations. Thus disability is a complex phenomenon, reflecting an interaction between features of a person's body and features of the society in which he or she lives.[4]

These definitions reflect the progress made since disabled people were referred to officially as spastics, imbeciles and cripples. However, they also obscure the vital distinction established by the disability movement between individual impairment and disability as social discrimination.[5] Leaving aside terminology for the moment, WHO figures do indicate the extent of impairment globally:

> Hearing loss, vision problems and mental disorders are the most common causes of disability... Worldwide, an estimated 650 million people (10 percent of the total population) live with disabilities, the vast majority in low-income and middle-income countries... A significant proportion of disabilities are caused by traffic crashes, falls, burns, and acts of violence such as child abuse, youth violence, intimate partner violence, and war...up to one quarter of

---

4:   www.euro.who.int/violenceinjury/20080519_1
5:   This distinction informs the terms used throughout this article, except where quotes are used. In preferring the term "disabled people", for example, to "people with disabilities" (the term most used in the US), disability is seen primarily as a social phenomenon rather than something directly arising from each individual's impairment.

disabilities may result from injuries and violence. [These] include: physical and/or cognitive limitations due to neurotrauma; paralysis due to spinal cord trauma; partial or complete amputation of limbs; physical limb deformation resulting in mobility impairments; psychological trauma; sensory disability such as blindness and deafness.[6]

The WHO's 2008 report also highlights mental disorders as among the 20 leading causes of disability worldwide, with depression alone affecting around 120 million people. Fewer than 25 percent of those affected have access to adequate treatment and healthcare. In 2004 the Labour government estimated Britain's disabled population to be 10 million. The statistics show beyond doubt that a very large number of people are disabled. Second, many of their impairments are socially caused, and third, a large majority of disabled people are poor.

## The creation of disability

Weaker, older or impaired members of pre-class societies were more likely to survive with the development of settled agricultural production and surplus crops. Feudal societies saw impairment in religious terms, as a mark of either good or evil, which meant those affected often faced persecution. However, the rural production process, and the extended nature of the feudal family, allowed many to make a genuine contribution to daily economic life. Families living and working as large groups were able to provide networks of care for children and the elderly. This way of life, typical for much of the world's population for thousands of years, was to virtually disappear in the last three centuries.

The rise of capitalism forced people off the land. In Britain production for the market began on a scale sufficiently small as to be carried out in the home, and therefore impaired people could still play a role. However:

> the rural population was being increasingly pressed by the new capitalist market forces, and when families could no longer cope the crippled members would have been most vulnerable and liable to turn to begging and church protection in special poor houses. Market forces soon favoured machinery which was more efficient and able to produce cheaper more plentiful woven material. Those working larger looms would more likely survive and cripples would have had greater difficulty working such equipment.[7]

---

6:    http://www.euro.who.int/violenceinjury/20080519_1
7:    Finkelstein, 1981.

The Industrial Revolution accelerated the pace of change enormously. Larger-scale machinery concentrated in factory towns increasingly destroyed the old cottage industries as well as traditional family structures, with members forced to find work away from the home or patch of land. The new factory worker "could not have any impairment which would prevent him or her from operating the machine. It was, therefore, the economic necessity of producing efficient machines for large-scale production that established ablebodiedness as the norm for productive (ie socially integrated) living...production for profit undermined the position of physically impaired people within the family and the community".[8]

Working lives previously shaped by the hours of daylight and the seasons were now determined by the rhythm of the factory—even more so with the invention of gaslight and round the clock working. People's bodies were now valued according to their ability to function like machines:

> Factory discipline, time keeping and production norms broke with the slower, more self-determined and flexible work pattern into which many disabled people had been integrated. As work became more rationalised, requiring precise mechanical movements of the body, repeated in quicker succession, impaired persons—the deaf or blind, and those with mobility difficulties, were seen as—and without job accommodations to meet their impairments, were—less "fit" to do the tasks required of factory workers, and were increasingly excluded from paid employment. [The Industrial Revolution] removed crippled people from social intercourse and transformed them into disabled people.[9]

Specialisms were developed to help maintain and reproduce the new working class. Poor Law officials and an expanding medical profession developed pseudo-scientific categories to identify those of the poor who were unfit for work—"the sick, the insane, defectives, and the aged and infirm". Dependence on others was now identified as a social problem and impairment equated with sickness and illness. Throughout the 18th and 19th centuries those identified as disabled were segregated into workhouses, asylums, prisons and special schools. This had "several advantages over domestic relief: it was efficient, it acted as a major deterrent to the able-boded malingerer, and it could instil good work habits into the inmates".[10]

---

8:  Finkelstein, 1981.
9:  Russell and Malhotra, 2002.
10:  Barnes, 1991.

Isolating disabled people in institutions—barbaric and oppressive as they were—led to the intensive study and treatment of impairments, creating the basis for clearer scientific understanding and classification. Mental impairment, for example, was seen as a single category until Langdon Down's reports for the London Hospital in 1866. These identified, among other conditions, what later became known as Down's Syndrome.[11]

With labour power now a commodity whose components were separately identified and valued, people with mental health problems were also increasingly categorised and placed in segregated institutions. In 1826, the first year for which statistics are available, fewer than 5,000 people were confined in asylums throughout England. By 1900, this had increased to 74,000.[12]

Capitalism represented a huge advance from previous societies in many ways. For the first time in history the productive capacity existed to feed, clothe and house the entire global population, while scientific and medical advances offered the prospect of understanding and curing diseases. But the new working class creating this wealth were excluded from any say over what was produced and how, suffering for their pains physical and mental impairment on an unprecedented scale. Those marginalised or excluded from production, either by injury or already existing impairments, also became marginalised or excluded from wider society. In this way capitalism created disability as a particular form of social oppression.

## Reform and reaction

Life expectancy in the industrial towns was incredibly short. Manchester's Medical Officer of Health reported in 1875 that "the average age at death of the Manchester upper middle class was 38 years, while [for] the labouring class [it] was 17; while at Liverpool these figures were represented as 35 against 15".[13] Cholera epidemics, poor hygiene and sanitation were not only a threat to the poor, and social reformers increasingly saw an unregulated free market as counter to the interests of British capitalism. Charities such as Barnardo's and the Spastics Society took a growing role in caring for disabled people. Their often wealthy patrons lobbied for state intervention, better standards of treatment, and education for their disabled children.

---

11:  Stratford, 1989, chapter 4. Although a reformer, Langdon Down's views were shaped by Victorian prejudices. He followed his predecessors in ideintifying those with Down's Syndrome as "Mongolians", a supposed racial group considered "degenerate" by those running the British Empire.

12:  Appignanesi, 2008, p25. A recent TV documentary put the total UK figure for 1958 at over 150,000. See *Mental: A History of the Madhouse*, BBC Four, 17 May 2010.

13:  Marx, 2003, p795.

The years of explosive strikes and growth in trade unions known as "New Unionism" also saw the formation of the British Deaf Association and the National League of the Blind and Disabled (NLBD). Founded as a trade union in 1899, the NLBD affiliated to the Trades Union Congress three years later.[14] Its members (including blind war veterans), mainly working in sheltered workshops, campaigned for better working conditions and state pensions. The league organised a national march of blind people on Trafalgar Square in 1920, carrying banners with a new slogan—"Rights Not Charity". Despite the small numbers, its aims were widely supported. The first legislation specifically for blind people was passed in the same year, followed by more in 1938.[15]

The upsurge of reforms also led to a reaction from the right. Eugenicists believed that, just as weaker or "inferior" members of a species weren't meant to survive in nature, they were not meant to survive in a competitive human society. From the late 19th century,

advocates of eugenics...propagated the myth that there was an inevitable genetic link between physical and mental impairments and crime and unemployment. This was also linked to influential theories of racial superiority, according to which the birth of disabled children should be regarded as a threat to racial purity. In the notorious Buck v Bell decision of 1927, the US Supreme Court upheld the legality of the forced sterilisation of disabled people... By 1938, 33 American states had sterilisation laws and between 1921 and 1964 over 63,000 disabled people were involuntarily sterilised... Whether or not codified into law, the sterilisation of disabled people was common in a number of countries in the first half of the 20th century, including Britain, Denmark, Switzerland, Sweden, and Canada.[16]

Eugenics theory advocated the enforcement of a new concept, "normalcy", through the elimination of "defectives". It attracted widespread establishment support in Europe and the US, but was taken to its logical and genocidal conclusion by Hitler's fascist regime. The extermination of disabled people was the first stage in its plans to "purify" the Aryan race of those considered weak or unproductive:

---

14: The NLBD merged with the old ISTC trade union in 2000 to form Community.
15: Campbell and Oliver, 1996, p40.
16: Russell and Malhotra, 2002. Sweden's sterilisation programme was only ended in 1975.

Nazi ideology considered disability to be a sign of degeneracy and viewed nearly any disabled person as a "life not worthy of life" [or] as [a] "useless eater"... Compulsory sterilisation for people with disabilities became German law in 1933. More than 400,000 people with disabilities were forcibly sterilised... A formal killing operation known as Aktion T-4 quickly followed, designed specifically for people with disabilities. The Nazi mechanisms for mass extermination of Jewish victims, such as carbon monoxide poisoning in "shower rooms", were first developed and perfected through the disability programme. As a result, more than 275,000 people with disabilities were murdered in the Aktion T-4 programme, not counting all those who lost their lives in the concentration camps and after the formal phase of T-4 ended.[17]

The Holocaust was unique in its scale and barbarity, but it was also the product of a system that sees human beings as commodities to be bought and sold—or discarded as insufficiently profitable. As for eugenics, the theory fell from favour only after the nature and scale of Nazi atrocities became known in the years following the Second World War.

## The rise and fall of the disability movement
The war economy had seen disabled people as well as women—previously considered respectively as incapable of or unsuitable for factory work—play a substantial role in wartime production. The need to reha-bilitate huge numbers of wounded servicemen prompted legislation that in practice led to the expansion of existing sheltered workshops, usually paying below minimum wages. The post-war decades, however, brought virtually full employment and high levels of social spending. The founda-tion of the National Health Service and the expansion of the welfare state boosted further specialism within the professions. Medical advances led to more people living longer, and enabled others to carry out activities of which they were previously incapable:

Of particular importance was the availability of domestic appliances which could be operated with the minimum of physical energy and skill. Teaching a physically impaired person how to go to a well, fetch a pail of water, collect firewood and light a fire to make a pot of tea may have been impossible last century, but teaching a similarly impaired person to fill an electric kettle with

---

17:   Disability Rights Advocates, 2001.

water, switch on a button, etc to make a pot of tea today is well within the accepted aims of modern rehabilitation practice.[18]

The long economic boom created space to challenge institutionalisation and the patronage of charities, with significant numbers of disabled people joining the workforce. By the 1960s some had begun to reject their labelling by the professions as deviants or patients, and to speak out against discrimination. Inspired in particular by the black civil rights struggle, the disability movement began in the US.

The "Rolling Quads", a group of student wheelchair users at the University of California, established the first Independent Living Centre in 1971. Within a few years hundreds more were created across the US and other countries including Britain, Canada and Brazil. Its opposition to institutionalisation and stress on the self-reliance of disabled people was to give the independent living movement an enduring influence.

Jimmy Carter's 1976 election campaign pledged his presidency to signing Section 504 of the 1973 Rehabilitation Act. These regulations, incorporating anti-discrimination law into the public sector, were partly the result of years of campaigning by disabled people, which had attracted Vietnam War veterans such as Ron Kovic.[19] In April 1977, as part of a series of nationwide protests against the refusal to ratify Section 504, a group of disabled people occupied the San Francisco Health Education and Welfare Department. The sit-in, whose numbers grew to around 120, attracted widespread support (including from the local branch of the Black Panther Party). After 25 days Carter caved in. It was a stunning victory. The protesters left en masse, singing "We Have Overcome".[20] The US disability movement, however, had focused so much on campaigning for Section 504 that it virtually fell apart once it was finally implemented. It was a pattern that was to be repeated.

The UN declared 1981 the International Year of Disabled People. For reasons little to do with the UN, that year turned out to be a turning point. Disabled Peoples' International (DPI) was formed by 250 disabled people at a conference in Canada, advocating "equal opportunity and full participation of handicapped people in all aspects of society as a matter of justice rather than charity".[21] DPI urged disabled people to unite in

---

18:  Finkelstein, 1981.
19:  Kovic, subject of his autobiography and Oliver Stone's film *Born on the Fourth of July*, has been a key figure in the US anti-war movement for over 40 years.
20:  For an accessible history of the disability movement in the US, see Shapiro, 1994.
21:  Driedger, 1989, p36.

multi-impairment coalitions, and by 1989 had 69 members, each representing national organisations of disabled people.[22]

The coalition that emerged in the UK, the British Council of Organisations of Disabled People (BCODP), had by its mid-1990s peak grown to 106 affiliated organisations representing 400,000 disabled people.[23] Its protests, sometimes involving several thousand people, included a "Rights Not Charity" demonstration at the Department of Health and Social Security in 1988, and two mobilisations against ITV's "Telethon" in 1991 and 1992—the latter putting an end to the notoriously patronising charity fundraiser. BCODP activists were from the outset hostile to organisations "for" (as opposed to "of") disabled people—primarily the professions and the hugely better-funded disability charities. This was even truer of smaller, more radical organisations such as the Direct Action Network (DAN). However, these principles rapidly gave way to joint campaigns with the big disability charities, on the grounds that the overriding priority was now to secure anti-discrimination legislation similar to that passed in the US in 1990.

John Major's weakened Tory administration formed a task force to draft new laws. The BCODP refused to participate as a body, but some activists argued they could exert more influence by being involved. [24] The result, 1995's Disability Discrimination Act (DDA), was widely criticised as both narrow and toothless. New Labour's landslide election in 1997 led to a new Disability Rights Commission (DRC), which the government pledged would publicise, strengthen and enforce the DDA. The DRC successfully absorbed much of the remaining leadership of the disability movement.[25] The truth is that few activists had an alternative strategy.

The alliance with the charities and New Labour seemed for many disabled people the only way to achieve broader social change. Single impairment charities had long been a vital source of welfare support or social networks. To many, disability was simply a human rights issue: "The principal thing is that we're getting together...to make it different in terms of the politics of disability, which is about the rights of individuals; it is about the right to control our own lives".[26] Many activists saw "able-bodied

---

22: Driedger, 1989, p89.
23: According to former BCODP director Richard Wood—Campbell and Oliver, 1996, p188.
24: The BCODP merged a number of existing disability organisations, and is now the UK Disabled People's Council. See http://www.ukdpc.net
25: Including Jane Campbell and Bert Massie, well-known figures in disability politics. Massie (who had already joined the Tories' Disability Task Force in 1994) chaired the DRC from 2000 until its disbandment in 2007.
26: Campbell and Oliver, 1996. p101.

society" in general as the problem, believing that people who were disabled had different and separate interests from those who were not. DAN activists were most explicitly separatist, seeing all able-bodied people as oppressors. This led to even more divisive notions such as who was "really disabled". Meanwhile, blacks, gays and women pointed to discrimination against them by fellow disabled activists.

New Labour's promised reforms effectively neutered the movement.[27] As Oliver and Barnes put it at the time:

> [We have seen] the growing professionalisation of disability rights and the wilful decimation of organisations controlled and run by disabled people at the local and national level by successive government policies despite rhetoric to the contrary. As a result we no longer have a strong and powerful disabled people's movement... Since the late 1990s the combination of government and the big charities have successfully adopted the big ideas of the disabled people's movement, usurped its language, and undertaken further initiatives which promise much yet deliver little.[28]

The crucial difficulty, however, was that the disability movement grew in Britain (and elsewhere) during and after a period of defeats for the working class, when other movements of the oppressed had already passed into decline (a fact reflected in the title of one early history, "The Last Civil Rights Movement").[29] Few activists saw any evidence then that the working class could successfully unite struggles of the oppressed with a shared interest in more fundamental change. As left and right alike within the movement agreed that disabled people needed firstly to organise for themselves, it was inevitable that the politics of identity would increasingly come to dominate those of class.

All this said, the disability movement helped win a wider understanding of the inequalities faced by disabled people, and in doing so achieved legislation addressing that inequality. How successful were these reforms in achieving this aim?

### Reforms and neoliberalism
The most significant and best-known anti-discrimination laws of the last

---

27: Which is not to suggest there has been no further significant activism. For example, several thousand deaf people marched on parliament in 2003, winning full government recognition of British Sign Language.
28: Oliver and Barnes, 2006.
29: Driedger, 1989.

20 years are the Americans with Disabilities Act (ADA) of 1990 and in Britain the Disability Discrimination Act (DDA) of 1995 (with its subsequent amendments). However, the record since their implementation is not impressive. One US observer noted in 1999 that "the unemployment rate of disabled people has barely budged from its chronic 65-71 percent...in the first eight years [of the ADA], defendant-employers prevailed in more than 93 percent of reported ADA employment discrimination cases decided at the trial court level".[30]

In 2005 Tony Blair went so far as to pledge full equality for all disabled people within 20 years.[31] Two years later—and 12 years after the passage of the original DDA—the UK government had to acknowledge continuing and "unacceptable" levels of inequality among disabled people. It found that disabled workers earn between 6 and 17 percent less than non-disabled workers.[32] More recent government figures show that among those of working age, fully 50 percent of disabled people are unemployed (compared with 20 percent of non-disabled people) and 23 percent have no qualifications (compared with 9 percent of non-disabled people). People with mental health problems have the lowest employment rates of all impairment categories, at only 20 percent.[33]

The ADA and the DDA share key weaknesses. Both require individuals wishing to pursue a legal complaint to prove first that they have a recognised impairment, with tribunals placing a primacy on medical evidence. Both also place the onus on individual disabled people pursuing—usually at their own expense—court cases which carry no guarantee of success, far less legally binding change.

The fault did not and does not lie solely in the legislation. A report produced by the Public Interest Research Unit on the effectiveness of the DRC found that "neglect of its enforcement powers, along with the difficulties individuals face in taking action themselves, has helped ensure that the majority of discriminators have got away with committing unlawful acts".[34] There is little evidence that the DRC's successor, the Equality and Human Rights Commission (EHRC), has performed any better. When

30: Russell, 1999.

31: Prime Minister's Strategy Unit, 2005.

32: Equalites Review 2007, http://archive.cabinetoffice.gov.uk/equalitiesreview

33: Office for National Statistics Labour Force Survey, January-March 2009. See www.shaw-trust.org.uk/disability_and_employment_statistics

34: Public Interest Research Unit, 2004. An even more damning report on all three equality commissions prior to the EHRC can be found at www.leeds.ac.uk/disability-studies/archiveuk/harwood/tuwnov9.pdf

Trevor Phillips (notorious for his claims that multiculturalism in Britain was not working) was reappointed as EHRC chair in July 2009, six board members resigned, several blaming the new body's ineffectiveness under his leadership.[35]

## The politics of independent living

We are often told that the gains of the post-war years have led to "a demographic time bomb". That so many people are now living longer lives should be a cause for celebration. However, the concern to capital is that a rising proportion of the population cannot be exploited, and constitute a growing economic burden. The huge public spending cuts expected in the wake of the current recession are therefore likely to include further attacks on the living standards—and lives—of old age pensioners, who comprise by far the biggest proportion of the disabled population.

With the closure of the hated institutions and the onset of community care, subsequent debates have focused on how appropriate care can be provided at home, and how disabled people can get more control over the services they use. The disability movement therefore campaigned for government policies based on this philosophy.

John Major's dying government conceded a system of "direct payments" alongside the DDA in the mid-1990s. The scheme was championed by figures such as Colin Barnes and Jenny Morris, on the basis that disabled people must have choice over how their personal care needs are met—even if this meant further privatisation.[36] Low take-up by local authorities, however, led to a rebranding under New Labour. "Personalisation" obliged the former, from 2003 onwards, to offer "individual budgets" to any applicants for disability-related services. Hopes that user-led organisations controlled by disabled people, particularly Centres for Independent Living, would provide the infrastructure and expertise to help run these schemes proved unfounded. Contracts have instead gone mainly to local authorities, charities or the private sector.[37]

These initiatives have so far led to little real change. One 2009 study

---

35: Those who resigned included Sir Bert Massie and Baroness Jane Campbell. The remaining members of the board include a CB, another baroness, two CBEs and two OBEs.
36: Barnes, 2007, and Morris, 2005.
37: Contracts to provide services replaced grants as the basis for funding at local and national level. This led to the collapse of many campaigning groups of disabled people (eg Greater London Action on Disability, Greater Manchester Coalition of Disabled People and Derbyshire Coalition of Disabled People). Some turned themselves into service providers, particularly Centres for Independent Living, in an attempt to survive.

found that 60 percent of disabled people with social care needs rely on informal help from relatives or friends to meet those needs.[38]

> Over 70 percent of local authorities provide services only to those whose needs are considered "critical or substantial"; the rest are left to go it alone. While our politicians have adopted the language of the Independent Living Movement, users receiving services are lucky to get anything extending beyond being washed and fed.[39]

Labour's approach has been adopted with a vengeance by the new government. In a keynote speech in July 2010 health secretary Andrew Lansley adopted a familiar slogan of the disability movement: "[Our] guiding principle will be 'no decision about me without me'... We will extend personal budgets, giving patients with long-term conditions real choices about their care".[40] But the rhetoric is accompanied by budget cuts which threaten the widespread closure of existing services such as day centres and respite care. The cuts are also likely to mean that "the trend towards narrowing the eligibility criteria for support will continue, as demand for social care grows and budgets are increasingly restricted".[41] Many local care agencies have already been privatised, staffed by typically low-paid and unskilled workers. With further restrictions on disability benefits, individual budgets and/or personalisation are likely to promise meaningful choice or independence only to those who can afford to pay. For most disabled people, they offer instead an increasingly impoverished existence, atomised and isolated in their own homes.[42]

Health and social care services are increasingly provided by "third sector" bodies (voluntary organisations, charities and businesses), with government funding of around £7 billion a year. In 2008 Barnardo's total income was £253 million, while in 2008-9 Scope received over £100 million and Leonard Cheshire (running care homes and supported accommodation) over £145 million.[43] But these figures are dwarfed by public sector spending: the NHS budget in 2008-9 alone was £100 billion.[44]

---

38: 2009 Disability Review, Leonard Cheshire. See www.lcdisability.org/?lid=11009
39: Campbell, 2008.
40: Speech on NHS reforms, 16 July 2010. See www.dh.gov.uk/en/MediaCentre/Speeches/DH_117366
41: Beresford, 2008.
42: For a more detailed critique of personalisation, see Ferguson, 2007.
43: See www.guidestar.org.uk/gs_aboutcharities.aspx
44: Government figures—www.nhs.uk/NHSEngland/thenhs/about/Pages/overview.aspx Both these figures are set to fall significantly with government cuts.

The fact that most welfare services in Britain are still both free at point of use and (in the main) universally available is considered a major problem by many in the ruling class. The neoliberal solution, which US writer Marta Russell has aptly called "free market civil rights", is a society of individualised consumers forced to shop around for services no longer run by public authorities, but by charities or private businesses. Much of the present UK cabinet may favour this solution—but they are a long way yet from achieving it.

## The social model of disability

The pioneering distinction between impairment and disability was first made explicit by a group of disabled socialists in 1976, including anti-apartheid activist Vic Finkelstein. The tiny Union of the Physically Impaired Against Segregation (UPIAS) declared that disability, far from being biologically determined, was a social creation that could be challenged and eliminated:

> In our view, it is society which disables physically impaired people. Disability is something imposed on top of our impairments by the way we are unnecessarily isolated and excluded from full participation in society. Disabled people are therefore an oppressed group in society.

> Thus we define impairment as lacking all or part of a limb, organ or mechanism of the body; and disability as the disadvantage or restriction of activity caused by a contemporary social organisation which takes little or no account of people who have physical impairments and thus excludes them from the mainstream of social activities.[45]

These "Fundamental Principles" were later developed, principally by Oliver, into the social model of disability. He described it as a "tool for action" rather than a thoroughgoing theory:

> [If disability] is seen as a tragedy, then disabled people will be treated as if they are the victims of some tragic happening or circumstance. This treatment will...be translated into social policies which will attempt to compensate these victims for the tragedies that have befallen them... If disability is defined as social oppression, then disabled people will be seen as the collective victims of an uncaring or unknowing society... Such a view

---

45: UPIAS, 1997.

will be translated into social policies geared towards alleviating oppression rather than compensating individuals.[46]

As he put it later, this oppression "is ultimately due to our continued exclusion from the processes of production... The social model of disability is concerned with the personal and collective experiences of disabling social barriers and how its application might influence professional practice and shape political action".[47]

These ideas turned received wisdom on its head and had a hugely liberating impact on many disabled individuals. The social model played an important role in helping activists, particularly in Britain, understand and challenge discrimination. It won widespread acceptance as the disability movement grew under the Tory governments of the 1980s until the mid-1990s.[48] As the movement receded, however, and hopes increasingly centred on a future New Labour government, the social model of disability began to be identified with a "rights" model centred on achieving legislative change. This "reclaiming" or "rectifying" of the social model often turned into its outright rejection, not least in the growing academia of Disability Studies departments.

The social model met increasing criticism (largely, it is true, from the right) on the grounds that it ignores impairment, a problem claimed to be at least as important, if not more than discrimination in the lives of disabled people. Oliver replied that the social model is "a campaigning aid concentrating on the collective experience of disablement, not the individual experience of impairment". This wish to avoid divisions is understandable. Drawing on the precedents of the struggles for black, gay and women's liberation, and rejecting biological explanations of social inequality, Oliver insists that "there is no causal relationship between impairment and disability".[49]

In his influential book *The Politics of Disablement*, Oliver attacks the "medicalisation" of disability. This refers to the way disabled people have for many decades been made the objects of oppressive medical practice and research, focused on individual cures and treatment. Refusing to integrate

---

46: Oliver, 1990, p2.
47: Oliver, 1996.
48: Internationally, terminology and detail of definitions have varied and continue to vary. That adopted by the DPI at its 1982 World Council was "a. Disability is the functional limitation within the individual caused by physical, mental or sensory impairment, and b. handicap is the loss or limitation of opportunities to take part in the normal life of the community on an equal level with others due to physical and social barriers"—Driedger, 1989, p92.
49: Oliver, 1996.

impairment into the social model, Oliver argues the former is a less useful campaigning focus. However, this is to overlook struggles such as those in South Africa for affordable drugs to combat AIDS, as well as others against drugs such as thalidomide or ritalin, which have actually caused impairment. There continue to be fierce debates on the subject of medical cures or therapy among disabled people. The point here is that they are neither the whole answer to impairment nor "incompatible with social change and civil rights", but that each should be taken on its merits.[50]

Other critiques of the social model highlight its lack of relevance to other forms of oppression, cultural issues or those of representation. These arguments miss the central issue—the social model's aim was to outline a materialist understanding of disability as a form of oppression that could be fought against and overcome.[51] It dealt a huge blow to the idea that disability was simply about personal tragedy or individual medical conditions. It pointed to major social and economic change as the cause of disability and to further change as its solution. It is therefore on this basis—as a starting point in any theory of disability liberation—that the social model should be examined.

## Disability and oppression

The idea that disabled people are less productive and "able", and more dependent in general remains common sense, and in capitalist terms is largely correct. Without some form of assistance to compensate for the particular impairment or lack of function, many disabled people are likely to be less economically productive as individuals.

The advanced capitalist societies invest heavily in health, education and social services that help reproduce the labour force (keeping workers skilled, fit and healthy enough to work). Rehabilitating back into the workforce people with short-term impairments or illnesses is relatively inexpensive. But those with more severe long-term illnesses or impairments receive far less priority, as meeting their needs often carries no guarantee of future profits.

All forms of oppression share similarities but also important differences. Discrimination against black people, women, or gays and lesbians is not directly rooted in the way work is organised. Gender, ethnic origin and sexual orientation have no direct bearing on how productive individuals

---

50: Shakespeare, 2006, p109. Previously a passionate advocate of the social model, Shakespeare became one of its main critics, especially in this nevertheless useful book.

51: Although Oliver himself has stressed that the social model is "not a substitute for social theory" or a "materialist history of disability"—Oliver, 1996.

are under capitalism. Other oppressed groups were not and often still are not considered capable of particular kinds of work. But this is not the same as employers wishing to avoid paying the additional costs of hiring a disabled worker, whether in the form of work station adaptations, interpreters, readers, environmental modifications or liability insurance:

> [The] root of our oppression is the fact that capitalism sees everything in terms of profit and profitability—and this colours how capitalists view disabled workers. Most employers see disabled employees as a "problem"—something difficult, something different, something that will cost them more to employ. That isn't to say that capitalists are incapable of realising that disabled people can be a source of cheap labour. So the oppression of disabled people is a reflection of the way in which capitalism reduces everything to profit—effectively, capitalism says disabled people are surplus to requirements. This is especially true in periods of economic crisis—provision for disabled people is always one of the first things to be hit.[52]

Disability discrimination is a distinct but complex form of oppression, based on the (negligibly to substantially) greater expense to capital of the labour power of impaired people. This oppression was not particular to the Industrial Revolution. Disability continues to be rooted in the way the capitalist mode of production subordinates concrete labour (and the concrete labourer) to abstract, interchangeable and homogeneous labour. The very nature of work in capitalist society constantly undercuts any potential for liberation.

The social model's weakness in relation to impairment needs to be addressed. Limitations or lack of "part of a limb, organ or mechanism of the body" or mental function are the raw material on which disability discrimination works, and as such cannot be divorced from the latter. We have seen how disability is historically and socially determined. But this is also true of impairment. The "particular social and historical context...determines its nature... Where a given impairment may be prevented, eradicated or its effects significantly ameliorated, it can no longer be regarded as a simple natural phenomenon".[53]

The nature and heterogeneity of impairment distinguishes disability from other forms of oppression. Impairments may be physical or mental (or both), single or multiple, temporary or permanent, and acquired before

---

52: Stack, 2007.
53: Abberley, 1996, pp61-79.

or after birth. They may be mostly invisible, severely disfiguring or incapacitating, painful or even terminal. "The limitations which individual bodies or minds impose...vary from the trivial to the profound... The majority of disabled people do not have stable, congenital impairments... or sudden traumatic lesions (such as spinal cord injury), but instead have rheumatism or cardio-vascular disease or other chronic degenerative conditions associated with ageing".[54]

Most people don't fit neatly into two categories of able-bodied or disabled. People with slight visual or hearing defects, for example, can render these almost irrelevant by using spectacles or hearing aids (although they may need to pay for them), but those who are completely blind or deaf face far greater obstacles to social integration. The most severely impaired people are highly dependent on able-bodied support, provided in Britian by six million carers.

Finkelstein raises an associated problem. Disabled people "constantly fear that they may become associated with those that they see as less employable and more dependent. By trying to distance themselves from groups that they see as more disabled than themselves they can hope to maintain their claim to economic independence and an acceptable status in the community".[55] A more recent study shows that "[both] disabled and non-disabled people regard those with a learning disability or a mental illness as the least desirable groups".[56]

The issue of who is "really" disabled can be highly divisive. Mike Barratt of the NLBD recalls being told that blind people are not disabled.[57] The disability movement in Britain primarily organised around a fairly narrow stratum of physical impairment and was led mainly by wheelchair users.[58] As one activist with learning difficulties complained, "We are always asked to talk about advocacy and our impairments as though our barriers aren't disabling in the same way".[59]

Most disabled people do not actually consider themselves disabled. Department of Work and Pensions research in 2006 found this was true of

---

54: Shakespeare, 2002.
55: Finkelstein, 1993.
56: *Guardian*, 21 March 2007. See www.enham.org.uk/pages/research_page.html
57: Campbell and Oliver, 1996, p96.
58: Campbell abd Oliver write that this is because "the obstacles to political participation... are less severe than for people with other impairments"—Campbell and Oliver, 1996, p96.
59: Campbell and Oliver, 1996, p97. The issues around mental impairment are complex, and can only be touched on in this article.

"around half of those covered by the DDA".[60] Deaf people pose a particular problem in these terms. Many whose first language is sign see themselves as a linguistic minority, and regard integration as a threat to a history and culture at least 250 years old.[61] Other disabled people may see themselves as impaired, for example, some of those identified as having behavioural or mental health problems who arguably are not, but still suffer discrimination. This highly subjective element is partly why disability, to use a cliché, means different things to different people.

The extent and nature of these differences are other reasons (besides the more fundamental one of timing) why the disability movement attracted neither the opposition nor the scale of mobilisations and involvement experienced by other movements of the oppressed. Disability has no comparable equivalent to Stonewall or the great marches for black civil rights.

Capitalism in general does not scapegoat disabled people in order to divide and rule in the way it does with other forms of oppression. Such discrimination plays a less central ideological role than that of homophobia, women's oppression or racism. Neither is it generally popular. A recent UK survey, for example, found that 91 percent of people believe disabled people should have the same opportunities as everyone else.[62] Disabled people are often the victims of prejudice and ignorance, but they are rarely targeted solely because of their impairment. Even where this was true, for example, with the mass murder of disabled people in Hitler's gas chambers, this was not central to the Nazi movement in the way that scapegoating the Jews was. Similarly, bigotry against those with AIDS remains largely linked to anti-gay prejudice. Disability is fundamentally about neglect and marginalisation. Those who defend it ultimately do so using a much more central ideology—capitalism's need to extract the maximum profit from labour with the minimum possible expense.

David Cameron's government echoes its predecessor in its approach

---

60: Quoted in "Time to drop the 'disabled' label?", *Disability Now*, November 2006, p28.
61: Campbell and Oliver 1996, p120. Sacks, 1990, provides a fascinating introduction to the history of sign language and deafness, as well as addressing the issue of deaf people as a linguistic minority. I see no contradiction between accepting this view and still seeing deaf people's social exclusion as a disability.
62: Much was made of the report's other main finding—that "90 percent of Britons have never had a disabled person in their house for a social occasion". While it is true that many disabled people remain socially marginalised, this finding could equally be held to demonstrate how hidden or unacknowledged disability can be. See www.scope.org.uk/news/comres-poll

to "equalities" with a "corporate approach to diversity" which projects an inclusive image but in reality changes little.[63] The DRC, before its recent demise, largely portrayed discrimination in terms of unacceptable attitudes (for example, "See the person not the disability" advertisements). Many disabled people also see individual prejudice and social barriers as the central problem. Some believe further progress depends on strategies such as cultivating "disability pride" or urging more people to "come out" as disabled.

If disability is rooted in the economic organisation of society, real change must involve a new economic organisation of society. If it is not primarily a political or ideological construct, the key cannot be to change attitudes or language, important as these are. Achieving real change requires a power which disabled people alone do not possess.

While the differences may be significant, the experience of other social movements has shown that the common and fundamental problem in attempting to unite an oppressed group is the issue of class. The huge struggles for black liberation turned into demands for black businesses, while the fight against sexism has been appropriated by raunch culture on the one hand and concerns about the "glass ceiling" for a minority of high-achieving women on the other. For gays and lesbians too, genuine equality, despite (as well as because of) the rise of the "pink economy", remains elusive. Despite legislation outlawing discrimination against these oppressed groups, inequality remains deeply entrenched within the system.

## Class and disability

Like its counterparts in the US ruling class, the *Economist* complained about the potential costs of anti-discrimination legislation:

> Everyone agrees that it is desirable to cater for [disabled people's] needs. But if those needs are treated as rights, the obligation to help them could become limitless... Rights for the disabled must be balanced against the goal of a competitive economy.[64]

After these initial warnings about its alleged unaffordability, objections to anti-discrimination legislation focused on limiting its provisions, excluding "scroungers" (including alcoholics or drug addicts) and "fakers" deemed undeserving of rights or benefits. This issue of cost underpins most debates about disability, as well as those more generally around the

---

63: Younge, 2010.
64: "The price of rights", *Economist*, 13 August 1994.

"social costs of labour".[65] British capitalism needs some social spending in order to compete on the world market. But in recessions this conflicts with demands for reductions in spending, leading to arguments over what and how much is to be cut.[66]

Disability does not impact on all individuals equally. The incidence of impairment is much higher in poorer families.[67] In England people living in the poorest neighbourhoods die on average seven years earlier than those in the richest. The average difference in impairment-free life expectancy is 17 years. So working class people not only die sooner, but will also spend more of their shorter lives as disabled.[68] Secondly, wealthy disabled people can afford to pay for goods and services to compensate for the effects of oppression, in the same way that rich women employ nannies or cleaners. The majority of disabled people have no such option. Their lives are dominated by poverty, poor education and housing—as is the case for most other workers. As Glynn Vernon once said, "[My main problem is] I don't have enough money, and I don't have enough sex".[69]

The greater visibility of disabled people in the labour force means they are more likely to be accepted as workmates, rather than social or economic burdens. In Britain the first disability trade union conference (organised by Nalgo, one of Unison's predecessors) took place in Hull in 1988. Today disabled members' sections exist in most British trade unions, with notable efforts to unite able-bodied and disabled workers. Recent trade union campaigns (for example, the PCS's Public Services Not Private Profit campaign and Unison's against the Private Finance Initiative/Public Private Partnerships), as well as others such as Keep Our NHS Public or Defend Council Housing, have brought unions together with service providers and user groups, including those of disabled people.

Aids and adaptations originally designed for disabled people have often proved to have much wider benefits. The typewriter, for example, was first invented over two centuries ago to help blind individuals communicate more effectively, while e-mail and internet chat rooms

---

65:  This is reflected in the DDA itself, with the mainly cost-based justifications for refusing "reasonable adjustments".

66:  At time of writing these have led to government U-turns over axeing free milk for under-fives and the freeze on school rebuilding programmes.

67:  *Guardian*, 21 April 2010. See www.biomedcentral.com/content/pdf/1471-2431-10-21.pdf

68:  "Fair Society, Healthy Lives: A Strategic Review of Health Inequalities in England Post-2010", February 2010. See http://www.marmotreview.org

69:  Vernon was the subject of the excellent disability awareness film *Stand Up The Real Glynn Vernon* (1988).

originated with inventions made for the deaf in the 1960s and 1970s. Today dropped kerbs on pavements benefit parents with pushchairs or shoppers with trolleys, closed captions on TV allow hearing viewers to watch in silence, and automatic doors in local supermarkets make access easier, not just for wheelchair users, but for everyone.[70] The principles of "universal design" (products and environments usable by all which need no adaptations) are now increasingly popular in education.[71]

Disability rights for socialists must be part of building a collective working class consciousness. The provision of aids and adaptations in schools, universities and workplaces both helps disabled individuals to participate on an equal basis and builds unity in practice. This means ensuring, for example, that the Disability Equality Duty (DED), limited as its provisions may be, is fully implemented wherever possible.[72] It may also mean defending sheltered workshops such as Remploy, even though we oppose segregation, and defending "special needs" education against cuts, though we believe everyone's needs are special.[73] Social reforms must be defended—not least in order to show the possibility of winning greater change in the future—but without illusions. Working class disabled people cannot afford to pay for their rights, either in the form of services or legal proceedings to secure access to them. While individual rights are important, they are in the final instance no substitute for collective liberation.

Other social movements helped achieve important legal change, while leaving intact fundamental inequalities. Over three decades after the British Equal Pay Act women's earnings are still on average 21 percent less than men's.[74] Disability discrimination too can never be simply legislated away, because, like women's oppression, it is embedded deeply in the structures of capitalist society.

In its earlier days the disability movement represented and organised those who saw social change—no matter how narrowly conceived—as the key to a better life for all. As UPIAS recognised, disabled people are a

70: Johnson, 2003, pp214-217. Johnson describes the US backlash against disability rights since the ADA.

71: Center for Universal Design, NC State University: www.design.ncsu.edu/cud/about_ud/udprinciples.htm

72: The DED requires that all public bodies '"give due regard'" to the promotion of disability equality. See www.dotheduty.org/. It is as yet unclear how the DED will be affected by the new Equality Act.

73: This is a hotly debated area. The socialist principle is that every need can be fully provided for through fully resourced mainstream education—an important building block towards a properly integrated society.

74: Fawcett Society report quoted in the *Guardian*, 30 October 2009.

minority in society who lack the power to achieve lasting change on their own. Disabled people often in practice express a broader political or class identity, rather than one based purely on disability. The biggest demonstrations on record, the huge mobilisations against the Iraq war, were also the biggest demonstrations of disabled people.

The "festival of the oppressed" has been a feature of every major period of working class struggle, where previously demonised or marginalised groups have championed a common cause. Immigrant workers helped lead movements such as the Chartists and the Wobblies. At the peak of the struggle in Poland in 1980 one hospital doctor related how working class patients discharged themselves, suddenly well enough to join the Solidarność workers' movement.[75] The Russian Revolution of 1917, which saw women and Jews elected as its leaders, producing new ideas about disability many decades ahead of its time.[76] Just as oppressed minorities rose to the forefront of these struggles, disabled people will be among those leading the revolutions of the 21st century.

## An end to disability?

The horrors of the past are not simply abstract history lessons. The assumptions of eugenics are still present in claims that human society and behaviour are determined by our genes. Discussing online the death of David Cameron's disabled son Ivan, senior British National Party activist Jeffrey Marshall complained about "an excess of sentimentality towards the weak and unproductive", adding later that "there is not a great deal of point in keeping these people alive".[77] Although such ideas remain largely confined to the margins, this can change quickly.[78] Cuts on a scale unseen since the 1930s are likely to rapidly polarise society, as the media and the government round on the latest scapegoats for the crisis. The coalition's plans to privatise workplace safety inspections, increase its predecessor's restrictions on disability benefits and promote the expansion of "special" (segregated) schools will create more impairment and more disability. But attacks on social services, pensions and benefits risk provoking generalised resistance.

From Mumbai to Mexico City, slums similar to those Marx, Engels

---

75: Barker and Weber, 1982, p148 .
76: Vygotsky's pioneering and influential work, for example, on the education of disabled children.
77: *Observer*, 31 May 2009.
78: BBC Radio 4 recently hosted a debate featuring arch-reactionary David Marsland proposing that "The morally and mentally unfit should be sterilised"—"Iconoclasts", 25 August 2010.

and Dickens exposed 150 years ago now house an estimated 1 billion people, with poverty creating more disease and opening pathways for epidemics like HIV/Aids. Much of modern capitalism, with its ageing population, service industries and technological advances, differs markedly from the Industrial Revolution. Today's workforce is as likely to be affected by repetitive strain injury or depression as by other workplace injuries. But the remorseless global drive to accumulate continues to cause disabling accidents and conditions at an unprecedented rate. The essence of humanity, our capacity to reshape ourselves and our world through social labour, remains controlled by a small minority whose sole interest in production is profit. The removal of this exploitation—the most fundamental divide in society—is a prerequisite if humanity is to achieve its liberation.

Marx provided a new definition of meaningful labour:

> In a higher phase of communist society, after the enslaving subordination of individuals under division of labour, and therewith also the antithesis between mental and physical labour, has vanished; after labour, from a mere means of life, has become the prime necessity of life...society [can] inscribe on its banner: from each according to his abilities, to each according to his needs.[79]

A socialist society will not liberate disabled people from their impairments. But eradicating competitive accumulation, the basis for capitalism's wars, waste and pollution, will also eradicate the source of so much impairment. Simple measures implemented globally, for example, could prevent or cure the vast majority of all visual defects and blindness.[80] In an economy planned and controlled by the majority, science, medicine and social care will be socialised and restructured by providers and users alike. Cooperation on a scale unprecedented in history will provide the basis for a real individualism celebrating diversity difference, and mutual interdependence. Only such a society can significantly reduce both the causes and the effects of impairment—as well as providing an end to disability.

---

79: Marx, 1875.
80: For the measures and the figures, see www.who.int/mediacentre/factsheets/fs282/en

# References

Abberley, Paul, 1996, "Work, Utopia and Impairment", in Len Barton (ed), *Disability and Society: Emerging Issues and Insights* (Longman).

Appignanesi, Lisa, 2008, *Mad, Bad and Sad: A History of Women and the Mind Doctors from 1800 to the Present* (Virago).

Barker, Colin, and Kara Weber, 1982, "Solidarność: from Gdansk to Military Repression", *International Socialism 15* (winter).

Barnes, Colin, 1991, *Disabled People in Britain and Discrimination: The Case for Anti-Discrimination Legislation* (Hurst).

Barnes, Colin, 2007, "Direct Payments for Personal Assistants for Disabled People: a Key to Independent Living?", www.independentliving.org/docs7/barnes20070605.html

Beresford, Peter, 2008, "Whose Personalisation?", *Soundings*, number 40.

Campbell, Jane, 2008, "Joined up thinking", *Guardian* (30 April).

Campbell, Jane, and Michael Oliver, 1996, *Disability Politics* (Routledge).

Crow, Liz, 2000, "Helen Keller: Rethinking the Problematic Icon", *Disability and Society*, volume 15, number 6.

Davis, John, 2003, *Helen Keller* (Ocean Press).

Deal, Mark, 2006, "Attitudes of disabled people towards other disabled people and impairment groups", www.enham.org.uk/pages/research_page.html

Disability Rights Advocates, 2001, *Forgotten Crimes: The Holocaust And People With Disabilities*, www.dralegal.org/downloads/pubs/forgotten_crimes.pdf

Driedger, Diane, 1989, *The Last Civil Rights Movement* (St Martin's Press).

Ferguson, Iain, 2007, "Increasing User Choice or Privatizing Risk? The Antinomies of Personalisation", *British Journal of Social Work*, 37.

Finkelstein, Vic, 1981, "Disability and the Helper/Helped Relationship. An Historical View", in Ann Brechin, P Liddiard and J Swain (eds), *Handicap in a Social World* (Hodder Arnold).

Finkelstein, Vic, 1993, "The Commonality of Disability", in John Swain, Sally French, Colin Barnes and Carol Thomas (eds), *Disabling Barriers, Enabling Environments* (Sage).

Johnson, Mary, 2003, *Make Them Go Away: Clint Eastwood, Christopher Reeve and the Case Against Disability Rights* (Avocado Press).

Marx, Karl, 2003 (1867), *Capital*, volume 1 (Lawrence & Wishart), www.marxists.org/archive/marx/works/1867-c1

Marx, Karl (1875), *Critique of the Gotha Programme*, www.marxists.org/archive/marx/works/1875/gotha/ch01.htm

Morris, Jenny, 2005, "Independent Living: The Role of Evidence and Ideology in the Development of Government Policy", www.leeds.ac.uk/disability-studies/archiveuk/morris/cash%20and%20care%20conference.jennymorris%20paper.pdf

Oliver, Michael, 1990, *The Politics of Disablement* (Palgrave Macmillan).

Oliver, Michael, 1996, "Defining Impairment and Disability: Issues at Stake", in Colin Barnes and Geof Mercer (eds), *Exploring the Divide—Illness and Disability* (The Disability Press 1996).

Oliver, Michael, and Colin Barnes, 2006, "Disability Politics and The Disability Movement in Britain: Where Did It All Go Wrong?", www.leeds.ac.uk/disability-studies/archiveuk/Barnes/Coalition%20disability%20politics%20paper.pdf

Pagel, Martin, 1988, "On Our Own Behalf" (Greater Manchester Coalition of Disabled People), www.gmcdp.com

Public Interest Research Unit, 2004, "Teeth and their Use", www.leeds.ac.uk/disability-studies/archiveuk/harwood/tuwnov9.pdf

Prime Minister's Strategy Unit, 2005, "Improving the Life Chances of Disabled People", www.cabinetoffice.gov.uk/media/cabinetoffice/strategy/assets/disability.pdf

Rogers, Ann, 1993, "Back To The Workhouse?", *International Socialism* 59 (summer).

Russell, Marta, 1999, "Productive Bodies and the Market", *Left Business Observer* (9 November).

Russell, Marta, and Ravi Malhotra, 2002, "The Political Economy of Disablement: Advances and Contradictions", *Socialist Register 2002: A World of Contradictions* (Merlin).

Russell, Marta, and Jean Stewart, 2001, "Disablement, Prison and Historical Segregation", *Monthly Review*, volume 53, number 3 (July-August), www.monthlyreview.org/0701russell.htm

Sacks, Oliver, 1990, *Seeing Voices* (Picador).

Shakespeare, Tom, 2002, "The Social Model of Disability: An Outdated Ideology?", *Research in Social Science and Disability*, 2.

Shakespeare, Tom, 2006, *Disability Rights and Wrongs* (Routledge).

Shapiro, Joseph, 1994, *No Pity: People with Disabilities Forging a New Civil Rights Movement* (Three Rivers Press).

Stack, Pat, 2007, "Why are disabled people oppressed?", *Socialist Worker* (28 July), www.socialistworker.co.uk/art.php?id=12549

Stratford, Brian, 1989, *Down's Syndrome; Past, Present & Future* (Penguin).

UPIAS, 1997 (1976), "Fundamental Principles of Disability", www.leeds.ac.uk/disability-studies/archiveuk/UPIAS/fundamental%20principles.pdf

Younge, Gary, 2010, *Who Are We?* (Viking).

# Decoding capitalism

*Joseph Choonara*

*A review of David Harvey,* **The Enigma of Capital** *(Profile, 2010), £14.99*

David Harvey ranks today among the world's most renowned Marxist theoreticians. His fame is thoroughly deserved. Few red professors have his gift for presenting sophisticated ideas with such clarity or his commitment to exploring the central questions of the moment. In recent years he has been most strongly associated with a growing interest in Marxist political economy, notably through his talks on *Capital*, which are available free online and now in book form.[1]

In these talks, Harvey combines a thorough and serious engagement with *Capital*, first demonstrated in his classic 1982 work, *The Limits to Capital*,[2] with a refreshing willingness to treat Karl Marx as a human being, capable of digressions, mistakes and the odd off-day.[3] Where Marx's writings are incomplete and unfinished, and this includes the second and third volumes of *Capital*, it is not enough simply to repeat passages as revered scripture. It is necessary to extend Marx's method to seek to complete his account of capitalism, while always bearing in mind that the novelties capitalism throws up as it evolves necessitate the "perpetual recasting of the conceptual apparatus".[4]

---

1: http://davidharvey.org/reading-capital/ and Harvey, 2010b.

2: Harvey, 2006a, henceforth *Limits*.

3: For instance, he writes in his guide to *Capital* that chapters 17 and 18 "do not pose any substantial issues", consisting largely of repetition, and ignores "odd passages" in the preceding chapter that "echo 19th century thinking on environmental determinism and the domination of nature"—Harvey, 2010b, pp239-240.

4: Harvey, 2006a, p446.

*The Enigma of Capital* is therefore a work we should take very seriously indeed.[5] The winner of the 2010 Isaac and Tamara Deutscher Memorial Prize, it represents Harvey's most sustained attempt to grapple with the current economic crisis. In addition, it highlights his commitment to translate his theoretical perspectives into political answers to Lenin's question, "What is to be done?"[6] As Harvey recently demonstrated at a series of hundreds-strong meetings in London and Athens, this involves reviving once unfashionable terms such as "revolution" and "communism".[7]

## Exploring the crisis

*Enigma* opens with a 40-page account of the current crisis, written in a narrative style, charting the mutation of the subprime housing crisis in the US into a full-blown global recession. At this level there are strong parallels between Harvey's account and that of writers associated with this journal.[8]

He charts the growth of finance over recent decades, seeing this as reflecting shifts and problems in the wider system, rather than as an autonomous process. Financialisation develops out of the increasingly global nature of capitalism, which requires the formation of a global financial system to support flows of capital; wage repression, which necessitates growing consumer credit to maintain demand; and a shift from investment in production towards investment in "asset values" that can be driven up in price for speculative gain.[9] Harvey writes, "Less and less of the surplus capital has been absorbed in production (in spite of everything that has happened in China) because global profit margins began to fall after a brief revival in the 1980s".[10] The creation of a series of asset price bubbles helped to keep the economy driving forwards, so it was no coincidence that the collapse of these bubbles led to the stalling of the system, both through the freezing of credit markets and the collapse of global trade.

Harvey then moves from his narrative account of the crisis to a theory of capitalist crises in general. He first presented a sophisticated and extremely influential account of crisis in *Limits*, and it is worth considering this, both in order to compare it with that in *Enigma* and because

---

5:   Henceforth *Enigma*.
6:   Harvey, 2010a, p227.
7:   Harvey's talk at King's College London is available in video from http://davidharvey. org/2010/05/ and an MP3 of the talk is available from http://kclreadingcapital.blogspot.com/
8:   See, for instance, Callinicos, 2010, pp20-94; Harman, 2009a; Harman, 2009b, pp277-304; Choonara, 2009a; Choonara, 2010.
9:   Harvey, 2010a, p23.
10:  Harvey, 2010a, p28.

the latter book is far more popular in form, leaving the theoretical underpinnings largely unelaborated.

In *Limits* crisis theory is presented in three stages. The "first cut" theory is derived mainly from Marx's writings on the "law of the tendency of the rate of profit to fall" and the "counteracting tendencies" in the third volume of *Capital*.[11] Abstracting from complexities such as interest rates or land rent, this first cut theory, Harvey suggests, involves "periodic crises" that may be intensified and deepened by "secular decline".[12]

Many political economists prior to Marx had pointed out an apparent long-term tendency for profit rates to fall. Marx sought to explain this fall as a consequence of the "rising organic composition of capital". Capitalists, spurred by competition, tend to accumulate capital in the form of "dead labour"—machinery, equipment, greater quantities of raw materials, etc— at the expense of employing and exploiting more "living labour" (wage workers). Because it is only living labour that creates new value for the capitalists, this drive to accumulate dead labour can only undermine profitability in the long run. Harvey is at pains to point out in *Limits* that Marx also elaborated a series of counteracting tendencies that offset the tendency for profit rates to fall. By far the most important is the potential cheapening of dead labour, which can lower the value of investment, thus driving up profit rates.

Harvey suggests that this can take the form of a gradual depreciation, with the resulting shift in values constantly disturbing the capitalist economy, or it can take the much more violent form of crisis:

> The gentle imagery of "depreciation" gives way to the more dramatic and violent imagery of "destruction" when it comes to describing the devaluations that occur in the course of crises. At the moment of crisis, all of the contradictions inherent in the capitalist mode of production are expressed in the form of violent paroxysms which impose "momentary and forcible solutions" and "for a time restore the disturbed equilibrium" (*Capital*, volume 3, p249).[13]

Already, at the time he wrote *Limits*, Harvey was sceptical about the law of the tendency of the rate of profit to fall, although he does accept that it was central to Marx's account.[14] In *Enigma*, although he does not engage

---

11: Those unfamiliar with these concepts can consult Choonara, 2009b, or Harman, 2007.

12: Harvey, 2006a, p191.

13: Harvey, 2006a, p200.

14: Discussion with the author.

with these questions with anything like the same degree of rigour, he is much more definite: "It is hard to make Marx's theory of the falling rate of profit work when innovation is as much capital or means of production saving...as it is labour saving".[15] While Harvey believes that the rate of profit has in fact fallen during the post-war period, he rejects Marx's explanation. But there is no need to go down this road. Harvey seems to accept the writings of theorists such as Nobou Okishio, who sought to prove that investment will always take place in such a way as to raise profitability, provided the standard of living of workers remains fixed.[16] But this is based on a static equilibrium model of capitalism. Once the system is conceived as a temporal one, with investments by particular capitalists happening at one point in time, production and sale subsequently, Okishio's "proof" vanishes into thin air.[17]

There are good theoretical reasons to believe that capitalists would operate in such a way as to raise the organic composition of capital. "Capital saving" investments are certainly possible, but this is not the end of the story. Insomuch as they liberate additional surplus value, they create the potential for further investment. Even when capitalists have made all the capital saving investments available to them, there will be opportunities for additional labour saving ones, provided they can amass the surplus value required. Once one capitalist makes such an investment, raising the productivity of their labourers and undercutting rivals through price competition, there will be a powerful pressure on other capitalists to replicate the investment.[18] Despite such arguments, Harvey has long argued that it is necessary to replace Marx's law of the tendency of the rate of profit to fall with something more general:

> Marx, in his anxiety to straighten out the political economists, is lured into an erroneous specification of what should have been a synthetic model of the contradictions of capitalism. More specifically, by taking over the problem of the inevitability of a falling rate of profit from the political economists of the time and treating it as a question, Marx diverts from the logic of his own argument to such a degree that what should have been a tangential proposition appears fundamental while the fundamental proposition gets interred in a mass of tangential argument.[19]

---

15: Harvey, 2010a, p94.
16: See Harvey, 2006a, pp185-188 and the references therein.
17: See Harman, 2007; Harman, 2009b, pp68-75; Kliman, 2007, pp113-136; Carchedi, 1991, pp139-141.
18: Harman, 2007; Choonara, 2009b, pp80-82.
19: Harvey, 2006a, p180.

In Harvey's view the imperative to innovate and accumulate instead leads to a "surplus of capital relative to the opportunities to employ that capital. Such a state of overproduction of capital is called the 'overaccumulation of capital'."[20] It is this account, and with it an associated "disposal of surplus problem", that Harvey carries over into *Enigma*.

But if the problem capitalism faces is the disposal of surplus, this can imply either of two possible theoretical frameworks. The first is that held by authors such as Paul Sweezy, Paul Baran and John Bellamy Foster associated with the US-based periodical *Monthly Review*. This is that monopolies are able to manipulate prices such that they receive "surplus profits" (a rather vague term) that they struggle to dispose of. This is not, as far as I can tell, Harvey's position.[21] The second version is to see overaccumulation as the generation of a mass of profit (which may in absolute terms be vast, even if the rate of profit is low) under conditions where there are few profitable outlets. In this version Marx's law of the tendency of the rate of profit to fall can strengthen the analysis, provided it is argued theoretically and empirically guided.[22] This would explain why, in conditions of low profitability, money flows to geographical locations where capitalists expect, rightly or wrongly, that they can make a healthy profit (Harvey discusses the enormous over-capacity in China[23]) and into assets where they can make short-term paper profits without generating new value.

Is this a fundamentalist position? It has certainly been subjected to a sustained attack along those lines for several decades (Okishio's critique was published in 1961). But if, for Marx, capital is essentially value set in motion to expand, and if the system is based on capital, then any factor that undermines this process from within seems worthy of special status. In fact, in *Enigma* Harvey seems to slip into some rather sweeping claims of his own about capital's expansion, for instance, his insistence that capitalism requires a 3 percent rate of compound GDP growth.[24] But this point is never subjected to any serious investigation, nor is the relationship between GDP growth, profitability and rates of

---

20: Harvey, 2006a, p192.
21: See, for instance, Harvey, 2006a, p141, where he argues that Sweezy and Baran's account means "abandoning the law of value—which, to their credit, Baran and Sweezy are fully prepared to do". While *Enigma* is more complimentary, it treats their analysis of monopoly as pertinent only at a particular point in history—Harvey, 2010a, p113.
22: See, for instance, Harman, 2010; Kliman, 2010.
23: Harvey, 2010a, p222.
24: Harvey, 2010a, pp26-27.

accumulation explored. This is unfortunate given how frequently the concept is deployed.[25]

Whatever one makes of all this, Harvey is correct to argue that crisis cannot be simply reduced to a single factor, whether "profit rates" or the "disposal of surplus". There are two ways in which he seeks to broaden the theory of crisis.

The first is to see the potential for capital's circuit to break down, even if only momentarily, at any point where a "blockage" arises.[26] If capitalists cannot harness the money they require to invest, or if the labour power, equipment or raw materials are not available, the circuit will be interrupted. Similarly, crisis can erupt if goods cannot find a market with sufficient effective demand either from other capitalists or workers. The possibility of crisis is ever-present. Harvey also adds various "natural" limits to capital—ecological destruction or shortages of oil, for example—though, as he points out, the environment and its limits are rarely "natural" in some "pure and pristine" manner.[27] This is all true, and indeed Marx sets out a much more general theory of potential breakdown prior to looking at the specific mechanisms involved.[28] But this cannot substitute for an analysis of the concrete processes driving the system into crisis, as it sometimes seems to in *Enigma*.

In going beyond the formal possibility of breakdown, the second way that Harvey seeks to broaden his account of crisis is far more fruitful. This involves integrating additional features of capitalism through what he calls in *Limits* his "second" and "third" cut theories of crisis. The "second cut" involves something Marx never fully achieved in his drafts for the third volume of *Capital*—the integration of his account of production with that of credit and finance. Consequently, Harvey's attempt to do this is one of the highlights of *Limits*.[29] Here finance is seen as a force driving capital beyond its limits, coordinating different aspects of the capitalist cycle through the movement of interest rates, and causing it to erupt into speculative bouts and frenzied monetary or stockmarket crises. Wholly new forms of crisis now become possible, and our understanding of existing ones is dramatically reshaped. One suggestive possibility is that problems developing in a particular sphere of a capitalist economy may be displaced into another, delaying the onset of crisis, only for it to resurface in a new form. One such example might be the way that the prolonged period of fraught accumulation faced

---

25: See, for example, Harvey, 2010a, pp45, 50, 70, 86, 112.

26: Harvey, 2010a, pp116-118.

27: Harvey, 2010a, pp84-85.

28: Harvey mainly draws on Marx's Grundrisse, but see also Marx, 1975, pp492-535.

29: Harvey, 2006a, pp324-329.

by capitalism in recent decades, rather than leading directly to crisis, helped create an increasingly bloated and unhealthy financial system, which is where, in 2007-8, crisis ultimately erupted. As Harvey writes in *Enigma*:

> The problem of falling profits and devaluations due to lack of effective demand can be staved off for a while through the machinations of the credit system. In the short term, credit works to smooth out many minor problems, but over the long term it tends to accumulate the contradictions and the tensions. It spreads the risk at the same time as it accumulates them... When one limit is overcome accumulation often hits up against another somewhere else... The crisis tendencies are not resolved but merely moved around.[30]

One of Harvey's claims is that categories such as credit, which Marx developed very late in the manuscripts for *Capital*, need to be deployed from the outset to understand the system's concrete development.[31] This also applies to categories that barely feature in *Capital* such as the state.[32] And, as Harvey stresses in *Enigma*, the "state-finance nexus", the arrangement of central banks, treasuries and monetary systems in particular nations, is crucial to grasping the unfolding crisis.[33] Indeed, the emergence of the sovereign debt crisis in Europe, which developed largely after the book was written, reinforces his argument.[34]

## Geography matters

The "third cut" theory of crisis adds another dimension—the development of capital in space. Harvey's concern with the geography of capitalism is one of his ongoing contributions to Marxist theory.[35] This provides *Enigma* with two of its most thought-provoking chapters, "The Geography of it all" and "Creative Destruction on the Land". Capital, for Harvey, always evolves in space and time, creating as it does so distinctive geographies. Capital clusters together to avoid the frictional costs of transportation, and is embodied in landscapes through urbanisation and the development of communication networks. This process is both uneven and never-ending, abhorring any equilibrium. Because the logic of accumulation is to seek profit wherever it is to be found, capitalist development means the

---

30: Harvey, 2010a, pp116-117.
31: Harvey, 2006a, pp187-188.
32: Harvey, 2009.
33: Harvey, 2010a, p54-57.
34: Harvey, 2010a, p222.
35: See Harvey, 2006a, pp373-445; Harvey, 2006b; Harvey, 2005a, pp94-101.

periodic ripping up and reorganisation of the geography of capitalism, and potential shifts in its foci:

> The geographical landscape is…shaped by perpetual tension between the economies of centralisation, on the one hand, and the potentially higher profits to be had from decentralisation and dispersal on the other. How that tension works out depends on the barriers posed to spatial movement, the intensity of agglomeration economies and divisions of labour.[36]

His desire to understand these patterns led Harvey to devote a large section of *Limits* to attempts to understand Marx's theory of land rent, and he continues to insist that as in "the case of interest and credit, rent has to be brought forward into the forefront of the analysis, rather than being treated as a derivative category of distribution as happens in Marxist as well as in conventional economic theories".[37] Harvey charts the spread of the current crisis from a localised glitch in the US subprime mortgage market to a global cataclysm through this uneven space. But the space is not just the terrain of capital; it is also constituted by a system of rival states. As in his earlier works, he sets out a vision of imperialism as constituted by the intersection between two logics—that of capitalism and a "logic of power" driven by "territorial imperatives and political interests".[38]

Of course, this is simply to pose the problem in a formal sense. The test is whether theory can grasp the concrete ways that these "two logics" work together, dialectically and in tension with each other, in the course of the development of capitalism. Much of Harvey's work is devoted to just such an effort—notably *The New Imperialism, A Brief History of Neoliberalism* and now *Enigma*. He is aware of the enormous difficulties of his endeavour: "The reason that it is so difficult to integrate the making of geography into any general theory of capital accumulation…is that this process is not only deeply contradictory but also full of contingencies, accidents and confusions".[39]

Generally, Harvey's attempts are impressive, and all of his flair as a story teller is on display in these chapters. However, issues with Harvey's account of accumulation resurface in his attempt to weave the two logics together. He tends to emphasise "push" factors spurring the spread of

---

36: Harvey, 2010a, p165.
37: Harvey, 2010a, p183.
38: Harvey, 2010a, p204. See also Harvey, 2005a; Callinicos, 2009, pp71-73.
39: Harvey, 2010a, p214.

capital—in particular the need for a "spatial fix" to solve the "surplus capital disposal problem". At times this can make capitalist globalisation and imperialism seem like a conscious attempt by the ruling class to stave off crises of overaccumulation.[40] This credits our rulers with too great an understanding of their system. I would prefer to emphasise the "pull factors", which at times Harvey also stresses, such as the search for greater potential profits, the need to establish control over territories, resources and markets to bolster the economic fortunes of particular states and so on.

## Theorising social change

One of Harvey's most ambitious goals in *Enigma* is his quest to develop a wider theory of social evolution. Here he manages to be both incredibly incisive and, at times, infuriating. He constructs what seems to me a peculiarly schematic model of social development involving:

> Seven distinctive "activity spheres" within the evolutionary trajectory of capitalism: technologies and organisational forms; social relations; institutional and administrative arrangements; production and labour processes; relations to nature; the reproduction of daily life and of the species; and "mental conceptions of the world". No one sphere dominates even as none of them are independent of the others. But nor is any one of them determined even collectively by all of the others".[41]

Seven is certainly an evocative number. (Seven hills of Rome, seven wonders of the ancient world, seven sleepers of Ephesus, seven deadly sins, seven days of creation, seven seals in the *Revelations*...) But why seven? Why not eight spheres or 80 or 800? Why are the organisational forms of capitalism part of the same sphere as the technologies? Are they not also worthy of the kind of autonomy that separates institutional relations from social relations? Harvey claims to derive his list, at least in part, from a footnote to chapter 15 of the first volume of *Capital*. This is certainly a fascinating chapter, detailing the wider social, economic and political implications of the development of machinery. But I think Harvey gives too much weight to the footnote. According to Marx:

---

40: Here Harvey's overaccumulationist theory is the flip side of Lenin's underconsumptionist account of crisis in *Imperialism: The Highest Stage of Capitalism*, where Lenin argues, "The need to export capital arises from the fact that in a few countries capitalism has become 'overripe' and...capital cannot find a field for 'profitable' investment"—cited in Callinicos, 2009, p47.

41: Harvey, 2010a, p123.

A critical history of technology would show how little any of the inventions of the 18th century are the work of a single individual. Hitherto there is no such book. Darwin has interested us in the history of Nature's Technology, ie, in the formation of the organs of plants and animals, which organs serve as instruments of production for sustaining life. Does not the history of the productive organs of man, of organs that are the material basis of all social organisation, deserve equal attention? And would not such a history be easier to compile, since, as Vico says, human history differs from natural history in this, that we have made the former, but not the latter? *Technology discloses man's mode of dealing with Nature, the process of production by which he sustains his life, and thereby also lays bare the mode of formation of his social relations, and of the mental conceptions that flow from them.* Every history of religion, even, that fails to take account of this material basis, is uncritical. It is, in reality, much easier to discover by analysis the earthly core of the misty creations of religion, than, conversely, it is, to develop from the actual relations of life the corresponding celestialised forms of those relations. The latter method is the only materialistic, and therefore the only scientific one. The weak points in the abstract materialism of natural science, a materialism that excludes history and its process, are at once evident from the abstract and ideological conceptions of its spokesmen, whenever they venture beyond the bounds of their own speciality.[42]

As Harvey writes elsewhere, when it comes to relating the different spheres of activity mentioned in the italicised passage, "Though his language is suggestive, Marx leaves the question open, which is unfortunate since it leaves lots of space for all manner of interpretations".[43] But Marx does provide plenty of material in other works from which an account of social change can be derived.[44] And the challenge Marx makes immediately after the italicised passage of the footnote is to see mental conceptions of the world, in this case religion, as arising out of historically determined material conditions.

This requires that we view society as a structured totality of dialectically interrelated elements, but this is not the same as seeing each element as occupying an equal and equivalent position. Harvey, by insisting on this, comes very close to poststructuralist accounts of society,

42: Marx, 1970, p352 (my italics).
43: Harvey, 2010b, p192.
44: See, for instance, Marx's famous "preface" to his *A Contribution to the Critique of Political Economy*—Marx, 1977.

even at one point embracing Gilles Deleuze and Felix Guattari's concept of the "assemblage" as a method.[45]

This leads to all sorts of odd claims. For instance, Harvey argues that the Russian Revolution of 1917 was derailed because of the failure of Lenin (and later Stalin) to "engage politically across" each of the "seven spheres". The Bolshevik Revolution "inevitably failed" because "a single-track programme in which the productive forces (technologies) were placed in the vanguard of change" led to "stasis, stagnant administrative and institutional arrangements, turned daily life into monotony, and froze the possibility to explore new social relations or mental conceptions. It paid no mind to the relation with nature, with disastrous consequences".[46] Harvey adds:

> Lenin, of course, had no option but to strive to create communism on the basis of the configuration given by the preceding order... He plausibly argued that if the transition to socialism and then communism was to work it had to be initially on the basis of the most advanced technologies and organisational forms that capitalism had produced. But there was no conscious attempt, particularly after Stalin took over, to move towards the construction of truly socialist, let alone communist technologies and organisational forms.[47]

There are three problems with this kind of account. First, for a Marxist so acutely aware of the international, to ignore Lenin's view that revolution in Russia was a prelude to a necessarily European-wide revolutionary process is strange. Lenin's argument was not that aping Western style technological innovation would lead to socialism, but that the material means for socialism did not exist on the Russian terrain. Following Leon Trotsky, he argued that revolution had to be an international process in order to become permanent. Second, Harvey is guilty of a reductionism that sees all of the factors he describes as flowing from what he perceives to be the misguided political theory of the Bolsheviks. There is no attempt to trace the rise of the bureaucracy in the context of the civil war that followed the revolution, or to consider the degeneration of the workers' democracy that had been, far more than technology, the basis for the cultural and political liberation that flowered in the early years. Third, he does

---

45: Harvey, 2010a, p128. See Brennan, 2003, for an excellent critique of Michael Hardt and Antonio Negri's adoption of the same term and method in their work *Empire*.
46: Harvey, 2010a, p136.
47: Harvey, 2010a, p136.

not sufficiently or clearly distinguish between those forces that claimed to be attempting to establish socialism from the top-down (in this case Stalin) and the forces at the bottom of society seeking to bring about socialism from below through a process of self-emancipation (the workers who provided the motive force of the revolution).[48]

This means, more generally, that Harvey cannot distinguish between splits that reflect the sectarianism of sections of the left, and splits that reflect more substantive issues, such as that between Stalinism and Trotskyism.[49] He lumps together such varied experiences as that of the "Bolivarian movement in Venezuela" and "the workers' party in Brazil" (and even throws in "the Communist Party in China"), ignoring the explosions of popular struggle that gave the first of these its much more radical edge.[50] While his call for a broad movement challenging capitalism is welcome, this does not mean disregarding important historical lessons, some of them very hard won.

Whatever the limitations and ambiguities, Harvey's emphasis on strategy is both timely and extremely welcome. Few academics, even left academics, today are prepared to assume the role of public intellectuals, using their prestige to champion the oppressed and excluded. Fewer still are capable of descending from the ivory tower to address directly and clearly movements that challenge the logic of the system. Harvey's embrace of militant struggle and the possibility of revolution make easier the task of all those on the left who wish to respond to the current crisis. And his is a full-blooded vision of revolution, involving the dispossession of the powerful, which he insists cannot be purely pacific.[51] Towards the end of *Enigma* he writes, "Capitalism will never fall on its own. It will have to be pushed".[52] The more we debate the themes Harvey raises, the greater will be our clarity over the lessons thrown up by the past, and the more effective will be our efforts to ensure that in the struggles ahead we can push in the same direction at the same time.

---

48: Draper, 1966, is the classic statement of this position.
49: Harvey, 2010a, pp252-253.
50: Harvey, 2010a, p256.
51: Harvey, 2010a, p250.
52: Harvey, 2010a, p260.

# References

Brennan, Timothy, 2003, "The Italian Ideology", in *Debating Empire* (Verso).

Callinicos, Alex, 2009, *Imperialism and Global Political Economy* (Polity).

Callinicos, Alex, 2010, *Bonfire of Illusions: The Twin Crises of the Liberal World* (Polity).

Carchedi, Guglielmo, 1991, *Frontiers of Political Economy* (Verso).

Choonara, Joseph, 2009a, "Marxist Accounts of the Current Crisis", *International Socialism 123* (summer), www.isj.org.uk/?id=557

Choonara, Joseph, 2009b, *Unravelling Capitalism: A Guide to Marxist Political Economy* (Bookmarks).

Choonara, Joseph, 2010, "The Crisis: Over or Just Beginning?", *Socialist Review* (May), www.socialistreview.org.uk/article.php?articlenumber=11255

Draper, Hal, 1966, "The Two Souls of Socialism", *New Politics 5* (winter), www.marxists.org/archive/draper/1966/twosouls/

Harman, Chris, 2007, "The Rate of Profit and the World Today", *International Socialism 115* (summer), www.isj.org.uk/?id=340

Harman, Chris, 2009a, "The Slump of the 1930s and the Crisis Today", www.isj.org.uk/?id=506, *International Socialism 121* (winter),

Harman, Chris, 2009b, *Zombie Capitalism: Global Crisis and the Relevance of Marx* (Bookmarks).

Harman, Chris, 2010, "Not All Marxism is Dogmatism: A Reply to Michel Husson", *International Socialism 125* (winter), www.isj.org.uk/?id=613

Harvey, David, 2005a [2003], *The New Imperialism* (Oxford University).

Harvey, David, 2005b, *A Brief History of Neoliberalism* (Oxford University).

Harvey, David, 2006a [1982], *The Limits to Capital* (Verso).

Harvey, David, 2006b, *Spaces of Global Capitalism: Towards a Theory of Uneven Geographical Development* (Verso).

Harvey, David, 2009, "Interview: David Harvey—Exploring the Logic of Capital", *Socialist Review* (April), www.socialistreview.org.uk/article.php?articlenumber=10801

Harvey, David, 2010a, *The Enigma of Capital and the Crises of Capitalism* (Profile).

Harvey, David, 2010b, *A Companion to Marx's Capital* (Verso).

Kliman, Andrew, 2007, *Reclaiming Marx's "Capital": A Refutation of the Myth of Inconsistency* (Lexington).

Kliman, Andrew, 2010, *The Persistent Fall in Profitability Underlying the Current Crisis: New Temporalist Evidence* (Marxist-Humanist Initiative).

Marx, Karl, 1970 [1867], *Capital, volume 1* (Lawrence and Witshart), www.marxists.org/archive/marx/works/1867-c1/

Marx, Karl, 1975 [1863], *Theories of Surplus Value, volume 2* (Progress), www.marxists.org/archive/marx/works/1863/theories-surplus-value/

Marx, Karl, 1977 [1859], *Preface to A Contribution to the Critique of Political Economy* (Progress), www.marxists.org/archive/marx/works/1859/critique-pol-economy/preface.htm

# What's wrong with school history?

*Andrew Stone*

"The moment I understand history as possibility, I must also understand education in different way".[1]

The huge student protests over tuition fees and the Educational Maintenance Allowance beginning in November 2010 were an inspirational challenge to the coalition government's far-reaching plans for marketising education. Alongside attempting to slash public funding, Tory education secretary Michael Gove has also attempted to undermine comprehensive education with unaccountable "free" schools and to profoundly alter the school curriculum.

Within weeks of the election Gove approached the right wing historian Niall Ferguson to take part in yet another reform of the school history curriculum.[2] Describing to an audience at the Hay Festival his intention that children be taught the "big story" of the last 500 years—"the rise of Western domination of the world"—he denounced critics in the audience who suggested a less nationalistic approach as "the militant tendency". This article will attempt to put his project in historical context—as another stage in a long-running battle to shape the pedagogy, methods and content of school history—and argue that the militancy he disparages is precisely what is required in the face of his reactionary proposals.

---

1:  Darder, 2002, px.
2:  *Guardian*, 31 May 2010.

## A short history of school history

But what is the state of school history? Is Ferguson right at least to consider it in need of reform? To try to answer these questions adequately it is necessary to consider a brief history *of* school history in the UK.

School history was first introduced in the sixth form of Rugby School in the 1820s.[3] This was a time when the best hope of education for most working class children (if the meagre, heavily gendered fare on offer could be described as such) was via the factory or the workhouse. School history took some time to become established, but when it did it was firmly within the Whig tradition, celebrating the progress of constitutional government. When elementary schooling was made compulsory in 1870, the central goal was to foster patriotic sentiment.[4]

The 1902 Education Act (passed under a Tory administration) created the very Local Education Authorities (LEAs) which the Tories are now doing their best to undermine with academies and "free" schools. Although more recently LEAs have sometimes been seen as a refuge from government edicts, they were originally created to facilitate greater central control of schooling than the patchwork of provision and curricula previously allowed. The history taught was dominated by what has often been described as the "Great Tradition".[5] In a school system conciously formed as a lever of social control, this tradition glorified hierarchy and empire. This was the top-down Great Man theory of history supposedly typified by the 1905 children's book *Our Island Story*, recently re-released to gushing praise from Tory historians such as Andrew Roberts and Lady Antonia Fraser.[6] John Slater memorably parodied the content of this style of history, which he said was "based largely on hidden assumptions, rarely identified, let alone publicly debated", as:

Largely British, or rather Southern English; Celts looked in to starve, emigrate or rebel, the North to invent looms or work in mills; abroad was of interest once it was part of the Empire; foreigners were either, sensibly, allies, or, rightly, defeated. Skills—did we even use the word?—were mainly those of

---

3:   Historical Association, 2005, p12.
4:   Historical Association, 2005, p12.
5:   Phillips, 2004, p12.
6:   Marshall, 2005. Edward Vallance argues that *Our Island Story* is in fact "a subtly subversive text" with pacifist and feminist sympathies—Vallance, 2009, p5. His evidence does suggest that Marshall was less of a gung-ho imperialist than some of her admirers have painted her as, although I'm not convinced that this goes far beyond an essentially Whiggish appreciation of a constitutionally limited monarchy. Thanks though to Christian Høgsbjerg for pointing out this discussion.

recalling accepted facts about famous dead Englishmen, and communicated in a very eccentric literary form, the examination-length essay.[7]

One such assumption, as indicated, was that this was overwhelmingly content-driven, to be taught didactically and obediently learnt, often by rote, eg as a call and response catechism.[8]

Slater has disparagingly dubbed this Great Tradition an "inherited consensus".[9] However, this is something of a misnomer as it was never entirely unchallenged. For example, mavericks such as MW Keatinge in 1910 outlined a rationale and method for the classroom use of historical evidence.[10] In 1908 even the Board of Education made a series of proposals warning against written work merely "as a test of memory" and suggested a spiral curricular model where topics were returned to in greater detail, and even working in reverse chronological order. As the Historical Association notes, "many methods and approaches often criticised nowadays as 'trendy' or 'novel' have in fact a heritage almost as long as school history itself".[11] Nevertheless the depressingly staid approach of the Great Tradition would remain hegemonic, at least in the secondary sector, until the 1960s.

The tripartite system (of grammar, technical and secondary modern schools) introduced by the 1944 Butler Act reinforced history's status as an "academic" subject, and therefore its shape remained the prerogative of independent and grammar schools. The growth of comprehensive schooling—driven by parental and teacher demand—throughout the 1960s and early 1970s and the delay of the school leaving age until 16 opened up the history O-level to large layers of working class students. This combined with wider societal pressures to challenge the dominance of the Great Tradition. This was also a period of expansion for higher education, resulting in more graduates from working class backgrounds becoming teachers. They did so at a time when the New Left was challenging established orthodoxies about class, nation and latterly gender. Chris Husbands cites the influence of EP Thompson, Eric Hobsbawm and Sheila Rowbotham along with the "reprographics revolution" (the ability to photocopy resources and thus reduce reliance on textbooks) in widening the content and conceptual fields available to teachers.[12]

---

7:   Slater, 1989, p1.
8:   Historical Association, 2005, p12.
9:   Slater, 1989, p1.
10:  Husbands, 2003, p9.
11:  Historical Association, 2005, p13.
12:  Husbands, 2003, p10.

Primary schooling was the first to innovate. As far back as 1931 the Board of Education's Hadow Report had recommended that "the curriculum is to be thought of in terms of activity and experience rather than of knowledge to be acquired and facts to be stored".[13] The formation of the Schools' Council and the commissioning of the Plowden Report in 1963, finally reporting in 1967, fully established progressive methods in the sector, influenced by the work of Jean Piaget. Piaget was a developmental psychologist who theorised the gradual refinement of the child's cognitive structure, primarily through a combination of interaction with the environment and biological maturation. Although his constructivist theories have rightly been criticised for their formulaic correlation of "ages and stages", at the time his focus on child-centred learning was an important step away from teacher didacticism.[14] More project-based group work was encouraged and students were encouraged to discover history rather than be told it.

However, change in secondary history was frustrated for several more years, until Mary Price's 1968 essay "History in Danger" drew attention to the widespread attitude that school history was both boring and useless, and that there was a real prospect of it disappearing from the timetable as a discrete subject.[15] It is probably no coincidence that this notorious "year of the students", in which the film *If...* presented a violent insurrection at a public school, was the watershed which allowed a far more radical history pedagogy to emerge. This was formalised in the Humanities Curriculum Project, the Place, Time and Society Project and the Schools' Council History Project (known on many a textbook since as SHP). Each of these advocated a profound shift away from the notion of history as a fixed (and essentially reactionary) body of knowledge towards a more contested framework in which evidential skills were nurtured.

As part of this re-evaluation, the pioneering studies of the Russian Marxist Lev Vygotsky were rediscovered and popularised. Vygotsky graduated from Moscow State University, appropriately enough, in 1917, and worked at the Institute of Psychology in the mid-1920s before his death from tuberculosis in 1934, by which time Stalinist orthodoxy had denounced his "idealist aberrations". His diverse and groundbreaking work on developmental psychology and pedagogy deserves an article in its own right. To summarise, he built on the simple insight that we learn in interrelationship with others—and that this included peers, parents and

---

13:  Harnett, 2004, p25.
14:  Kyriacou, 2001, pp29-31.
15:  Price, 1968, pp342-347.

other adults, as well as teachers. Therefore the key to true understanding is communication between the student and others—"the zone of proximal development" in which learning is fostered. Paired and group work thus has an important role in supporting the linguistic skills and "procedural habits" on which intellectual progress depends.[16]

Vygotsky's influence in the 1960s was bolstered by the largely complementary work of American cognitive psychologist Jerome Bruner. He theorised three flexible stages of developmental representation—enactive (ie "learning by doing"), iconic (eg using diagrams to represent concepts) and symbolic (eg how language depends on assigning meaning to words). To assist them in negotiating these processes, Bruner proposed the use of "scaffolding" in providing students with contingent "levels of support" appropriate to the child's development. In the history classroom this might mean showing a student how to build a model medieval siege machine, making a mind-map of causes or providing sentence starters for an essay.

Both Vygotsky and Bruner shaped history specialist Martin Booth's influential research into enabling students to construct and critique historical arguments. This posited that, contrary to Piagetian orthodoxy, given the right scaffolding school students could use sources as more than just imaginative stimuli, rather as a tool to generalise and interpret how historians construct arguments.[17]

This "New History" therefore stressed the importance of conceptual understanding rather than facts presented out of context. It promoted student enquiry and the development of skills in analysing sources and evaluating interpretations. Although rooted in the historical method, these skills can also be utilised much more broadly to criticise representations of the dominant ideology. A student who is regularly considering the nature, origin and purpose of a historical source is much better prepared to question contemporary "spin". It is no surprise that elites are so distrustful of such skills, or that they denigrate New History or subjects such as Media Studies and Citizenship when they help to decode and challenge myths, propaganda and stereotypes.

Most contentiously, New History also promoted historical empathy. While the Great Tradition had invariably emphasised a ruling class view of the world, New History allowed teachers and students to reflect on the experiences of the exploited and oppressed. Not all teachers or schools took full advantage of this opportunity, but in retrospect many have seen New

---

16: Phillips, 2005, p25.
17: Phillips, 2005, pp25-28.

History's period of dominance in the late 1960s and the 1970s as a "golden age" of teacher autonomy.[18]

## New history, new danger?

The conservative backlash was not long in coming. As with many of the attacks mounted under Margaret Thatcher, the preceding Labour administration paved the way. In 1976 the then Labour prime minister James Callaghan made a speech at Ruskin College arguing that parents, industry and government should have greater influence on the school curriculum.[19] Initial caution in Thatcher's first term gave way to arrogance once the wars in the Malvinas and against the miners were won. From the mid-1980s the New Right extended Callaghan's rhetoric of public accountability, exploiting the growing distrust of authority figures to create a dichotomy between teachers as truculent "producers" and parents and businesses as "consumers".[20]

As the government planned to impose the National Curriculum, New Right pressure groups (such as the Hillgate Group and the Centre for Policy Studies established by Keith Joseph and Margaret Thatcher) launched a media campaign against "trendy teaching methods", particularly in history, which Stephen Ball has described as a "discourse of derision".[21] They argued that historical methodology had squeezed out content, and that children were too immature to utilise these skills anyway; that British history was being ignored because of a random mix of topics; that empathy was a nebulous or "woolly" concept which was difficult to assess; and that history in general had been hijacked by the left, obsessed with class conflict and multiculturalism.

Many of the proposals in the Hillgate Group's 1986 *Whose Schools? A Radical Manifesto*—a national testing policy (SATs), grant maintained schools, "parent influence" and a national curriculum—were enacted in Thatcher's third term.[22] As education writer Ted Wragg argued in a pamphlet for the National Union of Teachers (NUT) in 1988, this programme represented a wholesale embrace of the market. Even the language reeked of it: "Instead of children being 'taught', a curriculum is 'delivered', fine for the morning papers, milk or next week's groceries, but somewhat alien for the nurturing of human talent".[23] Terry Wrigley has commented that "the

---

18:  Lawton, 1980.
19:  Phillips, 2004, p13.
20:  Wrigley, 2006, p29.
21:  Ball, 1990.
22:  Phillips, 2005, p20.
23:  Reprinted in Wragg, 2005, p204.

National Curriculum seemed a perfect solution for capitalism—technologically advanced but socially reactionary".[24]

History was perhaps the most controversial of the subjects under review. The deliberations of the History Working Group (HWG), established by the secretary of state for education, Kenneth Baker, to make recommendations for English schools, prompted shrill media debate and interventions from cabinet ministers up to and including Margaret Thatcher. Given Baker's terms of reference—that British history, in particular its political, constitutional and cultural heritage, should form the core of the curriculum—and that he appointed a retired naval officer and castle owner, Commander Michael Saunders-Watson, to chair it, the Final Report could have been much worse.[25]

British history was interpreted widely (see below) and a careful balance of knowledge, skills and concepts was advocated, with no precise syllabuses mandatory. Incensed that her cultural legacy was being watered down, Thatcher demanded that the report go out to further consultation, and the resulting "MacGregor" proposals increased the stress on historical knowledge and British history.[26] After a further round of consultations, Baker's successor, Kenneth Clarke, directly intervened to ensure that modern history should focus on "the first half of the 20th century...to draw some distinction between the study of history and the study of current affairs".[27] Here was a clear attempt to curtail the potentially radical conclusions to be drawn from well-taught school history.

The initial version of the curriculum, introduced in 1991, stipulated that political history should end at least 20 years before the present. It was overloaded with content ("Programmes of Study") and assessment requirements, which when they proved unmanageable were slimmed down and simplified in revisions in 1995 and 1999.[28] The prospect of changing required content back to indicative content (as originally envisaged by the HWG) led, among other overblown headlines, to the *Sun* screaming: "Britain's glorious past banished from history lessons".[29]

## Localism, nationalism and multiculturalism

In fact, even ignoring optional GCSEs and A-levels, most students still

---

24: Wrigley, 2006, p8.
25: Phillips, 2005, pp20-21.
26: Phillips, 2004, pp16-17.
27: Quoted in Phillips, 2004, p17.
28: Haydn and others, 2003, p23.
29: Quoted in Phillips, 2004, p17.

learn about the defeat of the Spanish Armada, the growth of English exploration, the formation of "Great Britain", the Agricultural and Industrial Revolutions, the expansion of the British Empire, and Britain's victories in the First and Second World Wars. But short of an entirely micromanaged curriculum—which would require an even more heavily policed education system than that enabled by Ofsted, league tables and performance-related pay—it's very difficult for any government to dictate the precise values fostered in the process. Teachers, students and, in the best schools, parents too can ensure that the topics taught do not glorify capitalism and imperialism but criticise it, by listening to the voices of the oppressed, exploited and marginalised, both within and outside the British Isles.

The tensions in the characterisation of "Britishness" complicated the ideological counter-offensive by the New Right. Many would have hankered after the pre-war elision between England and Britain, as this typical statement of Great Tradition ideology did in 1908:

> [The purpose of history was] to bring before the children the lives and work of English people who served God in church and state, to show that they did this by courage, endurance and self-sacrifice, that as a result the British Empire was founded and extended and that it behoved every child to emulate them.[30]

However, by the time the National Curriculum was being written, attempting to submerge Welsh, Scottish and Irish history into an Anglocentric narrative was politically untenable. This was partly because of the growth of local history during the preceding two decades, particularly social "history from below". But it also reflected the growth of Welsh and Scottish nationalism, influenced by social democratic opposition to a Tory government with little representation outside of England. This would bolster the support of the Scottish National Party and Plaid Cymru and lead towards devolution.

Thus National Curriculum deliberations included distinct advisory groups for Wales, Scotland and Northern Ireland. The History Committee for Wales recommended a broadly similar outline to England, with some specifically Welsh content, but within a British, European and world context. Scotland's was less prescriptive, but did insist on the importance of Scottish history as part of a wide curriculum, with extra funding put into developing textbooks. Northern Ireland included compulsory

---

30: Willis Bund, quoted in Haydn and others, 2003, p18.

cross-curricular themes on "Education for Mutual Understanding" and "Cultural Heritage"—in this case the contemporary relevance of history (to "the Troubles") was embraced, although this was no guarantee that it would always be used for progressive ends.[31]

In England the HWG's advice to define British history as containing "a range of interpretations" based on its multicultural "inheritances" (rather than a singular "heritage") also sanctioned a continuation of local history and history which reflected Britain's post-colonial diversity.[32] There was no specific commitment to anti-racism (that would have been anathema to the New Right), but a space remained open for teachers prepared to take the initiative. After pressure from the Historical Association the most recent revision of the curriculum (2008) has made explicit current good practice by adding "cultural, ethnic and religious diversity" to the key concepts students are required to investigate and understand.

## The state we're in

The 1988 Education Reform Act briefly made history a compulsory subject between the ages of five and 16. However, policy reviews and curriculum changes made it voluntary after 14 from 1991. This contrasts with much of Europe—including France, Germany, Italy, Spain and Russia—where history is compulsory until the age of 16.[33] New Labour's 1998 literacy and numeracy strategies then squeezed time for history within primary schools as part of a general narrowing of the curriculum.[34] Without any change in legislation, some schools are also now teaching a truncated Key Stage 3 curriculum (normally taught over three years between 11 and 14—the rationale is to have a whole three years working on GCSEs!), meaning many students now finish studying history at 13.

A recent survey by the Historical Association suggests that the picture is continuing to worsen, with 35 percent of academies and 20 percent of comprehensive and grammar schools reporting an overall decrease in teaching time for history at Key Stage 3. Furthermore, 48 percent of academies reported that 11 and 12 year olds were spending less than one hour a week learning history.[35] This may not always be a negative development— at my previous school we taught an integrated humanities curriculum for students' first year in secondary school. This combined skills from history,

---

31: Phillips, 2004, pp18-21.
32: Phillips, 2004, p16.
33: Historical Association, 2005, p17.
34: Husbands, 2003, p15.
35: Historical Association, 2009, pp5-6.

geography, religious education and citizenship and was allocated a generous six hours a week. However, the survey also reflects a general pressure on schools, particularly those serving inner cities (where there is a greater proportion of state comprehensives and, up until now, academies) to increase hot-housing around English and maths.

This is one impact of the recent alteration of school league tables. Whereas previously schools were primarily competing over the percentage of students achieving five or more A* to C grades at GCSE, the new "gold standard" requires English and maths to be among them. Because vocational BTEC diplomas are counted as the equivalent of four GCSEs for the purposes of league tables, many schools have also begun to impose "student pathways", where students are directed into either academic or vocational subjects. When these pathways are being decided for students, often by senior managers who don't personally teach them, they rely heavily on predicted grades extrapolated from student performance in Key Stage 2 SATs (ie taken when they were 11). Phrases such as "educational apartheid" may seem hyperbolic, but when colleagues describe being told to hand different coloured prospectuses to different 13 and 14 year olds at options evenings, who see their "choices" essentially made for them, it certainly feels like that.

While theories of "assessment for learning"—where weaknesses are identified and remedied through the actual process of learning—have provided useful insights into education, [36] in practice they are always trumped by the demands of "levelling" and "grading", which are delivered by high-stakes tests under formal conditions. The impact for history is that students who may love historical drama and fiction, or contribute astutely to class discussions and debates, or excel at making historically accurate models, or have a love for historical sites and artefacts, can be denied the opportunity to continue to learn history because they do not have the necessary formal exam skills. "Summative assessment" (high-stakes tests under formal conditions) trumps holistic teacher "formative assessment" (where weaknesses are identified and remedies attempted). Otherwise the threat of Ofsted, with its increasingly reductionist results-driven criteria, will be there to punish. [37]

A recent survey showed that 69.8 percent of students found history "quite enjoyable" (compared to 41 percent in 1967) and that 69.3 percent thought it "quite useful", up from only 29 percent when history was "in danger" because of the Great Tradition. [38] Yet only 30 percent take history

---

36: Black and Wiliam, 2001.
37: Stone, 2009.
38: Harris and Haydn, 2008, pp44-46.

GCSE, a proportion likely to fall if current trends continue. This figure goes down to just 18 percent for students entitled to free school meals due to low parental income.[39]

## Niall Ferguson—a very Cameronite historian

If the brazenly jingoistic Andrew Roberts is the Norman Tebbit of history, then Niall Ferguson is the David Cameron. Both are aggressively pro-market, but whereas Cameron has a long family history in finance, Ferguson has spent much of his career writing about it, including his recent books *The Ascent of Money* (2008) and *High Financier* (2010). Both are keenly interested in media presentation—Cameron was director of corporate affairs at Carlton Communications for seven years while Ferguson is an adept documentary presenter. This has encouraged both men to make some rhetorical conces-sions to social liberalism in order to make their essential conservatism more palatable. Ferguson's 2003 book *Empire: How Britain Made the Modern World* is an interesting example of this. He revealingly admits that in 1982, "young and foolish", he "rashly opposed" an Oxford Union motion regretting colo-nialism, which "prematurely ended [his] role as a student politician".[40] Given Cameron's Bullingdon Club exploits, perhaps he need not have worried so much. Nevertheless, he claims "the penny dropped" and he began to also consider empire's costs. As Chris Bambery wrote in a review article:

> While accepting "the ugly side of empire", Ferguson argues that "in economic terms it was a positive force. It encouraged global free trade, investment in underdeveloped countries, labour migration and non-corrupt governments." This is set within a contemporary context in which Ferguson sings the joys of capitalist globalisation.[41]

Even in his introduction to *The Ascent of Money*, when the impact of the debt crisis was first rippling through the world economy, Ferguson stressed the positive role of financial capital:

> Poverty is not the result of rapacious financiers exploiting the poor. It has much more to do with the *lack* of financial institutions, with the absence of banks, not their presence... This point applies not just to the poor countries of the world. It can also be said of the poorest neighbourhoods in supposedly

---

39: Maddern, 2010.
40: Ferguson, 2004a, p xvii.
41: Bambery, 2003.

developed countries—the "Africas within"—like the housing estates of my birthplace, Glasgow.[42]

Of course, not many of those residents attended the private Glasgow Academy, as Ferguson did (though he was described by a gushing Michael Gove as coming "from a typical Scottish educational background"), or work as hedge fund consultants, as he does.[43] But then a dubious form of philanthropy (providing credit) appears to be Ferguson's only suggestion for ameliorating the poverty endemic in the Darwinian financial system he describes with general approval in *The Ascent of Money*.[44] This is not unlike Cameron's "big society" vision of replacing public services with Victorian charity.

In *Colossus: The Rise and Fall of the American Empire* (2004) Ferguson rejected the increasingly absurd denial of many American commentators that the US practises imperialism. However, he reiterated, "I am in favour of empire. Indeed, I believe that empire is more necessary in the 21st century than ever before".[45] What was important was whether it would be a *liberal* empire, "one that enhances its own security and prosperity precisely by providing the rest of the world with generally beneficial public goods".[46] Apparently this was what Britain was attempting to do after the Great Irish Famine and the Indian Mutiny made its old model unviable, though as usual Ferguson vastly overstates the "enlightened" part of this enlightened imperial self-interest.

## Ferguson's vision for school history

In a 2006 blog singing Ferguson's praises, Michael Gove hinted at the paranoia that pervades much of the right about a liberal media Mafia, when he bemoaned how "those historians who are most prepared to tell our island story in a way that doesn't turn it into a chronicle of unredeemed oppression tend not to be academics". He then went on to pontificate on how:

> Most of us who take an interest in our country's past, who harbour a curiosity about our ancestors, who wish to discover what moved them and understand the conflicts of their times, are not searching for reasons to feel ashamed of our culture.

---

42: Ferguson, 2008, p13.
43: Gove, 2006. Gove also attended a private school.
44: Ferguson, 2008, pp348-358.
45: Ferguson, 2004b, p24.
46: Ferguson, 2004b, p25.

Furthermore:

It is hugely unfashionable now to confess to a liking for the sort of history produced by Victorians such as Macaulay, who presented our national story in richly personal terms as one of progress, albeit troubled, and achievement, albeit compromised. But I defy anyone who picks up Macaulay now not to be engaged by his story and not to feel that his narrative speaks to our natural appetite for empathetic engagement with those who made us what we are.[47]

Be afraid. Be very afraid.

Yet there is a (small) section in Ferguson's introduction to *The War of the World* (2006) which appears to bode well for his role as curriculum adviser. It recounts how his old school history books

told the story of the 20th century as a kind of protracted, painful, but ultimately pleasing triumph of the West. The heroes (Western democracies) were confronted by a series of villains (the Germans, the Japanese, the Russians) but ultimately good always triumphed over evil. The world wars and the Cold War were thus morality plays on a global stage. But were they?[48]

However, as the above discussion on New History suggests, such simplistic narratives are not now the norm. This is a straw man he's fighting. Notwithstanding the regular compromises teachers necessarily grapple with to make complex topics accessible, the emphasis on both teachers and students actively evaluating interpretations is much stronger than in the days of the Great Tradition.

At the time of writing, Ferguson has made some curriculum suggestions but has not outlined a detailed set of proposals. However, he has said that "we need to use television. The reason I do TV is because I think it's a more accessible way of teaching".[49] Leaving aside the suspicion that he wants all students to be forced to watch *his* shows, it's certainly not true that teachers don't currently use video stimuli. But unless used sparingly it can encourage student passivity, and though it may be more entertaining than teacher talk it is not necessarily pedagogically superior. Documentaries can have a role in providing an overview of a topic, but should always be approached critically as an interpretation.

---

47: Gove, 2006.
48: Ferguson, 2007, p xxxvii.
49: Quoted in Vasagar, 2010.

Ferguson has also collaborated with a US software developer (no doubt providing its services for entirely altruistic motives) to create a Second World War computer game for classroom use. The aim of the game (called, coincidentally, *The War of the World*) is to explore imperial strategy through role-play. This ties in with Ferguson's long-standing interest in counter-factual history.[50] Although there is certainly a place for historical role-play, and in a recent survey it was the most popular activity among history students,[51] his choice of protagonist is very ideological and encourages students to identify with national leaders and their imperial priorities. It also requires a good grasp of the actual course of events and the factors involved if it is to be meaningful, and unless carefully constructed and debriefed, risks exaggerating the role of individuals at the expense of wider economic and social forces.

Ferguson's appointment was followed by that of fellow US-based documentary maker Simon Schama as "narrative history tsar" (clearly coined by someone with a sense of historical irony). Michael Gove told the Tory party conference in October 2010 that "children are growing up ignorant of one of the most inspiring stories I know—the history of our United Kingdom".[52] Therefore Schama is assigned to deliver these stories, though his superficial *A History of Britain* (2000) series was far inferior to Michael Wood's *Story of England* (2010) both in novelty of research and depth of analysis. But perhaps the "inspiring stories" told by Wood—in which rebellion, protest and dissent were treated sympathetically—were not what Gove had in mind.

The exact contours of Simon Schama's blueprint remain blurry, despite articles waxing lyrical about children's receptiveness to "the epic of long time; the hunger for plenitude".[53] He advocates the virtues of chronology, though this is hardly innovative—most secondary schools still begin in the Middle Ages and end in the latter part of the 20th century. His allusions to the popularity of the *Harry Potter*, *Lord of the Rings* and *His Dark Materials* serials as models are problematic for a number of reasons—not least in that children generally choose to read them. Instead Schama apparently proposes the creation of a school history canon, which while advertising its multicultural credentials (look, we include Indians, Chinese and the Irish!) does so through the eyes of the British Empire. This has the potential to make the curriculum more prescriptive and even less

---

50: Ferguson, 1999.
51: Harris and Haydn, 2008, p45.
52: Vasagar and Sparrow, 2010.
53: Schama, 2010.

responsive to the needs and interests of students.

Ferguson claims that his own grand narrative of the rise of the West is not intended to be triumphalist, and cites the geographical factors explored in Jared Diamond's *Guns, Germs and Steel* in support.[54] Nevertheless there is a real likelihood of his approach essentialising national, regional and religious groups, as Colin Jones, the president of the Royal Historical Society, warns:

> The history that he has in mind has the risk of making the distinctions between different groups appear more real than they really are. It homogenises culture, so French culture is characterised by shrugging and having revolutions and the British by being phlegmatic and not having revolutions.[55]

Short of having that revolution, what alternatives can socialists provide to Ferguson's proposals?

## There are many alternatives

Despite the many constraints, teachers can play an important role in inspiring students. My own history teacher conveyed a passionate interest in social justice through her teaching, which didn't stop at the classroom door. When she spotted two National Front members leafleting at the school gate, she single-handedly chased them off. As Christopher Hill wrote, "History properly taught can help men [and women!—AS] to become critical and humane, just as wrongly taught it can turn them into bigots and fanatics".[56]

Clearly, depending on the commitment of individuals is insufficient. The Historical Association made some helpful recommendations in its 2005 curriculum development report. These included ending the determination of content and assessment by factors such as "the need for history departments to 'sell' the subject through the options system at 14+, commercial competition between awarding bodies and between publishers, the availability of resources in school and on the open market, and an understandable desire on the part of teachers to keep to what they are familiar with".[57] It also advised an end to the use of source work in exams—which it described as "dull, formulaic and divorced from the context of genuine historical investigation"—to be replaced by their use

---

54: Diamond, 1998.
55: Vasagar, 2010.
56: Quoted in Haydn, 2003, p18.
57: Historical Association, 2005, p9.

within the context of genuine enquiries.[58] The subsequent GCSE specification shows some movement in this direction. The Historical Association also called for greater cross-curricular overlaps between different subjects.

This thematic approach is encouraged in the new Key Stage 3 specification. While positive in theory, in practice it is often seen as a burden, another imposed initiative requiring more planning for already overworked teachers (who on average work over 50 hours per week, and significantly more in many of the most challenging schools).[59] One reason for the relative success of the integrated humanities initiative at my school was that in the term before it was implemented all the teaching staff involved were given a week off timetable to meet and plan the schemes of work. But in the three years since many teachers have reported a greater rigidity from school managers in allowing time for training and development, mainly resulting from New Labour's failure to fund the reform that contracted teachers should "rarely cover" for absent colleagues.

Perhaps though we should go much further? As Michael Rosen rightly points out, the division of education into "subjects" largely corresponds to a mixture of medieval and Victorian ideas. He suggests therefore that ultimately we should aim to do away with subject boundaries altogether.[60] The radically different basis of a socialist society might make this a real possibility. However, Bruner's concerns about the "structures of subjects"—their particular skills, concepts and methodologies—would still need to be considered.[61]

Many history teachers will have winced, as I have, when non-specialist colleagues used a historical topic in a banal or inappropriate way—role-plays in what it was like in a death camp, or simplistic Martin Luther King = good, Malcolm X = bad dichotomies, for example. Likewise I'm sure my own teaching of geography and religious education themes within integrated humanities lacked rigour at times. One solution is much more time granted for continuing staff training and cooperation. The recent initiative to make newly-qualified teachers take a master's degree might be helpful in this regard if they were not in the midst of one of the most intensive periods of work in their life. What is needed is more teachers, enabling smaller classes and more learning time for all concerned.

More fundamentally though, it would require a change in the relationship between education workers, students and parents. Teachers would

---

58: Historical Association, 2005, p10.
59: Gray, 2009.
60: Rosen, 2004.
61: Cited in Phillips, 2005, p28.

need to feel freed from the constant policing of Ofsted, league tables and performance management to be more explorative, starting from students' current interests, strengths and needs rather than predetermined assessment objectives and schemes of work. Only then could Vygotsky's notion of "the zone of proximal development"—where the teacher acts as a guide between the child's current and potential level of development—become a realistic prospect.[62] It is not likely to happen while secondary history teachers see 200 or more students a week, and while that situation remains talk of "personalised learning" is just another unrealisable goal making teachers feel guilty and inadequate.

Terry Wrigley has researched a range of schools and systems world-wide that have instituted progressive reforms we could learn from and fight for in the short term. These include Danish schools being advised not to over-plan in advance as this could undermine negotiations with students about what and how to study;[63] the Beutelsbach Consensus in Germany which encourages openness about the controversial nature of issues (the Historical Association has attempted something similar with its Teaching Emotive and Controversial History report, but it is often stymied in prac-tice by low-trust management and surveillance);[64] and Filton High School staff have organised week-long projects on topics such as the 2004 tsunami, Make Poverty History and climate change, where each subject teacher con-tributes from their own specialism.[65]

The 10 and 24 November student walkouts, protests and occupations have revived hopes that such alternatives can carry mass support. Extending and generalising such struggles is the key task for anyone wishing to trans-form education. The NUT's call for coordinated strike action over pensions holds great potential for enabling this. A more decisive strategy than seen previously in building a nationwide SATs boycott will also be important in weakening the deadening hand of assessment. The Tories' scandalous cuts to Building Schools for the Future projects, along with its elitist academies and "free" schools proposals are also all very unpopular, with a poll taken even before the outbreak of the student protests showing that 42 percent of voters thought the government was doing a bad job in "reforming" schools, against only 23 percent who believed it was doing a good job.[66] Among the unimpressed were many Liberal Democrat voters. They may remember

62: See Kyriacou, 2001, p31.
63: Wrigley, 2005, p134.
64: Wrigley, 2005, p135; Historical Association, 2007.
65: Wrigley, 2006, p100.
66: Clark, 2010.

that their education spokesman, David Laws, said in February 2010:

> The Tory position on the core curriculum is totally incoherent. On the one hand they are saying that all pupils should be learning British history, but then they propose to establish new schools in which there would be no requirement to have a basic knowledge of anything... The Conservative proposals are confused, ill thought-out and naive.[67]

It seems that it is the Liberal Democrats who are now confused, and increasingly reviled for it. They will need to be educated by a mass movement that unites education workers, students and parents in the fight for genuine comprehensives. In the process we can create a liberatory curriculum where all students are entitled to a historical education that helps them to shape their future.

---

67: Vaughan, 2010.

# References

Bambery, Chris, 2003, "Capital and Conquest", *Socialist Review* (February), www.socialistreview.org.uk/article.php?articlenumber=8311

Ball, Stephen, 1990, *Politics and Policy Making in Education* (Routledge).

Black, Paul, and Dylan Wiliam, 2001, *Working Inside the Black Box*, King's College London School of Education, www.collegenet.co.uk/admin/download/inside%20the%20black%20box_23_doc.pdf

Board of Education, 1931, "The Hadow Report", www.educationengland.org.uk/documents/hadow1931

Clark, Tom, 2010, "Coalition cracks could start to show over schools reforms, poll suggests", *Guardian* (18 August), www.guardian.co.uk/politics/2010/aug/18/coalition-cracks-education-reforms-poll

Darder, Antonia, 2002, *Reinventing Paulo Freire: A Pedagogy of Love* (Westview Press).

Diamond, Jared, 1998, *Guns, Germs and Steel: A Short History of Everybody for the Last 13,000 Years* (Vintage).

Ferguson, Niall, 1999, *Virtual History: Alternatives and Counterfactuals* (Basic Books).

Ferguson, Niall, 2004a, *Empire: How Britain Made the Modern World* (Penguin).

Ferguson, Niall, 2004b, *Colossus: The Rise and Fall of the American Empire* (Allen Lane).

Ferguson, Niall, 2007, *The War of the World* (Penguin).

Ferguson, Niall, 2008, *The Ascent of Money: A Financial History of the World* (Allen Lane).

Gove, Michael, 2006, "There's Only One Fergie in the History Game" (14 June), www.michaelgove.com/content/theres-only-one-fergie-history-game

Gray, Sadie, 2009, "Teachers call for 35-hour cap on working week", *Independent* (28 March), www.independent.co.uk/news/education/education-news/teachers-call-for-35hour-cap-on-working-week-1656168.html

Harnett, Penelope, 2004, "Curriculum Decision-Making in the Primary School", in James Arthur and Robert Phillips (eds), *Issues in History Teaching* (Routledge).

Harris, Richard and Terry Haydn, 2008, "Children's Ideas About School History and Why They Matter", in *Teaching History* (September).

Haydn, Terry, James Arthur and Martin Hunt, 2003, *Learning to Teach History in the Secondary School.* (Routledge Falmer).

Historical Association, 2005, *Curriculum Development Project: History 14-19.*

Historical Association, 2007, *TEACH: Teaching Emotive and Controversial History 3-19*, www.tellingfilms.netne.net/historicalasscnreport.pdf

Historical Association, 2009, *Findings from the Historical Association Survey of Secondary History Teachers*, www.history.org.uk/resources/general_resource_3249,3262_14.html

Husbands, Chris, and others, 2003, *Understanding History Teaching* (Open University Press).

Kyriacou, Chris, 2001, *Effective Teaching in Schools* (Nelson Thornes).

Maddern, Kerra, 2010, "Three-quarters of pupils in some English regions miss out on history", *Times Educational Supplement* (29 October), www.tes.co.uk/article.aspx?storycode=6061748

Lawton, Denis, 1980, *The Politics of the School Curriculum* (Routledge & Kegan Paul).

Marshall, Henrietta, 2005, *Our Island Story* (Civitas).

Phillips, Robert, 2005, *Reflective Teaching of History 11-18* (Continuum).

Phillips, Robert, 2004, *Government Policies, the State and the Teaching of History*, in James Arthur and Robert Phillips (eds), *Issues in History Teaching* (Routledge).

Price, Mary, 1968, "History in Danger", in *History*, 53.

Rosen, Michael, 2004, "Learning to Dream", *Socialist Review* (February), www.socialistreview.org.uk/article.php?articlenumber=8767

Schama, Simon, 2010, "My vision for history in schools", *Guardian* (9 November), www.guardian.co.uk/education/2010/nov/09/future-history-schools

Slater, John, 1989, *The Politics of History Teaching: A Humanity Dehumanised?* (ULIE).

Stone, Andrew, 2009, "An Inspector Galls", *Socialist Review* (December), www.socialistreview.org.uk/article.php?articlenumber=11048

Wrigley, Terry, 2006, *Another School is Possible* (Bookmarks).

Vallance, Edward, 2009, *A Radical History of Britain* (Abacus).

Vasagar, Jeevan, 2010, "Niall Ferguson Aims to Shake Up History Curriculum with TV and War Games", *Guardian* (9 July), www.guardian.co.uk/education/2010/jul/09/television-war-games-niall-ferguson

Vasagar, Jeevan, and Andrew Sparrow, 2010, "Simon Schama to Advise Ministers on Overhaul of History Curriculum", *Guardian* (5 October), www.guardian.co.uk/politics/2010/oct/05/simon-schama-ministers-history-curriculum

Vaughan, Richard, 2010, "Lib Dems Slam Tories' Curriculum Reform Plans", *Times Educational Supplement* (19 February).

Wragg, Ted, 2005, *The Art and Science of Teaching and Learning* (Routledge).

Wrigley, Terry, 2005, *Schools of Hope* (Trentham).

# Why we should be
# sceptical of climate sceptics
*Suzanne Jeffery*

C limate science came massively under attack in 2010. Leaked emails from the Climate Research Unit (CRU) at the University of East Anglia were spun by the right wing media to claim that climate scientists had hidden and manipulated data. The affair was dubbed "Climategate". Newspapers echoed right-wing politicians, claiming the emails questioned the whole theory of human caused global warming. Climategate and the cold winter gave an opportunity to both rehabilitate the idea that there is "scientific doubt" about human caused climate change and raise political doubt about the need for action to halt it. The emails were leaked weeks before the crucial UN climate change talks at Copenhagen. The speculation in the press about the veracity of climate scientists no doubt helped blunt the impact of the criminal failure of the world's richest countries to reach any deal to tackle climate change at Copenhagen.

Meanwhile 2010 was the hottest year on record.[1] Extreme weather events have affected millions of people. From the devastating heat in Russia, where a state of emergency was declared in 23 regions as temperatures reached close to 40 degrees and forest fires raged outside the cities, to the devastating floods in Pakistan. In the worst catastrophe of its kind, widespread flooding has left thousands dead and 20 million people homeless. The increase in such extreme weather events is a consequence of a

---

1:    Grey, 2010.

warming planet, and as we have seen with Hurricane Katarina in 2005, it is the poorest people who suffer most.

In the run-up to Copenhagen, the UK saw its largest ever climate protest. Over 50,000 people took to the streets calling for the UK government to take the lead in huge reductions in carbon emissions. The failure of market solutions to climate change and the spectacular failure of the banks in 2008 made the case for solutions to climate change that challenge the market much stronger. On the streets of Copenhagen itself, 100,000 people demonstrated, despite massive police repression, many under the anti-capitalist banner of "system change not climate change".

The climate sceptics have a political agenda rather than a scientific one. They want to defeat the argument that global warming requires action, regulation and legislation. But while they have been emboldened in their attempts to do this over the last year, the case for radical action to tackle climate change has become greater than ever.

## The truth about the leaked emails.

It is unclear who leaked the emails and loaded them onto a number of notorious climate sceptic websites ensuring they quickly became widely publicised.[2] It has been suggested that dissidents within the University of East Anglia may have been involved, or that climate sceptic bloggers with technical expertise may have been the culprits. Another possibility is that the hackers may have represented a corporation or a state wanting to undermine the talks at Copenhagen or the climate bill coming to the US Senate. This final theory would not be entirely inconsistent with previous efforts of lobby groups to whip up negative publicity about climate science before major climate negotiations. George W Bush used some of these "controversies" to justify his refusal to ratify the Kyoto protocol.

However, no clear evidence has emerged about who leaked the emails. It is a sign of how successful the climate sceptics have been in setting the agenda that little attention has been paid to how the emails were hacked and by whom.

Instead the focus of the right wing media has been on the claim that the emails reveal that the scientists involved "manipulated and hid data" to give the results they wanted and suppressed the work of other scientists who challenged their conclusions. A small number of quotes, from

---

2:    Websites such as Anthony Watt's "Watt's up with that", Jeff Id's "Air Vent" blog, Warren Meyers' "Climate sceptic" and Steve McIntyre's "Climate Audit" website all carried links to servers holding the emails.

over 1000 emails, are taken out of context and twisted from their original meaning, to support this claim. A handful of examples that hit the headlines illustrates the lack of substance in these arguments.

One of the most quoted passages from the emails is from Phil Jones, the director of the CRU, whose work has involved assembling the past 160 years of global temperature records from around the world. In one email Phil Jones says "I've just completed Mike's nature trick of adding in the real temps for each series for the last 20 years (from 1981 onwards) and from 1961 for Keith's to hide the decline".[3] The word and phrase "trick" and "hide the decline" have been blasted across front pages claiming that data was manipulated to hide a decline in global temperatures. Sarah Palin accused him and other scientists of being a "highly politicised scientific circle" who "manipulated data to 'hide the decline' in global temperatures".[4]

The comment made by Phil Jones in his email was not a conspiracy to hide temperature decline. The decline referred to was not in recorded temperature, but in data from modern tree rings. This data had historically correlated to temperature rises and has been used to plot temperature from years prior to thermometer records. However, some modern tree rings were no longer reflecting the recorded temperature rises—this is the "decline" that Jones was referring to. The break down in correlation between temperature and tree rings is something that scientists have no explanation for.

The "trick" Phil Jones refers to was a graphic technique to merge tree ring data from earlier times with thermometer data for recent decades. This was something Michael Mann had done in his famous 1998 paper for *Nature*,[5] and subsequently became known as the "hockey stick" paper. This was because of the way global temperatures took on the shape of a hockey stick, with the hook representing the rise in temperatures during the industrial period. Michael Mann had not hidden his "trick"—he explained the methodology he was using and the reasons why at the time.

The second most used comment from the emails is from Kevin Trenberth, a climate scientist at the National Centre for Atmospheric Research in Boulder, Colorado. He had previously drawn the wrath of climate sceptics after linking hurricane intensity with global warming after Hurricane Katrina in 2005. In one email Trenberth said, "The fact is we can't account for the lack of warming at the moment and it is a travesty that

---

3:   Pearce, 2010, p174. Pearce uses the CRU emails published online at www.eastangliaemails.com. This email is given the reference 942777075.txt.
4:   Washington Post, 9 December 2009.
5:   Mann and others, 1998, p779.

we can't".[6] The two quotes relating to the "trick to hide the decline" and Trenberth's "travesty" are often strung together implying one is a response to the other. In reality the comments have nothing to do with each other—they were ten years apart! Trenberth's comments relate to a very public discussion he was having with other scientists about how to understand the "natural variability" that produced a series of years cooler than earlier ones, within the overall picture of global warming. The "travesty" was that scientists could not explain variability, not a suggestion that global warming was not happening.

He had been arguing that better measures of the planet's energy budget were needed. This would allow scientists to distinguish between the increase of overall heat in the atmosphere and oceans and the short-term natural cycles of variability that merely redistribute heat. The issues raised were being debated in the pages of scientific journals.[7]

Three enquiries have now completely cleared the scientists involved of scientific malpractice and any question of the validity of their results and conclusions.[8] After the report of the Muir Russell Review, Myles Allen, head of the climate dynamics group at the University of Oxford said:

> What everyone has lost sight of is the spectacular failure of mainstream journalism to keep the whole affair in perspective. Again and again, stories are sexed up with arch hints that these "revelations" might somehow impact on the evidence for human impact on climate. Yet the only error in actual data used for climate change detection to have emerged from the whole affair amounted to a few hundredths of a degree in the estimated global temperature of a couple of years in the 1870s.[9]

## Who are the sceptics?

The climate sceptics were successful in restoring a "false balance" to the debate about global warming. Climate sceptics present a picture of an unresolved and contentious debate within the scientific community about climate change, with equally weighted camps still producing evidence that continues to contradict each other. They claim powerful and politically motivated scientists have unfairly and prematurely closed down this debate, and that a large

6:    Pearce, 2010, p175. Online reference 1255352257.txt.
7:    Trenberth, 2009.
8:    They were the Parliamentary Science and Technology Select Committee Report in March 2010, Lord Oxburgh's Scientific Assessment Panel in April 2010 and Sir Muir Russell's Review in July 2010.
9:    Adam, 2010.

number of eminent, dissident scientists have been prevented from publishing their work. The "dissidents" are often cast in the same mould as Galileo.

The picture painted by climate sceptics is not accurate. There is not an equal number on either side of the debate with relatively equally compelling evidence to support theories of global warming and theories that challenge it. A recent study by the Proceedings of the National Academy of Sciences shows that 97 percent of climate scientists agree that human activity is changing the climate. There is an overwhelming consensus based on the weight of evidence. The report also found that the relative expertise and scientific prominence of researchers unconvinced of anthropogenic climate change are substantially below that of the convinced researchers.[10]

The climate sceptics who have risen to prominence during Climategate, such as Steve McIntyre, often don't have a background in climate science. Steve McIntyre said in 2009 that he had "worked most of his life in business, mostly on the stock market side of mineral exploration deals".[11] His sometime collaborator Ross McKitrick, environmental economist at the University of Guelph, Canada, and senior fellow at libertarian think-tank the Fraser Institute, has a background in economics.

Nor are the "dissident scientists" facing the censorship of a powerful establishment. In fact, many mainstream climate scientists have faced politically motivated attacks on their work, funding and careers. Ben Santer, a climate modeller at the Lawrence Livermore National Laboratory, came under attack for his involvement with the 1995 Intergovernmental Panel on Climate Change (IPCC) report which stated that it was possible to see the hand of man in climate change. In Fred Pearce's *Climate Files* he claims that, "there is a strategy to single out individuals, tarnish them and try to bring the whole of science into disrepute." Trenberth told Pearce, "The attacks on me are clearly designed to get me fired or to resign".[12]

The Republican ex-chair of the Senate Committee on Environment and Public Works Republican, James Inhofe, who has consistently opposed environmental legislation and supported oil industry interests in the US senate, upped the stakes in response to Climategate, leading a "McCarthyite witch-hunt" calling for a criminal investigation of the scientists.[13]

There is a reasonably well documented history of some of the ways that the fossil fuel industry in particular has worked with specific scientists to

---

10: Anderegg and others, 2010.
11: McIntyre, 2008.
12: Pearce, 2010, p81.
13: Guardian, 1 March 2010.

try to influence public opinion and policy on the issue of global warming.[14] In 1998 the American Petroleum Institute, whose members include among others Exxon Mobil, Shell and Halliburton, aimed to find "independent scientists" so that "those promoting the Kyoto treaty on the basis of science would appear out of touch with reality".[15]

However, it has not been easy to find "independent" scientists who are willing to promote such a message. Instead big business has had to rely on a plethora of right wing think tanks who publish work, often not peer reviewed, challenging the work of climate scientists. A 2008 study published in the journal *Environment Politics* found that, of 141 English language "environmentally sceptical books published between 1972 and 2005, 92 percent have links to conservative think-tanks, 90 percent of which "espouse environmental scepticism".[16]

Greenpeace has examined some of the best-known right wing think tanks and the funding they receive. Between 2005 and 2008 Exxon Mobil and Koch Industries, a petroleum and chemical company ranked second behind Cargill as a privately run US business, donated $8.9 million dollars and $24.9 million dollars respectively to organisations involved with challenging the science and politics of climate change. According to Greenpeace, "Koch industries'....funding of the climate denial machine... through a combination of foundation-funded front groups, big lobbying budgets... and direct campaign contributions makes Koch industries...amongst the most formidable obstacles to advancing clean energy and climate policy in the US". [17]

Many of the research papers that make it to the front pages of right wing newspapers have been produced by these think tanks. Many have a history that precedes the debate over global warming and have a background in promoting science that challenges the link between cancer and smoking. Some, such as the Heartland Institute, have links to organisations that purport to present scientific reasons for anti-gay and anti-abortion ideas.[18]

Naomi Oreskes and Erik M Conway suggest in their book *Merchants of Doubt* that ideology rather than money has been the primary motivation for some scientists. They argue that some key figures in the climate sceptic camp were motivated to take on a scientific establishment which they saw as unsympathetic to the interests of capital and national security. These scientists

14: See, for example, Hoggan and Littlemore, 2009, Gelbspan, 1998, and Monbiot, 2007.
15: Pearce, 2010, p84.
16: Jaques and others, 2008, pp349-385.
17: Greenpeace—www.greenpeace.org/kochindustries
18: Hickman, 2010.

had originally cut their teeth politically and scientifically in a cold war environment which informed their opposition to government regulation promoted by those who had identified a link between cancer and cigarettes.[19]

According to Oreskes and Conway, these scientists, many of who had been drafted in to provide scientific backing for Ronald Reagan's "Star Wars" missile defence programme in the 1980s, believed government regulation equalled "communism" and was to be challenged. The methodology employed was to sow doubt about so called establishment consensus, whether over tobacco and cancer or, latterly, global warming and greenhouse gases. More public doubt meant less likelihood of government action. But as Conway argues:

> There is a second generation but not one that is nearly as respected," said Conway. "The think-tank network now exists and is self-perpetuating. They simply hire their own people who have some credentials, rarely actually climate scientists, who continue to do that kind of thing.[20]

There has been much debate about the motives of those who made the numerous freedom of information requests to scientists at the CRU. Judy Curry, a prominent climate scientist at the Georgia Institute, has argued that the old industry-funded scientists have been replaced by a new generation of "climate auditors" who "have no apparent political agenda, are doing this work for free, and have been playing a watchdog role, which has engendered them to the trust of a large segment of the population".[21] Curry has subsequently led the way in arguing that all data must be freely available. Refusing freedom of information requests and withholding data is not an answer to climate sceptics, who will, as indeed they have, claim this as evidence of "cover-up" and conspiracy. All data must be available for the professional scientist and lay-person in order to challenge and develop scientific research.

Nevertheless, unlike Curry, others such as Michael Mann are unconvinced of the independence of this new generation of fighters for open science: "I would imagine that much of what might appear to an outsider to be organic, to be grassroots, is actually connected, funded, and manned by those connected with the climate denial movement".[22]

As Oreskes and Conway argue, an absence of industry money does

19: Oreskes and Conway, 2010.
20: Quoted in Weber, 2010.
21: Pearce, 2010, pp227-228.
22: Pearce, 2010, p228.

not mean an absence of political motivation. Often the world view of many of the new breed of individual bloggers challenging the climate science is one which clearly sympathises with the notion that ideas of global warming have been cooked up by liberal scientists who want to see less individual freedom and more state control in people's lives. However, more often than not, the attacks come from think tanks and research institutes that are industry funded but *present* themselves as independent. The Global Warming Policy Foundation, launched by the former Tory chancellor Nigel Lawson with amazing timing just three days after the emails first appeared on the web, aims to play that role in Britain. Lawson may refuse to say where the funding for the foundation comes from but his commitment to the free market and opposition to trade unions are a matter of public record.

## Challenging the sceptics, challenging capitalism

There is no consistency to the arguments of the climate sceptics. Different arguments are deployed at different times, many of which contradict each other. They dispute whether global warming is taking place, suggesting that temperatures may be falling, yet also argue global warming is a good thing that will bring many benefits to human beings. They accept the science that increased concentration of greenhouse gases causes warming but argue that any warming taking place is caused by natural phenomena such as the activity of sunspots. They don't dispute the increase in greenhouse gases in the atmosphere, or the role of fossil fuels in producing greenhouse gases, but argue that rises in carbon dioxide are a consequence of warming rather than a cause of it. They accept some global warming is taking place because of human activity but claim the impact will be negligible because factors such as aerosol particles in the atmosphere mitigate warming by blocking the sun's radiation.

In contrast the science of global warming is consistent. There is a "greenhouse effect"—certain gases can trap the sun's heat in the atmosphere. Gases such as carbon dioxide, water vapour and methane do this. Human activity has massively increased the amount of "greenhouse gases" in the atmosphere. The burning of fossil fuels, which release carbon, and deforestation, which reduces the ability to absorb carbon dioxide from the atmosphere, has resulted in a 35 percent rise in the main greenhouse gases since pre-industrial times. Knowing this we would expect to see a warming of the atmosphere and the oceans. This has happened and is observable.

Global temperature has risen by just under one degree Fahrenheit over the last century. If the way society is organised is not fundamentally transformed, larger amounts of greenhouse gases will be produced. This will lead to greater warming. Within nature there are also feedback mechanisms that could amplify any warming that takes place. The most well known is the impact of a loss of arctic ice, which currently reflects the sun's heat (unlike the open sea that absorbs heat). Warming will alter our climate and weather systems, which will affect the habitats and ecosystems of all life on earth.

It can be difficult for those of us who do not have a scientific background to follow the various twists and turns of the debate, but it is no more difficult than other scientific debates that have had important political consequences, such as the debate over tobacco or HIV. Global warming is not simply a scientific question, in which the task for activists is to become greater and greater specialists in the scientific debate. Scientific debates are not abstracted from society, from political debate and from the balance of forces in society. As the environmental campaigner George Marshall argued in response to the Channel 4 documentary *The Great Global Warming Swindle* in 2007, "It would be entirely possible to put together a similar programme, with a string of credible former academics, to argue that smoking does not cause cancer, that HIV does not cause AIDS, or that black people are less intelligent. However, Channel 4 would not dare broadcast the programme and we would not believe them if they did".[23]

What concludes such scientific debates is not simply more and more scientific study, replicating and confirming previous ones, but political debate which shifts the balance of forces away from the interests of the rich and powerful to the wider interests of society. For example, increasing evidence about the relationship between smoking and cancer facilitated and framed a political debate about whether smoking was simply an individual act, in which regulation and government intervention should play no role, or a public health issue, requiring societal controls to protect both the individual and society.

Increasingly, the argument that smoking was a public health issue was won in the teeth of opposition from the tobacco companies (and many of the same think tanks that are now challenging the science on climate change). Various forms of regulation have now been introduced, including a ban on smoking in public places.

It is this political argument, which the sceptics feared they were losing, that has unleashed the campaign we have experienced. The leaking of the emails so close to the Copenhagen talks was clearly, as Michael Mann said, "an orchestrated smear campaign to distract the public about the nature of the climate change problem".[24] However, the absence of a powerful and united movement that recognises and identifies the right wing nature of the

---

23: Marshall, 2007.
24: Pearce, 2010, p180.

attack, and that is able to defend the scientists politically, not just scientifically, makes it possible for the agenda to be set by climate sceptics and the right wing rather than those fighting for action on climate change.

There often seemed little appetite amongst environmentalists to defend the scientists. A few days after the leak, leading environmental campaigner George Monbiot wrote in the *Guardian* calling for Phil Jones to resign.[25] He retracted the call after the enquiries took place. Perhaps such a response represented the frustration of environmentalists that, having turned a corner on public attitudes to the problem, progress appeared to be jeopardised by the words of leading climate scientists in their emails. But there is often a belief within the environmental movement that it is ordinary people and their ignorance that is the root of the problem. Sadly, for many within the environmental movement, the success of the sceptics in grabbing the headlines confirmed their prejudice that the perceived greed and self interest of individuals is the real block to action on climate change, rather than the powerful vested interests.

This approach seriously hinders the environmental movement. The deep well of public cynicism that the climate sceptics tap into comes not from individual greed, but from the hypocrisy and weakness of politicians who profess the urgency of action on climate change and then fail to provide real solutions. Perhaps one of the reasons why the climate sceptics have made headway is because the rhetoric over climate change has never been matched by radical policies aimed at solving the problem. Instead nearly all climate change policy has been based on market mechanisms, such as the European Emissions Trading Scheme, which have failed to halt emission rises and have redistributed wealth from the poor to the rich. No surprise then that the climate sceptics have found some resonance from ordinary people, already angry and cynical about politicians, and who find it easy to believe they may have been lied to again by the scientists the politicians quote.

In Britain, for example, New Labour was strong in its rhetoric about the necessity of tackling climate change. But government action did not match the rhetoric. This was most visibly demonstrated when workers at the Vestas wind turbine factory on the Isle of Wight occupied to stop the closure of the only such factory in Britain. They sparked a national campaign of support and solidarity. Yet despite a stated commitment to renewable energy, and after using billions of taxpayers' money to bailout the banks, the government refused to intervene to keep the factory open. An important opportunity to further the case for renewable energy and save jobs was

---

25: Monbiot, 2009.

squandered just months before the Copenhagen talks at which the government claimed it would be at the forefront of tackling climate change.

Meanwhile, the big corporate beasts of the oil, coal and nuclear industry were having a field day. The government's energy policy embraced nuclear and coal fired power stations. They continued to back dangerous expansion by oil companies such as BP. People's experience of seeing politicians fail to challenge the polluting companies while urging them to change aspects of personal and family lifestyle to help save the planet has created a political climate of cynicism in which the sceptics can find resonance for their dangerous ideas.

The climate sceptics do not need to disprove the science or even convince millions that the science is wrong. They simply need to muddy the water and raise doubts. This way they can make climate change seem less of a priority. They can ensure that even if people believe it is happening, they can hope that something can be done about it in the future or another part of the world. Such an approach can be even more persuasive in a recession.

The economic crisis is giving greater weight to those who want as little regulation as possible aimed at cutting carbon emissions. Many in the ruling class understand the dangers of climate change. But they are unwilling to shoulder the cost of dealing with it as individual corporations or collectively as nation states. Such unwillingness was the cause of the failure at Copenhagen. It is in this context that the political usefulness of climate scepticism becomes greater. There is a greater willingness to have the sceptics' position aired by certain sections of the ruling class. It has a political impact over demands for action.

In a poll carried out after Climategate it was revealed that the number of people who were concerned about climate change had fallen from 91 percent in 2005 to 78 percent. Meanwhile, 40 percent thought the issue of climate change was exaggerated.[26] For right wing governments like Cameron's this is useful. They have not taken an overtly climate sceptic position but they want to shelve an approach based on government and business targets. Instead, they seek increasingly to individualise the cost of climate change through insurance and personal misery, as well as promoting the market rather than government as the solution.

With the economic crisis set to worsen, efforts to dispute the science that human activity causes climate change will continue. Those of us fighting for change should ensure that we mount a political battle against the climate sceptics, not simply a scientific one. We need to ensure

26: *Guardian*, 11 June.

that those waging that battle recognise that the real enemy is the capitalist system, which puts profit before the lives of billions of humans and the planet. Equally importantly, we need to recognise who the real allies are in this fight—the millions of working people around the world who have no vested interest in a system that prioritises profit over the world's climate.

## References

Adam, David, 2010, "Climategate scientists cleared of manipulating data on global warming", *Guardian* (3 July), www.guardian.co.uk/environment/2010/jul/08/muir-russell-climategate-climate-science

Anderegg, William R L, James W Prall, Jacob Harold and Stephen H Schneider, 2010, "Expert credibility in climate change", *Proceedings of the National Academy of the Sciences of the United States*, volume 106, number 27 (July), www.pnas.org/content/107/27/12107.full

Gelbspan, Ross, (1998), *The Heat is on: Climate Crisis, the Cover-up, the Prescription* (Perseus).

Grey, Louise, 2010, "Cancun climate change summit: 2010 was hottest year on record", *Telegraph* (7 December), www.telegraph.co.uk/topics/weather/8175591/Cancun-climate-change-summit-2010-was-hottest-year-on-record.html

Hickman, Leo, 2010, "Climate sceptics and fringe political groups are an unhealthy cocktail", *Guardian* (4 June), www.guardian.co.uk/environment/blog/2010/jun/04/climate-sceptics-fringe-political-groups

Hoggan, James, and Richard Littlemore, 2009, *Climate Cover-Up* (Greystone).

Jacques, Peter J, Riley E Dunlap and Mark Freeman, 2008, "The Organisation of Denial: Conservative think tanks and climate", *Environmental Politics*, volume 17, issue 3, (June).

Marshall, George, 2007, "The Great Channel 4 Swindle", http://climatedenial.org/2007/03/09/the-great-channel-four-swindle/

Mann, Michael E, Raymond S Bradley and Malcolm K Hughes, 1998, "Global-scale temperature patterns and climate forcing over the past six centuries", *Nature*, 392.

McIntyre, Stephen, 2008, "How do we 'know' that 1998 was the warmest year of the millennium?", http://climateaudit.files.wordpress.com/2005/09/ohioshort.pdf

Monbiot, George, 2007, *Heat: How We Can Stop the Planet Burning* (Penguin).

Monbiot, George, 2009, "Global warming rigged? Here's the email I'd need to see", *Guardian* (23 November), www.guardian.co.uk/commentisfree/cif-green/2009/nov/23/global-warming-leaked-email-climate-scientists

Oreskes, Naomi, and Erik M Conway, 2010, *Merchants of Doubt: How a Handful of Scientists Obscured the Truth on Issues from Tobacco Smoke to Global Warming* (Bloomsbury).

Pearce, Fred, 2010, *The Climate Files* (Guardian Books).

Trenberth, Kevin E, 2009, "An imperative for climate change planning: tracking Earth's global energy", *Elsevier*, 1 (October), www.cgd.ucar.edu/cas/Trenberth/trenberth.papers/EnergyDiagnostics09final2.pdf

Weber, Gretchen, 2010, "Merchants of Doubt Traces Roots of Denial", KQED News (14 June), http://blogs.kqed.org/climatewatch/2010/06/14/merchants-of-doubt-traces-roots-of-denial/

# Tony Cliff's Lenin and the Russian Revolution

*John Rose*

In Tony Cliff's original four-volume series on Lenin published in the 1970s, the second volume was entitled *All Power to the Soviets* and the third *Revolution Besieged*.[1] Besieged may not mean destroyed, but the civil war, which began in May 1918, fundamentally altered the relations between the soviets and the ruling Bolshevik Party. Lenin described this as follows at the Eighth Congress of the Bolshevik Party in March 1919: "The soviets, which by virtue of their programme are organs of government *by the working people*, are in fact organs of government *for the working people* by the advanced sections of the proletariat but not by the working people as a whole".[2]

Clearly this was a retreat from the fundamental principle of soviet power. Of course this was not of their own making but forced on the Bolsheviks by the shocking circumstances of civil war that would drain the soviets of their leadership and much of their manpower. Nor did it necessarily mean that the principle of government by the working people could not be re-established.

1:  I would like to thank Ian Birchall, David Crouch and Ken Muller for reading and commenting on the first draft of this article. Almost all of their suggestions and additional references have been incorporated. Also thanks to Kevin Murphy for our very stimulating and positive email exchange about the second draft.
2:  Cliff, 1978, p174, emphasis in the original. See also "Decline of local power of soviets", Cliff, 1978, pp149-151.

Victor Serge has left us this fascinating description of the Petrograd Soviet meeting in October 1919. Trotsky and Zinoviev were reporting about the military situation, as the city itself was under siege. It's a soviet "for the working people": but it's not at all difficult to see how, even at this late stage, its original mandate might have been restored under transformed circumstances:

The meeting of the soviet is thinly attended. A number of its members are at the front. There are many army greatcoats, fur or leather jackets, revolvers on belts. Young women, workers, Bashkirs, Muslims from the southern Urals. Not a single intellectual in sight. It really is the people itself, the people which suffers, toils, labours, fights, the people with horny chapped hands, the people which is inelegant, rough, a little brutal, with clumsy movements, with faces not refined by civilisation.

Nobody speaks to reply or asks questions. This is not the time for debating; in any case, the soviet does not debate much—there is nothing parliamentary about it. As it is at the moment, it is nothing but a very simple apparatus for popular consultation and dictatorship...

Nonetheless, the assembly is not passive. Such acceptance on its own would be worrying. But now, as people are leaving, someone shouts out: The Internationale. The whole hall rises to its feet, bare-headed, and two thousand manly voices intone the song of the "last fight".[3]

However, this brief article questions to what extent soviet power could properly develop at all even during those first six months. Was there really any opportunity to implement mass-based workers' democracy?

The implications of the political and practical realisation of the call for all power to the soviets had been profound. Soviet power meant direct producer democracy, prelude to the abolition of social classes and potential breakthrough to a new era in human history. It was a dramatic realisation of the principles expressed by Marx and Engels in the *Communist Manifesto* in 1848, and built on the first practical experiment in workers' power during the Paris Commune of 1871. The revolutionary decrees issued in the soviet government's first weeks signalled the arrival in the world of a new type of politics of emancipation.[4]

3:   Serge, 1997, p56.
4:   Cliff, 1978, pp5-12. Serge, 1992, pp122-123. See Haynes, 1997, for a discussion about

Lenin had always anticipated this—the central goal of the revolution. The administration of the new workers' state was to be controlled by the mass of workers, not just their representatives. Expanding on his famous one liner that "every cook shall govern", Lenin writes:

> The conscientious, bold, universal move to hand over administrative work to proletarians and semi-proletarians will, however, rouse such unprecedented revolutionary enthusiasm among the people, will so multiply the people's forces in combating distress, that much that seemed impossible to our narrow, old, bureaucratic forces will become possible for the millions.[5]

The soviets were at the core of this new rank and file activist democratic state.[6] The immediate aftermath of the revolution, that festival of the oppressed, seemed to more than justify Lenin's optimism as famously recorded in John Reed's *Ten Days that Shook the World*. In the same spirit Lenin had predicted in *The State and Revolution*, effectively the foundation document of the October 1917 Revolution, the relative ease with which the soviets would control the defeated counter-revolutionary social classes, especially the bourgeoisie. The exploiters had been unable to exploit the people without a highly complex machine. But Lenin argued that when the formerly exploited people take power "they can suppress the exploiters even with a very simple 'machine', almost without a 'machine', without a special apparatus, by the simple organisation of the armed people".[7]

Reporting this passage, Cliff interjects that the "simple organisation of the armed people" would be the Soviets of Workers and Soldiers Deputies. But, of course, this proved completely inadequate in the face of the

the immediate threats to sabotage the new revolutionary regime from the Mensheviks and the peasants' party, the SRs, the Social Revolutionary Party, in alliance with the Right; the conservative role of striking civil servants and the railway workers' union; and crucially the split in the SRs, leading to the Left SRs entering a coalition with the Bolsheviks.

5:    Cliff, 1976, p331. And here is the answer to Simon Pirani. Whatever the merits of his argument with Kevin Murphy in this journal, he undermines his case with his assertion that it was the Bolsheviks' "vanguardism and statism that made them blind to the creative potential of democratic workers' organisations"—Pirani, 2008, p235. On the contrary the Bolsheviks' "vanguardism", an unnecessarily gratuitous way of describing their selfless and exhausted mainly working class cadre, was devoted to unleashing that democratic potential. Their "statism" was, as we shall see, a desperate defence of the revolutionary potential of the new state, the network of soviets, from the overpowering threat of counter-revolution.

6:    See John Reed's brilliant contemporary description of the structure of the soviets in Reed, 1974.

7:    Cliff, 1976, p322.

monstrous scale of attacks faced by the revolution even in its early days, as Cliff himself makes clear elsewhere. It was the highly complex machine of the Red Army, which Trotsky began to build at extraordinary speed just a few months later, that defended the revolution. The second volume of Cliff's biography of Trotsky, *The Sword of the Revolution,* is dominated by the centrality of the Red Army. A catastrophic price would be paid—the effective neutering of the soviets. But this is to run ahead of the argument.

According to a key chapter in the widely acclaimed *Year One of the Russian Revolution* by the former anarchist turned Bolshevik, Victor Serge, "the first flames of the civil war" threatened the revolution from the beginning. This took three forms and reflected the counter-revolutionary backlash over the three main demands of October: land, peace and bread. Control of the land forced the soviets into confrontation with the Constituent Assembly. The peace terms split the new revolutionary government, the Bolshevik Party and the soviets. Lack of bread came close to starving the revolution in its industrial heartlands. Here I adopt Serge's approach, though I have changed the order following Cliff's chronology, analysing these three sets of events separately, but recognising that "in reality they were aspects of a single process", sabotaging the revolution.[8]

## The constituent assembly and its dissolution

In retrospect, it seems quite astonishing that over the years writers in the International Socialist tradition have paid so little attention to the dissolution of the Constituent Assembly which followed the October Bolshevik Revolution. After all, from the vantage point of the 21st century, constituent assemblies and democratic parliaments seem rather more successful expressions of democracy than do soviets. For most people the word "soviet" is damned by associations with words like Stalin, Stalinist, totalitarianism, bureaucracy and terror, and for understandable reasons. How then can we defend the Bolsheviks dissolving the Constituent Assembly, especially since they had campaigned for it right up until the eve of the revolution?[9]

Workers and peasants may have made the October Revolution but at the same time the peasantry posed the most immediate threat to its working

---

8:   Serge, 1992, p122.

9:   John Rees mounted a robust "Defence of October", including the Bolsheviks' dissolution of the constituent assembly, against all the fainthearts, many of them former Communists like the leader of the South African Communist Party, Joe Slovo—Rees, 1991. In the aftermath of the collapse of "Communism" two years earlier, not only did they belatedly discover the evils of Stalinism but were keen to point the blame also at Lenin, Trotsky and the Bolsheviks. See also Trudell, 2000.

class content. Or, as Cliff put it in particularly stark form, "the enormous threat facing the proletarian dictatorship [came] in the form of the mass petty bourgeois peasantry. The island of industry in the hands of the proletariat might be engulfed by the vast seas of the backward peasantry".[10]

This potentially lethal division found its precise expression in the outcome of the elections for the constituent assembly, which were dominated by the success of the Social Revolutionary Party (SRs). The SRs were the main peasant party but had attracted, over the years, shopkeepers, minor "progressive" officials of the Tsarist state, large sections of the intelligentsia and as the revolution approached a few of the more liberal landowners, bourgeoisie and even army officers. Cliff returned to the complexities of the land and peasant question many times in the four volumes of his Lenin biography. Suffice to write here that the slogan "All land to the tiller", which the Bolsheviks adapted from the SRs, was riddled with ambiguity. It could mean collective land ownership by poor peasants. But it could equally mean small-scale, competitive private farming by individual peasant farm owners. Moreover a rural class system was developing in the countryside.[11]

A speech in the Constituent Assembly by the Menshevik Tseretelli, hostile to the Bolsheviks, inadvertently put his finger on the problem: "The land taken by the peasants has in reality been taken by the kulaks, the rich peasants who possess the farming equipment".[12]

It is in this context that Cliff provides a very bleak analysis of the threat posed to the revolution by the Constituent Assembly:

> The catchment area covered by the Constituent Assembly was far wider than that of the soviet. While the Second Congress of Soviets represented about 20 million people, the number of votes for the Constituent Assembly was more than 40 million. The Bolsheviks, together with the Left SRs, represented the overwhelming majority of the urban proletariat, the peasantry in the neighbourhood of the industrial centres, and the troops in the north and north west. These were the most energetic and enlightened elements of the masses, on whose active support the revolution depended for survival. The SRs who dominated the Constituent Assembly represented the political confusion and indecision of the petty bourgeoisie

---

10: Cliff, 1978, p76.
11: Cliff had an unpublished book on the subject of the collectivisation of agriculture—available as a manuscript at Warwick University http://www.marxists.org/archive/cliff/works/1964/xx/index.htm
12: Serge, 1992, p133.

in the towns and the millions of peasants relatively distant from the capital and the industrial centres.[13]

Lenin spelt out the implications in an article, "Constituent Assembly Elections and the Dictatorship of the Proletariat". While in terms of voting power the countryside outweighed the towns, in real social and political power the towns were far superior: "The country cannot be equal to the town under the historical conditions of this epoch. The town inevitably leads the country. The country inevitably follows the town...big commercial and industrial centres...decide the political fate of the nation".[14] Cliff comments: "Lenin was compelled to take refuge in the anti-democratic measure of counting one worker's vote as equal to five peasants' in the elections to the soviets".[15]

Despite this, Chernov, the SR leader and president of the Constituent Assembly, seemed desperate to blur the differences with Lenin in his opening address in what Serge describes as a "masterpiece of sweet evasiveness":

> Several times he touched on the nation's "will for socialism", remarking: "The revolution has merely begun... The people want actions not words...socialism is not equality among poverty... We desire controlled socialist construction... We shall pass from the control of production to the republic of labour..." Finally he endorsed the nationalisation of the land without compensation.

Chernov called for collaboration between the Constituent Assembly and the soviets. But Bukharin for the Bolsheviks "refuted his 'chatter' in a short speech, as brutal as the other had been unctuous. 'How,' he asked, 'can a man talk of the will to socialism and at the same time be the assassin of socialism?'"[16]

The SRs had a long record of violent hostility to the Bolsheviks. Even after October SR-led insurrectionary demonstrations and coup attempts against the Bolsheviks had been under active consideration. Kidnap and assassination attempts on Lenin and Trotsky were called off at the last minute. "Their reasons? The two leaders were too popular; their disappearance would have provoked terrible reprisals".[17]

---

13: Cliff, 1978, p34-35.
14: Cliff, 1978, p36.
15: Cliff, 1996, p61.
16: Serge, 1992, p133.
17: Serge, 1992, p130.

"Throughout the years of the civil war in Russia (1918-1920)," writes Cliff, "the slogan of the Constituent Assembly served as a screen for the dictatorship of the landowners and capitalists".[18] The Constituent Assembly would have been effectively dominated by representatives of the emerging peasant kulak class and backed by all the forces of reaction. For the Bolsheviks to tolerate it alongside the soviets would almost certainly have hastened the civil war by giving its leaders a rival political platform and hence a rallying point in the industrial heartlands.

On the other hand, its dissolution disenfranchised 20 million peasants in the outlying areas and institutionalised the split in the revolution between town and country. As we shall see, this immediately intensified the new and ominous threat to the revolution and the soviets: famine.

## The "peace" of Brest-Litovsk

The word "peace" has been placed in inverted commas here because of the terms insisted upon to end the war in the early months of 1918 by the German High Command negotiators with the Bolsheviks. They were so harsh that, despite the overwhelming desire and demand for a genuine peace, a continuation of the war suddenly seemed preferable to probably more than half of the Bolshevik Party and certainly to a majority in the soviets. "Peace" was one thing, abject humiliation and "peace" terms which could wreck the revolution something else.

Trotsky's outstanding role prolonging the negotiations while fanning anti-war sentiment amongst front line German troops, the first stirrings of a revolutionary German workers' strike movement against the war, the fascinating and intense arguments between Lenin and Trotsky on tactics, important though they were, unfortunately are secondary to Lenin's absolute insistence on ending the war as soon as possible.

Of course, like Trotsky and the rest of the Bolsheviks, Lenin viewed ending the war as the potential trigger for the expected German socialist revolution, the taken for granted precondition for the survival of the Russian Revolution. But he was adamant that the Bolsheviks could not wait for it.[19]

Nevertheless the idea of turning the war into a "Revolutionary War" swept through the ranks of the Bolsheviks. Lenin was furious at what he saw as "revolutionary phrase-making...the repetition of revolutionary slogans irrespective of objective circumstances". Lenin had only one argument. But it was decisive: "The old army does not exist. The new army is

18: Cliff, 1978, p38.
19: Cliff, 1978, pp39-40.

only just being born... It is one thing to be certain that the German revolution is maturing and to do your work helping it mature...it is another thing to declare...that the German revolution is already mature (although it obviously is not) and to base your tactics on it." The Bolsheviks were split down the middle. Only by threatening to resign both from the government and the party leadership could Lenin secure his position.[20]

It is essential to stress that this was an argument that tested the nerves, the intellectual, political and moral fibre to breaking point, of the most committed Bolshevik. It was finely balanced throughout. The terms of the Brest-Litovsk "peace" treaty were indeed designed to wreck the revolution and inevitably hastened the civil war—not least because so much of the territory lost undermined the industrial and agricultural supply base of workers' power in the centrally strategic cities and towns:

> It was estimated that by this treaty Russia lost territories and resources approximately as follows: 1,227,000 square miles, with 62,000,000 population, or one fourth of her territory and 44 percent of her population; one third of her crops and 27 percent of state income; 80 percent of her sugar factories; 75 percent of her iron and 75 percent of her coal. Of the total 16,000 industrial undertakings, 9,000 were situated in lost territories. [21]

And, as Mike Haynes has observed, "puppet regimes were set up (in the south) which attracted the revolution's opponents. Miliukov [the leader of Russian liberalism], Chernov later said, 'went quite calmly to the zone of German occupation to seek salvation in friendship with the enemy of yesterday'."[22]

The debate over the war in the Bolshevik Party dominates the relevant chapter in the writing of both Cliff and Serge. Cliff reports a referendum of the views of 200 soviets in February, with a majority for continuing the war. In the industrial cities, Cliff writes that the "majority in favour of war was overwhelming. Only two large soviets—Petrograd and Sebastopol—went on record as being in favour of peace".[23]

The argument in the party concluded with a specially convened Seventh Congress from 6 to 8 March 1918 that, after a bitter debate, voted by 30 to 12 in Lenin's favour. The final ratification of the treaty took place

---

20: Cliff, 1978, pp46-47, 48.
21: Cliff, 1978, p50.
22: Haynes, 2002, p36.
23: Cliff, 1978, p50.

at the Fourth Congress of Soviets on 15 March 1918 by a vote of 748 to 261.[24] What made a lasting impression on Serge was the flourishing, open and dynamic rank and file democracy of the Bolshevik Party itself and its honourable conduct in the debate about the war:

> This party, so disciplined and so little encumbered by abstract fetishism for democracy, still in these grave hours respects its norms of internal democracy. It puts its recognised leader in a minority: Lenin's tremendous personal authority does not hinder the militants in the central committee from standing up to him and energetically maintaining their point of view; the most important decisions are settled by vote, often by small majorities (a margin of one vote...) to which the minorities are willing to defer without abandoning their ideas. Lenin, when in the minority, submits while waiting for events to prove him right, and continues his propaganda without breaking discipline. Even though impassioned, the discussion remains objective. Neither gossip nor intrigue nor personalities play any important part in what is said. The militants talk politics, without trying to wound or discredit the comrades on the opposing side. Since the opposition is never bullied, it shows only the minimum of emotion that one would expect in events of this order, and soon recovers from its rash decisions...

At this hour the party really is the courageous "iron cohort" of Bukharin's later description. It is a living organism, teeming with initiative from the lowest to the highest ranks.[25]

## Famine and industrial breakdown

Analysing these tumultuous events immediately following the October Revolution, Cliff interrupts the historical flow with a reflective chapter, "The Transition from Capitalism to Socialism". It serves to prepare and warn the reader for the shock of what amounts to the industrial breakdown of the revolution in the early months of 1918. The chapter discusses the difficulty Lenin had as he searched the writings of Marx and Engels for revolutionary guidelines for managing a workers' state in its initial stages. Arguments, probably familiar to readers of this journal, are restated, distinguishing Utopian socialist futuristic blueprints from concrete practicalities.

But the main problem was the one that Lenin already understood only too well. Marx and Engels always took it for granted that socialist

---

24: Cliff, 1978, p51.
25: Serge, 1992, pp173-174.

revolution would build on the solid foundations of a developed capitalist industry. Socialist revolution was not, and could not be, a motor to industrialise a backward peasant country. This unique circumstance had only one remedy—socialist revolution in the advanced capitalist countries in Western Europe and North America. But meanwhile the Bolsheviks had to manage the economy and society in the here and now. Lenin reached for the only conclusion, however unpalatable: compromises with capitalism.

In this chapter Cliff raises the more general problem of how a workers' state would impose its will on capitalism, following the socialist revolution. In other words, capitalism most certainly does not disappear over night. But the problem for Lenin and the Bolsheviks was obviously of an altogether much greater magnitude. Cliff quotes Lenin at some length struggling to reconcile the released energies and creative potential of liberated workers with an argument for strict work discipline and the integration of, and coordination with, capitalist expertise.

The tension is palpable and is stunningly expressed in the title of the next chapter as well as some of the chapter's subheadings. The chapter is called "We Need State Capitalism", a quotation from Lenin.[26] Subheadings include "We Need Bourgeois Specialists" and even "One Man Management", where Lenin defends the use of "Taylorism", the principles of "scientific management" that used the stopwatch in industry as a means of extracting intensified labour from workers.

But the most shocking part of this chapter is its first two pages, summed up by the telegram Lenin and the food commissar dispatched to all provincial soviets and food committees on 11 May 1918:

> Petrograd is in an unprecedentedly catastrophic situation. There is no bread. The population is given the remaining potato flour and crusts. The Red capital is on the verge of perishing from famine. Counter-revolution is raising its head, directing the dissatisfaction of the hungry masses against the Soviet Government.[27]

---

26: Lenin saw "state capitalism" addressing both the problems of industrial and agricultural breakdown. His concept here needs to be distinguished from Cliff's own alternative usage as an analysis of the later, Stalinist state. Lenin means that the fledgling workers' state had to use private capital to develop the country: but under a tight regime of state regulation combined with some supervision of management by elected workplace committees (though he conceded that private management would also retain independent direction of the enterprise)—Cliff, 1978, pp69-71. Lenin saw measures like these "as a purely temporary retreat". See also the concluding paragraphs of this article.

27: Cliff, 1978, p67.

Cliff goes on to describe industry in a state of nothing less than "complete collapse".[28] There was no food to feed factory workers, no raw material or fuel for industry.

The opening of Soviet archives following the collapse of Stalinism in 1989 has provided powerful confirmation of industrial breakdown. In his ground-breaking study of a major Moscow metal factory, Kevin Murphy describes hungry workers leaving the factory in March 1918 and going home to their villages. Later management complains about their peasant backgrounds. At the same time Bolshevik organisation in the revolution's second city was disintegrating. Although Moscow party membership stood at 40,000, only 6,000 were in the factories and less than half of those were on the shop floor. The local Bolshevik leader complains that "cells are falling apart because comrades have left for the Red Guards... Comrades call each other saboteurs".[29]

But Murphy's most staggering statistic trumps even Cliff's night-marish description of famine, industrial breakdown and the threat to the revolution: "By the summer of 1918, Soviet Russia had shrunk to the size of the medieval Moscovy state and had lost almost all grain producing regions".[30] It is inconceivable that the soviets could have functioned effectively in such circumstances. A further factor touched on by Murphy reinforces this conclusion. Civil war was looming and Trotsky was recruiting for the Red Army the best Bolshevik workers from the industrial areas, and hence emptying the soviets of their most able cadres. Cliff reports that by 18 April the number of volunteers "numbered nearly 200,000 men, practically only from the urban proletariat".[31]

## Soviet Petrograd

The above arguments are powerfully tested by a microscopic case study of "Red Petrograd", in the first year of the revolution, based on recently released archival materials. Alexander Rabinowitch's hostility to Lenin and Trotsky offers us an unintended template of objective reporting. It is easy to see beyond, and despite, his ideological limitations.[32] A highly professional

---

28: Cliff, 1978, p68.
29: Murphy, 2007, p66.
30: Murphy, 2007, p64. Trotsky is the original source for the catastrophic scale of the shrinkage of the soviet state—http://www.marxists.org/archive/trotsky/1919/military/ch03.htm.
31: Cliff, 1990, p66.
32: Rabinowitch identifies with the so-called "moderate Bolsheviks" and their greater willingness to resolve the post-revolutionary crisis by seeking coalition with the Mensheviks and SRs—only to be thwarted by Lenin and Trotsky.

scholar, he provides a plethora of evidence that pinpoints with precision what we might call the Lenin/Cliff case for the strengths and weaknesses of the Petrograd Soviet, and of soviets more generally because he has thoroughly explored the local district soviet archives as well. Here, following the pattern of this article, I will concentrate mainly on the early months of 1918.

The administration of the soviets at first depended upon what Rabinowitch describes as "veteran civil servants". They were hostile to the revolution and had been on strike against it. They were not replaced "by freshly trained representatives of the revolutionary masses, as Trotsky advocated".[33] What makes this comment particularly interesting is both the author's implicit explanation and his later observations about the civil servants. The Bolsheviks did not have the cadre to facilitate and supervise the training of a new revolutionary "civil service". Why not?

Civil war was already looming in the Don Territory in the south:

> Beginning in late November, in response to Lenin's urgent appeals to suppress the bourgeois counter-revolution on the Don, thousands of Petrograd Bolsheviks, Red Guards, Baltic Fleet sailors, and ordinary workers, many of them mobilised by district party committees, joined the rag tag Soviet forces bound for the south... This first episode in the Russian Civil War was typical of the post-October period with respect to the drain of Bolshevik personnel from Petrograd... The record shows that during the first year of Soviet power in Petrograd massive outflows of the most effective party workers, leading to organisational dysfunction, were the rule in all districts.[34]

Nevertheless, we learn much later from this author that the civil service problem had at least partly resolved itself. We discover not only "lower ranking civil servants...positively disposed to Soviet power", but that in the words of one of their representatives, they considered themselves not so much employees but "faithful servants of the revolution".[35]

However, it would be foolish to gloss over the implications of "organisational dysfunction", the result of draining of the Bolshevik cadre from Petrograd, both in the soviets and in the Bolshevik Party itself. Despite the Brest-Litovsk peace treaty, Lenin still feared a German military invasion and occupation of Petrograd. Consequently he insisted that the government administration move from Petrograd to Moscow. This allowed the

---

33: Rabinowitch, 2008, p57.
34: Rabinowitch, 2008, pp59-60.
35: Rabinowitch, 2008, p234.

revolution's enemies in Petrograd to make claims about a cowardly retreat and reawaken the debate about the Bolsheviks' "capitulation" to Germany. The argument merged with crippling food shortages—a result noted earlier, at least in part, of the Bolsheviks' forced surrender of vital grain producing regions under the Brest-Litovsk treaty—and rocketing unemployment, 46 percent of industrial workers, with many factories lying idle.

The severely weakened Bolshevik Party was thus unable to prevent the emergence of the Extraordinary Assembly of Delegates from Petrograd Factories and Plants (EAD). Although this movement gained credibility from former and now deeply disenchanted Bolshevik supporters, it was in essence a cover for counter-revolution and would open the door to the extreme right, with "frustrated workers, in increasing numbers...venting their desperation in anti-Semitic pogroms".[36]

Over the months the EAD would pose an increasingly menacing threat to Bolshevik authority, including threats of strike action. An example of just how frightening the situation was becoming occurred in the Petrograd district of Kolpino with bread shortages over the Easter holidays. Furious housewives descended on the local soviet and a fight erupted with soviet officials. The local commissar and soldiers pulled their guns and some of the housewives were shot at and wounded. Later an electricians' union official was killed.[37] Trotsky once remarked about the danger to the revolution when the Bolsheviks had to police food queues. That danger had arrived.

This was the moment, noted earlier, that Lenin defined as "famine... and counter-revolution...raising its head". In desperation the Bolsheviks turned to the *prodotriady*, food procurement detachments. But this would shatter the degree of political stability in the Petrograd soviets' structure provided by the coalition between the Bolsheviks and the Left SRs.[38] According to Rabinowitch, "Lenin's policy of squeezing the peasantry to feed starving workers, and the resulting creation of a virtual state of war between town and country, was implemented on a large scale in the late spring and summer. At that time, armed worker and Red Army units, the ...*prodotriady*, were dispatched to farming regions to seize surpluses from the peasants at gunpoint".[39]

As we shall see, Cliff not only concurs with this description, but also defines it as an extremely dangerous signal, even a turning point for the

---

36: Rabinowitch, 2008, p228.
37: Rabinowitch, 2008, pp223-236.
38: Read critically, Rabinowitch provides a useful background to this coalition—2008, pp260-270.
39: Rabinowitch, 2008, p270.

worse, in the revolution. Petrograd once again was called upon to provide the shock troops for the *prodotriady*—20,000 "select" workers for, in Lenin's words, "a merciless assault on the rural bourgeoisie". By July 1918, Lenin was calling for another 10,000 workers. Very reluctantly, the Bolshevik organisation in Petrograd had to say no. They were fearful of wiping out entirely the party's base in the city and its soviets.[40]

The party was already in catastrophic decline and in the next three months would collapse even further, by half, to a mere 6,000 members. More worrying, nearly half were new recruits who had joined since October, including, according to Soviet officials from Zinoviev down, "many corrupt profiteers who belonged in jail".[41] The soviets might be surviving but they were in danger of hollowing out, with the vacuum filled with counter-revolution.

Meanwhile, the Left SRs' opposition to *prodotriady* was denounced by Lenin, describing them as accomplices to counter-revolution, the "party of the weak willed, apt to defend the kulaks".[42] The Left SRs had also been in national coalition with the Bolsheviks in the CEC, the Central Executive Committee of Soviets of Workers' and Soldiers' Deputies. And since January 1918 they had controlled the Peasant Section headed by the legendary Maria Spiridonova.[43]

Tensions were inevitably built into this arrangement because of a fundamental disagreement about the leading role of the working class, in relation to the peasantry, in the revolution. They were at boiling point after the Brest-Litovsk treaty, which the Left SRs vehemently opposed. Now they exploded. In an open letter to the Bolshevik Central Committee, Spiridonova exposed brutalities inflicted on peasants, many not just poor but often themselves victims of the famine. She described "villages battered by artillery. Whole villages set on fire." The Bolsheviks could not deny it. Lenin would later concede that indeed "terrible errors" had been made.[44]

Spiridinova was a complex political persona. On the one hand she and the Left SRs shared many of the Bolsheviks' central objectives. At first she refused to publicly condemn either the Brest-Litovsk treaty or the

---

40: Rabinowitch, 2008, p273.
41: Rabinowitch, 2008, pp343-344.
42: Rabinowitch, 2008, p271.
43: In 1906, as a student member of the SRs, Maria Spiridonova assassinated the governor of Tambov province, who had crushed peasant unrest with signal brutality. She spent 11 years in a Siberian convict prison, "a regime so harsh that suicide became the political inmates' final form of protest"—Serge, 1992, p411, n70. She became the Left SR leader in 1917.
44: Rabinowitch, 2008, pp285-286.

*prodotriady*. Like the Bolsheviks, she was convinced that Europe was on the brink of revolution. She called on her supporters to defend the Bolsheviks and not cave in to the Mensheviks and Right SRs, who were "exploiting the hunger to mobilise the masses against Soviet power".[45]

On the other hand, as the split with the Bolsheviks over *prodotriady* widened, she gave way to earlier and frankly irrational Narodnik pressures. She sanctioned the Left SRs' assassination of the German ambassador in Moscow in July, as a deliberate provocation to force Germany to break the Brest-Litovsk treaty.[46] The Bolsheviks obviously then had to ban the Left SRs. It was a measure of Spiridonova's persisting credibility that she was held in prison only until November. She would repudiate the assassination.[47]

## "The Peasants' Resistance Shapes the State"

This is the title Cliff gave to arguably one of the most important sections of his third volume of *Lenin*.[48] It deals uncompromisingly with the implications of the Bolsheviks' food requisitioning programme. He cites Engels to make a comparison of the attitude of the Russian peasantry to the Bolsheviks with that of the French peasantry to the Jacobin government in the French Revolution of 1789. The French peasants had acted "in a revolutionary manner just so long as was required by their most immediate...private interests; until they had secured the right of ownership of their land which had hitherto been farmed on a feudal basis... Once this was achieved, they turned with all the fury of blind avarice against the movement of the big towns".[49]

In the fourth volume of his biography of Lenin, Cliff repeats the same point even more forcefully. He is explaining how the Bolsheviks' attempt to feed the towns and cities by using armed force for food requisitioning in the countryside eventually threatened to destroy the revolution. The policy met such massive peasant resistance that it overwhelmed them.[50] Lenin had to reverse the policy, introducing the New Economic Policy (NEP), which economically enfranchised the petty peasant proprietor. He saw it explicitly as a resumption of the "state capitalist" policy that he had initiated in early 1918, but which had been suspended by the civil war:

---

45: Rabinowitch, 2008, p280.
46: Rabinowitch, 2008, p290.
47: Rabinowitch, 2008, p294, p308.
48: It is most unfortunate that this volume is out of print. Bookmarks must seriously consider republishing all four volumes of Cliff's *Lenin*.
49: Cliff, 1978, p139.
50: For a fuller discussion of the background and the double edged attitude of the peasantry to the revolution and its leadership, see Cliff, 1978, pp132-143.

Lenin wrote a note, *1794 versus 1921*. In 1794 in France, the beneficiaries of the revolution, especially the more prosperous peasants, pressed for relaxation of Jacobin control and demanded freedom of trade. This demand swept away Robespierre and the whole revolution moved to the right... Lenin's note showed he intended to carry out an economic retreat so as to avoid a head-on clash with the forces equivalent to those which broke Robespierre.

He still saw this as a purely temporary retreat, a manoeuvre by the workers' state encircled by capitalism and banking firmly on revolutionary developments in Europe.[51]

As noted earlier, Cliff distinguished Lenin's formulation of the need for a temporary "state capitalism", in which the soviet government used private enterprise, from Cliff's own later formulation of bureaucratic state capitalism, which he argues, after Lenin's death, became the firm foundation of Stalin's claims to be building "Socialism in One Country". Nevertheless we can see clearly the seeds of degeneration here: "The rise of the bureaucracy in party and state was a very long process starting during the period of civil war, accelerated during the NEP, and culminating at the time of Lenin's departure from the political arena. There was nevertheless a gap between the victory of the bureaucracy and the establishment of a bureaucratic state capitalist regime".[52]

That time gap provided the last opportunity for the wider European working class revolution and its rescue of the socialist content of the Russian Revolution. The soviets were by now bureaucratically controlled by the Bolsheviks. Workers' power had dissipated. But enough Soviet officials still understood themselves as Bolshevik cadres, vision battered but undimmed. They were perfectly capable of responding to the long anticipated European socialist revolution which would reinvigorate Soviet industry and an active working class. Alas, it was not to be.

So were the Bolsheviks justified leading the working class to take power in an overwhelmingly peasant country? Cliff writes: "In the last few weeks before he completely lost consciousness Lenin suffered not only from a complete sense of isolation but from a moral agony almost unprecedented in the history of men and movements. Feelings of personal guilt pervaded all his utterances. Was the Russian Revolution a false spring? Did the Bolsheviks take power prematurely?"[53]

---

51: Cliff, 1979, p141.
52: Cliff, 1979, pp216-217.
53: Cliff, 1979, p230.

Rosa Luxemburg, his old adversary in Germany, who had constantly worried about Lenin's and the Bolsheviks' "substitutionism", would provide the resounding answer. October had showed us the potentialities of the proletariat:

> Theirs is the immortal historical service of having marched at the head of the international proletariat with the conquest of political power and the practical placing of the problem of the realisation of socialism and of having advanced mightily the settlement of the score between capital and labour in the entire world. In Russia the problem could only be posed. It could not be solved in Russia. And in this sense, the future everywhere belongs to Bolshevism.[54]

The victory of the October 1917 Socialist Revolution was the single most important historical and political event of the last century. Its failure continues to cast a long shadow over this century. The deepening crisis of capitalism is presenting a new generation of radical activists with searching political questions. Yet workers' power and communism hardly seem a plausible democratic alternative. The left has to rise to the formidable intellectual as well as the political and public challenge that this now poses. In a different context Lenin once cited the virtue of "patient explanation". That's precisely what we need in defence of "October", that workers' power really did exist even if only momentarily. It offered a vastly improved future for the great majority with the realisable objective of a classless society, but simply could not survive confined to a mainly peasant society.

---

54: Cliff, 1979, p236. Ian Birchall, Cliff's biographer, adds a final footnote about Cliff and Serge and their approach to Lenin and the revolution:

"I think it's worth noting that the strength of Cliff—and Serge—is the way they catch the duality of the process—the terrible difficulties and hardships, but also the enormous creativity and hope unleashed by the Revolution. I would contrast Cliff with Jean-Jacques Marie's *Lénine* [Paris 2004], which gives a scrupulously honest account of post-revolutionary Russia, but which tends to see so much gloom that it loses sight of what the Revolution was all about."

# References

Cliff, Tony, 1976, *Lenin Volume 2: All Power to the Soviets* (Pluto), www.marxists.org/archive/cliff/works/1976/lenin2/index.htm

Cliff, Tony, 1978, *Lenin Volume 3: Revolution Besieged* (Pluto).

Cliff, Tony, 1979, *Lenin Volume 4: The Bolsheviks and World Revolution* (Pluto).

Cliff, Tony, 1990, *Trotsky 2: The Sword of the Revolution* (Bookmarks), www.marxists.org/archive/cliff/works/1990/trotsky2/index.html

Cliff, Tony, 1996 [1960], "Trotsky on Substitutionism", in *Party and Class* (Bookmarks), www.marxists.org/archive/cliff/works/1960/xx/trotsub.htm

Haynes, Mike, 1997, "Was There a Parliamentary Alternative in Russia in 1917?", *International Socialism* 76 (autumn), http://pubs.socialistreviewindex.org.uk/isj76/haynes.htm

Haynes, Mike, 2002, *Russia: Class and Power, 1917-2000* (Bookmarks).

Murphy, Kevin, 2007, *Revolution and Counter-Revolution in a Moscow Metal Factory* (Haymarket).

Murphy, Kevin, 2010, "Conceding the Russian Revolution to Liberals", *International Socialism* 126 (spring), www.isj.org.uk/?id=643

Pirani, Simon, 2008, *The Russian Revolution in Retreat, 1920-24* (Routledge).

Pirani, Simon, 2010, "Socialism in the 21st century and the Russian Revolution", *International Socialism* 128 (autumn), www.isj.org.uk/?id=687

Rabinowitch, Alexander, 2008, *The Bolsheviks in Power, The First Year of Soviet Rule in Petrograd* (Indiana University Press).

Reed, John, 1974 (1918), "Soviets in Action", *International Socialism* 69 (first series, May) www.marxists.org/history/etol/newspape/isj/1974/no069/reed.htm

Rees, John, 1991, "In Defence of October", *International Socialism* 52 (autumn).

Serge, Victor, 1992, *Year One of the Russian Revolution* (Bookmarks), www.marxists.org/archive/serge/1930/year-one/index.htm

Serge, Victor, 1997, *Revolution in Danger* (Bookmarks).

Trudell, Megan, 2000, "The Russian Civil War: a Marxist Analysis", *International Socialism* 86 (summer), http://pubs.socialistreviewindex.org.uk/isj86/trudell.htm

# Sex work: a rejoinder

*Gareth Dale and Xanthe Whittaker*

Productive debate requires engagement with the other's stronger positions. In her reply to us, Jess Edwards ignores this rule, relying instead upon insinuation, imputation and distortion.[1] She enlists enough Aunt Sallies and straw men to pack out a small stadium, and red herrings to collapse a fishmonger's slab. She misrepresents our argument in so many places that locating even a fraction of them may try the reader's patience. Yet we must attempt the task.

According to Edwards we claim:

● "Sex work is fundamentally the same as" other work. It can be "equated" with care work, is "socially useful", and "challenges the institution of the family.".

● "Prostitution is not damaging to people working as prostitutes."

● Women's oppression only influences the sex industry as an "external" force.

● One's "primary response" to the sex trade should be "to organise sex workers in their workplaces". Those who go beyond this are aligned with "bourgeois moralists".

We reduce the sex work debate, she concludes, to questions of economic exploitation and union organisation and are "ambiguous" in our opposition to the sex industry.

---

1: Edwards, 2010. This rejoinder is a much reduced version of a longer one available from xanthew@gmail.com

This is a cock and bull account of our case. It relies upon gross and culpable misrepresentation.[2] Consider, first, an example of Edwards's technique. After citing our reference to Sophie Day's argument that selling sex "confounds the separation" between public and private, Edwards implies we're suggesting that sex work "threatens" capitalism. If so, "presumably" we're "encouraging people to enter the sex industry", and this is "precisely what the IUSW [International Union of Sex Workers] does". One of its "leading spokespeople", Douglas Fox, runs an escort agency!

In fact, our citation from Day concerned a different question: *why sex work attracts stigma*. We claimed that sex work threatens only a *"particular moral economy" within* capitalism. Fox, a self-employed sex worker who runs an escort agency, is no longer an IUSW member. The IUSW does not only include wage labourers and the self-employed in its ranks, yet these are the majority. We regard it as we do any union: critically. Other unions engage in disreputable activity (sweetheart deals, graft, etc), and many include managers, but they remain unions.[3]

We repudiate Edwards's suggestion that we deny that prostitution can be harmful. It is an outlandish claim. What we say is that the degree of harm varies greatly according to individuals and circumstances.[4]

Edwards claims that "68 percent of *prostitutes* suffer from post-traumatic stress disorder", and elsewhere that this percentage applies to *all* sex workers.[5] She insinuates that we ignore that trauma, but she fails to disclose that the study of 130 individuals from which the figure is taken was of *street* prostitutes, a category that we singled out as "highly vulnerable" to rape and other assault. The experiences of outdoor and indoor prostitutes should not be equated. When asked if they had ever been beaten, raped or stabbed, one study found that 27 percent, 22 percent and 8 percent of street prostitutes responded "yes", compared with 1 percent, 2 percent and 0 percent of indoor prostitutes.[6]

---

2:   Given its morally charged nature, participants in this debate should show courtesy and, in this journal, comradeship. In responding to Jane Pritchard, whose article started this debate, we discussed our text with her before publication. On seeing a draft of Edwards's rejoinder, we sent her nearly all the misrepresentations listed here and requested she amend them. She refused to amend or to communicate.

3:   If Edwards is unaware of this she should consult websites that expose it, eg www.socialistworker.org.uk.

4:   For two ends of the spectrum, see Illiria, 2008; Ditmore, 2010, p93.

5:   "The post traumatic stress disorder that is suffered by such a large percentage of sex workers, is not caused simply by bad employers"—online discussion.

6:   Weitzer, 2005. On surveys of clients, Edwards responds to our citation of one that finds many clients to be polite with the snipe that "whether sex work damages sex workers is not a

When approaching studies of sex work, a critical awareness of source and methodology is indispensable. Edwards's 68 percent figure tells a plausibly horrifying story of the misery some prostitutes experience during their work (and elsewhere, for most of the 130 had suffered physical and/or sexual abuse when children). However, she borrows the figure from prominent abolitionist Melissa Farley (via Kat Banyard).[7] Farley's methodology has been completely discredited.[8] Her surveys should be contrasted with "Setting the Record", a study by police into prostitution,[9] Nicola Mai's research,[10] and, for lap dancing, that of Teela Sanders and Kate Hardy.[11] We're not asserting that these give "the" complete picture, but neither do we think that Farley's statistics should be cited uncritically.

The risk of violence, combined with stigma and illegality, lead some to suggest that street sex work is not "a job like any other".[12] Yet the link between illegality, stigma and violence is indeed common to other work, such as drug dealing. *Some* aspects of *some* sex work resemble aspects of care work, in particular the performance "of caring, affection, and even love".[13] ("I consider sex for money a lot like nursing," says one prostitute. "It helps people whose lives are incomplete. It is a bit like when you like someone but not enough to have sex, but you feel sorry for them so you let them have sex.")[14] Edwards insinuates that because we see a *few* commonalities between care work and *some forms* of sex work we "fundamentally equate" the NHS and the sex industry. This is a baseless assertion; it bears no relationship to our text.

This debate matters because, if recognised as work, unsafe practices faced by sex workers are dealt with as employment issues covered by regulation. Additionally, sex workers and their supporters are keenly aware that there is "a clear link between stigma and violence", feel that "the bad reputation attached to working in the sex industry implicitly legitimised violent and criminal behaviour towards them", and call for its decriminalisation.[15]

Stigma is a complex issue, for different forces act to destigmatise sex

question of how some clients view them". But this bears no relation to what we actually wrote.

7:   She seems to think it applies only to women, when a quarter of the sample of street prostitutes were men and transgendered.

8:   Schaffhauser, 2011; Weitzer, 2005; Ditmore, 2010, p47.

9:   Jackson, 2010; Ditmore, 2010, pp28-64.

10:  Mai, 2009.

11:  Cassidy, 2010.

12:  Jeffrey, 2006; Schaffhauser, 2011.

13:  Dittmore, 2010, p60.

14:  Illiria, 2008.

15:  Mai, 2009.

work. One is the sexualisation of culture, discussed below. A second is pressure from sex workers and their supporters. The third is the changing legal situation. In some countries it has become significantly easier for prostitutes to pursue complaints of rape in the courts.[16] By implication, prostitution is increasingly recognised as the hiring of a service, with prostitutes recognised as legally entitled workers, not objects. That some employers in the sex industry would welcome the legal and social recognition of sex work as work should not affect our stance. After all, the same applies to its decriminalisation, supported by all sides in the debate in this journal.

How sex workers perceive their work, and their identity, matters to us. Alluding to this, Edwards cavils that we "risk falling into a postmodern pick-and-choose conception of identity" that takes at face value the self-perception of individuals. If taking seriously the views of sex workers is "postmodern" we plead guilty as charged. That we listen to their opinions is not to make the claim, which Edwards sticks in our mouths, that our position should be based upon sex workers' views *rather than* on "analysis of social and economic relationships". (Indeed, we engage with many such relationships, and in greater depth than Edwards.[17])

Our inclusion of sex workers' voices contrasts with the media framing of sex work. This focuses on the outdoor variety, when engaged in by women and with emphasis on violence and abusive circumstances. But sex workers reveal a heterogeneous picture. While media voices shout about the "sex", they focus on the "work",[18] and while media narratives emphasise entrapment as the explanation for entry into the trade, they describe a variety of motivations—above all money, sometimes the exercise of some control over their conditions.[19]

In championing collective organisation we have been seduced by "trade unionism", according to Edwards. To this we make two points. First, our piece was a critique of Pritchard's article, so focused upon the area of disagreement.[20] It was not a treatise on sex work as a whole. Second, Edwards is casting aspersions. Nowhere do we say that union organisation offers a complete strategy vis-à-vis the sex industry (or women's oppression). As to

16:  Cowling and Reynolds, p134.
17:  Discussion around sex work pays insufficient attention to political and economic dynamics—the erosion of welfare (low pay, unemployment, homelessness, tuition fees), migration of women, the growth of inequality and with it a servant class cooking and cleaning for, and jerking off, the rich.
18:  Hallgrimmsdottir, 2006.
19:  See Roberts, 1993, p307; Hallgrimmsdottir, 2006, p277; Ditmore, 2010, pp147-170.
20:  Pritchard, 2010.

Edwards's direct questions: we support campaigns against the opening of lap dancing clubs (although we are very wary if they appeal to state power or see lap dancers as the enemy), and we don't think job centres should advertise pole dancing jobs (with the caveat that we aren't overjoyed about them advertising many other jobs, eg with poor pay and conditions). In general, we follow this two fold rule of thumb: reject all forms of sexism while supporting as many sexual freedoms as possible; oppose the sex industry and the commodification of sex while resisting the stigmatisation of sex workers and supporting their efforts to organise.

Edwards's final charge is that we don't discuss women's oppression. In fact we discuss it *on every page*, are unambiguous in our aspiration "for a world where women don't have to sell sex", and argue that the commodification of sex feeds into the general objectification of women and vice versa. She's right that "the woman's own" desires aren't taken into account during sex work, but this is less a symptom of gender oppression than of alienated labour, as male sex workers (and workers in other industries) will attest. We aren't convinced by her assertion that the sex industry owes its existence to the oppression of women.[21] From what we know of alienation, objectification and commodification (not to mention the gay sex trade—which Edwards, it might seem, sees as a mere emulation of its straight counterpart) we'd be surprised if sex work were absent in a hypothetical non-sexist capitalist society. Moreover, we remain unconvinced by her ideas on the link between the sex industry and raunch culture. Raunch culture evolved from the growing assertiveness of a sexist interpretation of women's sexuality *and* the intrusion of market forces into the private realm. It does feed off pornography, but the sexualisation of popular culture is not a simple product of the sex trade.

The sexualisation of culture contributes to the destigmatisation of sex work, and it is bound up with something disturbing that has been happening to the social construction of sex. Although gazing at images of naked women has long been popular in some quarters (19th century oil paintings, etc), sexual imagery has of late become more mainstream and overt. Sociologists talk of our "profoundly self-pleasuring society", a "striptease culture" preoccupied with self-revelation and exposure.[22] As culture becomes permeated with a narcissistic preoccupation with the cultivation of looks in general and the body in particular, sexiness becomes ever more central to what is marked as

---

21: "The existence of the sex industry is the result of women's oppression and the existence of the industry serves to perpetuate women's oppression."—online discussion.
22: Attwood, 2009.

good and worthwhile, and sexuality and the performance of intimacy become part of the obligatory repertoire for many workers. (For example, the recent announcement that Pizza Express waitresses are to be trained in flirting. "It's great", says the asinine trainer, "if you're a guy and a really gorgeous Italian girl comes to your table").[23] Sexualised body display and erotic performance connote not only glamour and youth but, increasingly, strength and independence too. Strippers are more likely to be represented as feisty free spirits than downtrodden victims, and burlesque gains prominence through high-profile performers such as Dita von Teese.[24] Above all, there's the use of explicit, even pornographic, poses in advertising.

What lies behind these trends? Women's oppression is a necessary part of the explanation but not a sufficient one. In *Critique of Commodity Aesthetics*, Wolfgang Haug studied the aestheticising tendencies elicited by commodity exchange.[25] Exchange value, he argues, generates a seductively glamorous aesthetic, as commodities on the shelves exaggerate their sensual qualities to attract the buyer, enticing consumers to engage with them in a voyeuristic relationship. This cosmetic, eroticised aesthetic spills out of the realm of merchandising and seeps throughout the fabric of contemporary human relations. In other words, the ubiquity of a para-pornography of impossibly perfect bodies is no simple sex-industrial spin-off; rather, it's rooted in commodification and sexism in general.

Amid the incessant glossy rain of stylised sexual imagery and the provocative sex-chatter that saturates the media, it is tempting to argue that permissiveness has become a shackle and/or that the sex industry is the key problem. The former would be misguided, for the problem is not sex but sexism, and not sexiness per se but the way it is wrought, by the commodified aesthetic and narcissistic culture (not to mention Pizza Express), into an imposition. The latter would be one-sided. It is true that pornography tends to envision women as passive objects. But this is more the channelling of a ubiquitous sexism than its constitutive cause—just as computer war games are more the product than the progenitor of war.

Our analysis, then, *is* political and not Lenin's "pure and simple unionism". We do not believe that going beyond "trade union concerns" need entail lining up with "bourgeois moralists" but neither would we agree with modern puritans who dismiss, for example, the provision of masturbatory fantasies as "socially useless". Whether or not collectively

---

23: *Independent*, 14 October 2010, p24. See also Ditmore, 2010, pp9-22.
24: Attwood, 2009.
25: Haug, 1986.

produced porn/erotica is "socially useful" is a red herring. (A great deal of paid human labour appears "useless" to those who don't have a taste for its output, whether it be poker websites or the novels of Dan Brown.) Our critique of the sex industry is not that it produces and distributes sexual fantasies but that it commodifies sex and reinforces the oppression of women.

## References

Attwood, Feona, 2009, *The Sexualization of Western Culture* (Tauris).

Cassidy, Sarah, 2010, "One in four lapdancers has a degree", *Independent* (27 August 2010), www.independent.co.uk/news/uk/home-news/one-in-four-lap-dancers-has-a-degree-study-finds-2063252.html

Cowling, Mark, and Paul Reynolds, 2004, *Making Sense of Sexual Consent* (Ashgate).

Edwards, Jess, "Sexism and Sex Work", *International Socialism* 128 (autumn), www.isj.org.uk/?id=688

Hallgrimmsdottir, Helga, 2006, "Media Narratives of the Sex Industry", *Canadian Review of Sociology and Anthropology*, 43:3.

Haug, Wolfgang, 1986, *Critique of Commodity Aesthetics*, Minneapolis.

Illiria, Justine, 2008, "I Don't Sell My Body Anymore Because I Can Sell Drugs", Mute, www.metamute.org/en/i_don_t_sell_my_body_anymore_because_i_can_sell_drugs.

Jackson, Keith, 2010, "Setting the Record", www.acpo.police.uk/asp/policies/Data/Setting the Record (Project ACUMEN) Aug 2010.pdf

Jeffrey, Leslie, 2006, "The Economy of Sex Work in the Maritimes", *Canadian Review of Sociology and Anthropology*, 43:3.

Mai, Nicola, 2009, *Migrant Workers in the UK Sex Industry* (London).

Pritchard, Jane, 2010, "The Sex Work Debate", *International Socialism* 125 (winter), www.isj.org.uk/?id=618

Roberts, Nickie, 1993, *Whores in History: Prostitution in Western Society* (HarperCollins).

Schaffhauser, Thierry, 2010, "The sex work debate—a response to Jess Edwards", *International Socialism* website, www.isj.org.uk/?id=696

Weitzer, Ronald, 2005, "Flawed Theory and Method in Studies of Prostitution", *Violence Against Women*, 11:7.

# Discussing the alternatives
*Grace Lally*

In the last issue of this journal Alex Callinicos invited discussion on the kinds of demand that might provide a "complete" and "universally valid" transitional programme for revolutionaries today.[1] This is somewhat of a new departure for the Socialist Workers Party (SWP) and most certainly requires more consideration by party members than I can give it here, but I want to take issue with a number of the points he makes.

Alex describes transitional demands as reforms that can "only be won over the fiercest resistance of capital". This is certainly one element of what would constitute a programme of transitional demands but is by no means the most important. I'm presuming for instance that Alex does not believe the Green Party manifesto is a transitional programme simply because it includes the call for one million climate jobs or any other particular radical reform.

The key questions are, who is making these demands? In what context? For what purpose? And crucially, how are these demands to be achieved? A classic formulation of transitional demands was the Bolsheviks slogan "Peace, bread and land" in 1917. These demands formed part of a transitional programme in so far as they were connected to another demand—"All power to the soviets". In a revolutionary period of dual power, this programme could both relate to the urgent desires of workers and raise their consciousness of the immediate tasks required to achieve the transition to socialism.

---

1:    Callinicos, 2010.

It only makes sense to talk about this programme as "transitional" because it was put forward *by revolutionaries*—in direct opposition to reformist leaders—seeking to gain the leadership of a mass movement to smash the bourgeois state. The Comintern report of 1921 that Alex quotes also argued for transitional programmes in what they assessed was a "transitional period" where "any confrontation may turn into a struggle for power".[2] As it became increasingly clear that the "ebb" of revolutionary struggles was more than just the temporary oscillation of a rising revolutionary wave, and that gaining leadership of the majority of workers in order to take state power was not an imminent prospect, Lenin and Trotsky placed ever greater emphasis on the tactic of the united front as a means to influence reformist workers in the course of *joint struggle* for immediate demands.

When Trotsky put forward his transitional programme in 1938, which included in the title a call to "Prepare the Conquest of Power", he believed the world was once again in a pre-revolutionary situation—"a transitional epoch".[3] Whatever the validity of Trotsky's assessment, given the very small forces of the Fourth International at the time, this programme was destined to be used more as a means for winning individuals to a genuinely revolutionary party than for winning the class to a revolutionary strategy.

Until now the SWP has tried to avoid the error of other Trotskyist groups who came to view the transitional programme as an end in itself without any reference to the forces it relates to or the context in which it is put forward.[4] Rather, we have attempted to incorporate the spirit of the transitional programme by relating in a concrete way to demands that emerge from the movement instead of drawing up abstract schemas.

The interview with Panos Garganas in the same issue seems to provide a very clear example of this method.[5] The SWP's sister organisation in Greece is taking part in the debt debate from an independent class standpoint of demanding default in order to "save jobs and pensions and wages in the here and now". They are countering those who see the elections as the key to winning these demands by raising the argument that "there's no other way but to fight back and build a strike movement". And they are preparing workers for continued crisis rather than stabilisation in the wake of any default—continued attempts to "make the workers pay"—that will require new demands that cannot as yet be determined.

---

2:  Communist International, 1921.
3:  Trotsky, 1938.
4:  See, for instance, Hallas, 1973.
5:  Garganas, 2010.

The reality is that not every demand around which we organise will be transitional in any respect. In Ireland at the moment calling for the government to go is hardly "transitional"—by the time of publication it will probably be a fact—but this seems beside the point when thousands of workers are prepared to come onto the streets to achieve this aim.

Whether or not we now break with past practice to launch a transitional programme, Alex is signalling a political shift of an entirely different magnitude when he proposes that we treat the programmes of People Before Profit (PBP) and Research on Money and Finance (RMF) as transitional.

He suggests that their programmes are qualitatively different to the left reformism of the Alternative Economic Strategy (AES) in the 1970s because they "advocate measures...that challenge the power of capital" whereas the AES was "a reformist attempt to rescue capitalism". This differentiation rests on a misrepresentation of both.

Arguably the AES, with its explicit aim of bringing an eventual transition to socialism, was to the left of RMF's more muted aim of achieving a "wholesale reversal of neoliberal economic policy".[6] The AES provided the same kind of "detailed outline" as RMF of the measures that would need to be taken to stop things such as capital flight after the introduction of import controls and the nationalisation of key industries and banking. But the AES also included demands for "workers' control" and its proponents were clear about the need to mobilise workers to achieve it.[7] On the substantive question of what "social power" would wrest these reforms from capital there is a complete convergence between RMF and the AES—it is the nation-state.

Alex clearly feels that to equate the RMF programme with the AES would be to "dismiss them". But surely we can relate to people who are putting forward radical left reformist ideas without collapsing into labelling them as revolutionary? How we relate to left reformism is of course a subject for debate in itself.

In 1980 Geoff Hodgson of the Labour left argued that revolutionaries should not "abandon the AES to the reformists". The fact that it was "endorsed by both the TUC and several major unions" created the possibility of "bringing thousands of workers into the experience of struggle", struggles which "could then be diverted in a revolutionary direction".[8] The Communist Party (CP) saw "the implementation of this programme as the first stage in a revolutionary *process* characterised by intense conflict

---

6:   Lapavitsas and others, 2010, p3.
7:   See Sparks, 1977.
8:   Hodgson, 1980, p87.

and struggle".[9] They proposed that this was a "third road" to socialism long before Labour championed a third way that had nothing to do with socialism at all. Our argument was that the political strategy of the AES, by proposing piecemeal national reforms and confining itself primarily to the methods of parliamentary legality, would *objectively* tie workers to the interests of capitalism and so disarm them politically in the fight for their own class interests.[10]

Of course, in contrast to their lofty ideals, the Labour left and the CP in the late 1970s played a treacherous role in collaborating with the Labour governments' attacks on workers. Their politics of supporting a national economic solution to the crisis played no small part in disorganising and disorienting the working class militants who looked to them for leadership.[11] The tragedy is not that we dismissed their ideas but that we were too small to challenge them effectively or to provide an alternative.

Today, RMF advise that "if peripheral countries were to adopt debtor-led default, they ought to do so on their own accord, decisively, in good time", in order to avoid the Argentinian situation where debtor-led default was only adopted "in the midst of social and economic chaos caused by failed austerity".[12] But the "chaos" they wish to avoid is the kind of mass uprising of workers and the poor that overthrew successive governments in Argentina in 2001-2. Defaulting on the debt did not push this process forward: it was a strategy pursued by the state to gain some breathing space within which to co-opt and suppress the movement. RMF argues that, after defaulting on its debt, Greece, like Argentina, could "regain credibility" with international capital markets "within a short space of time". This is predicated on the experience of a country where this was only made possible because the state was able to subvert popular resistance and restore a stable capitalist order.[13]

The RMF's call for "participation by organisations of workers and civil society in renegotiating debt" would be a recipe not for extending democracy but for class collaboration if, as they hope, default were to pave the way for a "recovery of competitiveness".[14]

Left reformist programmes are not transitional: they are utopian. They demand measures which capitalism will not easily grant but they believe that such measures can be achieved without an all-out conquest of

9: Rowthorn, 1980, p88.
10: See Cockerill, 1980, for a reply to Bob Rowthorn and Geoff Hodgson.
11: See Cliff, 1979.
12: Lapavitsas and others, 2010, p50.
13: Lapavitsas and others, 2010, p51.
14: Lapavitsas and others, 2010, pp5; 52.

political power by the working class—without a revolution to smash the capitalist state. Because of this, left reformism proves to be entirely reactionary in practice during periods of crisis.

Despite the "radically different context" from the 1970s that Alex notes, it is interesting to see that Tony Benn has committed the new Coalition of Resistance to developing and supporting "an alternative programme for economic and social recovery".[15] We need to engage in joint struggles with all those who are pulled into activity through this or any other anti-cuts organisation. But there is no less call to counter Benn's politics with the same conviction we did 40 years ago and to patiently explain that "there's but one solution, revolution".[16]

The case of PBP is more complex than RMF as its main component organisation is a revolutionary party, the Irish Socialist Workers Party, rather than a group of pseudo-Marxist academics. Its *raison d'être*, however, is to organise workers who are not yet revolutionary so it necessarily stops short of linking its immediate demands with the need to smash the state—it cannot put forward a transitional programme. Whether, through their involvement in this broad left alliance, our comrades in Ireland will have more success in building a stronger revolutionary party than we in Britain experienced in Respect remains to be seen.

The economic crisis will continue to create deep class conflict but also to create rifts between competing capitals. Austerity will hit workers and benefit some sections of capital but it will also disadvantage others. Each state will attempt to shift the burden onto other states as well as onto the working class. This is why Ireland is under pressure to raise its corporation tax or China to raise the value of its currency. The job of socialists is not to intervene in these debates to establish the best course of action for "our" economy. It is ruthlessly to resist the logic of a system which has no permanent solution to the crisis it faces and to argue for an independent class position—to put forward demands which place the burden of the crisis on the capitalist class and to give a lead in organising struggle to fight for them.

Alex argues that "the logic of resisting the cuts...demands the formulation of an alternative economic programme". I disagree. Thankfully it has never been necessary for people to have worked out a coherent alternative to the profit system in order to fight for "fair" pay or pensions, nor to completely reject the idea of a "national interest" in order to fight against racism or war. It is the contradictions in people's ideas that opens the possibility

15: Benn, 2010.
16: Green, 1981, p103.

for workers to engage in struggle and learn through their own experience that solving the problems they face demands challenging the entire capitalist system. But the existence of a substantial organisation of workers who *do* understand this in the here and now is indispensable to carrying forward those struggles through which the mass of workers can throw off "the muck of ages" and achieve the final victory of our class.

Millions of men and women all over the world in every generation have fought the bitter realities of life under capitalism and dreamed of a better alternative. They've never needed socialists to tell them what they want, they've needed revolutionary politics to help them achieve it.

## References

Benn, Tony, 2010, "The time to organise resistance is now", *Guardian* (4 August), www.guardian.co.uk/commentisfree/2010/aug/04/time-to-organise-resistance-now

Callinicos, Alex, 2010, "Austerity politics", *International Socialism 128* (autumn), www.isj.org.uk/?id=678

Cockerill, Sue, "Reply to left reformism", *International Socialism 8* (spring).

Cliff, Tony, 1979, "The balance of class forces in recent years", *International Socialism 6* (autumn), www.marxists.org/archive/cliff/works/1979/xx/balance1.htm

Garganos, Panos, 2010, "Greece: striking back", *International Socialism 128* (autumn), www.isj.org.uk/?id=695

Green, Pete, 1981, "'Alternative' and 'socialist' economic strategies", *International Socialism 13* (summer).

Hallas, Duncan, 1973, "Do we support reformist demands?" *International Socialism 54* (first series, January), www.marxists.org/archive/hallas/works/1973/01/reform.htm

Hodgson, Geoff, 1980, "Britain's crisis and the road to international socialism—a reply to Jonathan Bearman", *International Socialism 7* (winter).

Lapavitsas, Costas, A Kaltenbrunner, G Lambrinidis, D Lindo, J Meadway, J Michell, JP Painceira, E Pires, J Powell, A Stenfors and N Teles, 2010, "The Eurozone between Austerity and Default", Research on Money and Finance (September), www.researchonmoneyandfinance.org/media/reports/RMF-Eurozone-Austerity-and-Default.pdf

Communist International, 1921, "On Tactics", Third Congress of the Communist International, www.marxists.org/history/international/comintern/3rd-congress/tactics.htm

Rowthorn, Bob, 1980, "The Alternative Economic Strategy", *International Socialism 8* (spring).

Sparks, Colin, 1977, "The Reformist Challenge", International Socialism 97 (first series, April), www.marxists.org/history/etol/newspape/isj/1977/no097/sparks.htm

Trotsky, Leon, 1938, "The Death Agony of Capitalism and the Tasks of the Fourth International: The Mobilization of the Masses around Transitional Demands to Prepare the Conquest of Power", www.marxists.org/archive/trotsky/1938/tp/index.htm

# Book reviews

## A tangled tale
*Yuri Prasad*

*History Commission, CPI(M)* **History of the Communist Movement in India: Volume 1** *(Leftword, 2005), $25*

The 1917 Russian Revolution inspired millions of people living under colonial rule to take up the fight against empire. That workers and peasants in a backward country could throw off centuries of subjection led many Indian nationalists towards communist ideas and eventually to the founding of Communist Party of India in 1920. This anomous "authorised history" from the Communist Party of India (Marxist) of the early years of the party documents in impressive—if somewhat exhausting—detail, the way in which early Indian Communists grappled with illegality, the developing mass movement against British rule—and a series of damaging factional clashes.

Running through the volume is the question of how revolutionaries should relate to the movement for independence led by the Indian bourgeoisie. It was a recurring problem that would see Communists at times playing a central role in the struggle, but playing down their commitment to working class emancipation, while at others completely abstaining from the movement out of fear that they were merely providing "left cover" for the Indian National Congress.

The Russian leaders of the newly-formed Communist International, the Comintern, focused on the problem time and again. Lenin in particular was eager to engage in debates on the subject, and agreed to amend his 1920 *Theses on the National and Colonial Question* following an exchange with Indian communist MN Roy.

Lenin had originally argued that it was necessary for Communists to "enter into a temporary alliance with the bourgeois democracy in the colonial and backward countries". Roy believed that the colonial bourgeoisie played a reactionary role and that their aim was merely "to replace the foreign exploiters in order to be able to do the exploiting themselves". Following a debate, Lenin's draft was amended so that it recommended alliance with the "revolutionary movement in the colonies", rather than the "bourgeois-democratic movements" as originally proposed.

Unfortunately, readers of this book will be left largely unaware of the how seriously Lenin took Roy. This is in large part because, despite having founded both the Communist party of Mexico and the Communist Party of India, Roy was to fall foul of Stalin and was expelled from the Comintern in 1929. He was, according to the authors, suffering from "right reformist tendencies".

Despite vicious British repression, and some frankly useless advice from Moscow, Communism in India grew steadily from the late 1920s onwards. Trade unionism flourished, Gandhi's freedom movement gathered pace, and revolutionary nationalism emerged as a distinct current—and

Communist militants played a leading role in all three spheres. But sharp tactical changes forced upon the Indian party by Stalin's Comintern were to seriously undermine its success

Indian Communists, taking their cue from Lenin's *Theses*, had originally set out to constitute a "strong left wing within Congress to counter-act bourgeois nationalism". But by 1928, with the Comintern's adoption of the disastrous "Third Period" policy, they saw Congress as little more than a fig leaf for British imperialism. Those on the left of Congress, including the young Jawaharlal Nehru and Subhas Chandra Bose, both of whom were prepared to countenance the use of violence against the British, became particular targets of Communists because they created an "illusion of radicalism".

The authors freely admit that during the 1930s this sectarian approach cost the party dearly. But readers will search in vain for an explanation as to why Stalin imposed the policy, or why Indian Communists accepted it—except that the fight against Trotskyism in the international movement was the cause of some "distortions" in the application of Marxist theory. The real reason was that by 1928 Comintern policy no longer reflected the need to create a world revolution. It had become a simple extension of Russian foreign policy.

In the mid-1930s fear of fascism in Europe led the Comintern to kill off the Third Period and replace it with its polar opposite, the Popular Front. Now Communists were urged to put aside their differences with Congress leaders and place the needs of workers and peasants below those of their bosses and landlords—a strategy that would allow divisions between Hindus and Muslims to flourish.

The application of the Popular Front policy in India and the Communist Party's with-drawal from it when the Second World War began forms the backdrop to the next volume. These are twists and turns that even the most loyal of Communists will find hard to explain.

# Revolution rewritten
*Jack Farmer*

*Colin Jones, Josephine McDonagh and Jon Mee (eds),* **Charles Dickens, A Tale of Two Cities and the French Revolution** *(Palgrave Macmillan, 2009), £50*

Charles Dickens was not a writer who liked to sit on the fence. A passionate advocate of reform, his novels rail against all manner of social ills—from poverty (*Oliver Twist, Hard Times*) to misanthropy (*A Christmas Carol*) to the inanity of the legal system (*Bleak House*). He is perhaps the quintessential London author, his infamous night-time wanderings feeding his intense interest in the burgeoning capital of empire.

Yet *A Tale of Two Cities* occupies an awkward position in Dickens' oeuvre. It is one of only two historical novels Dickens ever wrote. Despite being one of his most popular novels (in Britain at least) it suffers from a serious flaw that has befuddled numerous critics over the years—it's just not very "Dickensian".

This response probably comes from the same line of critical thought that describes some of Shakespeare's best plays (*Merchant of Venice, Measure for Measure*) as "problem plays". The problem belongs to the critics and not to Dickens.

Nevertheless, there is something strange about this book. Its often-quoted opening line seems to betray a strange equivocation. On whose side stands the author who writes of a revolution that it was the best and worst of times?

This inter-disciplinary volume brings together essays from a number of academics grappling with Dickens' relationship with the French Revolution, and the effect of his peculiar vision on Anglo-French readings of the Revolution. In particular, the editors argue that the novel has been unfairly seen as a triumphalist polemic on the virtues of British gradualism over French radicalism.

Some of the most interesting essays discuss Dickens's sources. *A Tale* includes a dedication to Thomas Carlyle's "wonderful book", *The French Revolution*—a right wing account hostile to the revolution. But this influence may have been balanced by Dickens's reading of Thomas Paine's *The Rights of Man*, and also by less openly partial works. For example, Arthur Young's account, prosaically entitled *Travels in France During the Years 1787, 1788, 1789* contains a description of a peasant child being run over in the street by a coach—a scene which finds its way into *A Tale*.

Young's account seems almost painfully even-handed in its treatment of the insurrection. Mark Philp points out that "Young sits uncomfortably on what quickly becomes a fence dividing those responding to France, at once compassionate…and yet fearful of the populace, resistant to political innovation."

Along with the broader arguments about the Revolution and Dickens's take on it, this volume contains essays that tease out different aspects of the novel. While Dickens summons a relatively small cast of characters, they are subject to constantly shifting identities, double agents, and doubled faces. Kamilla Elliot explores the difficulties of cleaving together names and faces in the novel. This must have had obvious implication for the Jacobin's prosecution of Terror against counter-revolutionaries, but Elliot's essay also usefully elaborates on class and identity. The *"Jacques"* (ie Jacobins) of the novel seem to draw from a collective identity, and be largely interchangeable. At the same time the main characters (mainly middle class and English) are chased by the spectres of deadly identities, as they are variously accused of being members of French aristocracy or the English secret service.

Other essays here explore cinematic and theatrical reworkings of *A Tale*, the theorisation of revolutionary violence in the novel and beyond it, and many other elements that have made this novel both compelling and problematic. Though there is much of interest here, at times some of these essays lapse into formulations that are unnecessarily complicated, and prose that is unhelpfully dense and difficult.

The dozen or so academics represented in this volume do not attempt to formulate a consistent interpretation of the French Revolution, though they share many conclusions about Dickens's retelling. Michael Wood's afterword offers a typically cryptic decoding of *A Tale*'s moral message: "What is inevitable will happen—unless we prevent it. 1859 in England is just like 1789 in France, except for the difference in time and place."

The simplest response may be the best. In 1859 Dickens chose to intervene in what had long been a ferocious contest to define the legacy of France. The revolutions of 1848—which saw the barricades back in Paris, and a final Chartist surge in London—underlined the importance of these arguments. On the streets of Paris the *sans-culottes* had been replaced by the *proletaires*. Across Europe the remnants of feudalism faced a decisive challenge but, crucially, the bourgeoisie vacillated. The spectre of a new kind of revolution haunted the minds of any would-be Robespierres in the mid-19th century.

As the dust settled, Dickens penned a tale about the French revolution that seemed to embrace both sides of an ideological gulf—from Carlyle to Paine. As a result the novel itself resists simple interpretations. Dickens was not a revolutionary. But he was a zealous reformer for whom revolution was a reasonable response to unreasonable rule. *A Tale* was (and remains) a reminder to the bourgeoisie of its radical legacy and a warning about its possible future fate.

# Analysing honour
*Mark Harvey*

*Kwame Anthony Appiah,* **The Honour Code: How Moral Revolutions Happen** *(Norton, 2010),* £19.99

Kwame Anthony Appiah has had an idea: "appeals to reason, morality, or religion aren't enough to ring in reform. Practices are eradicated only when they come into conflict with honour." He explores three past "moral revolutions"—the eradication of duelling, footbinding and slavery—to draw lessons on how to end continuing insanities such as honour killing.

The Duke of Wellington, in challenging Winchilsea to an illegal duel in 1829, was asserting his right to settle matters according to the code of "gentlemen", the privilege of being above laws that only applied to inferiors. Appiah tries to link honour and slights against it to Hegel's "struggle for recognition", but that drama takes place between master and slave, not between two equally vain members of the ruling class. The first

moves made against duelling came from more political than moral momentum: attempts in the 17th century to stamp out duelling formed part of efforts to subordinate the nobility to absolutism. By the time Wellington himself joined an anti-duelling society, duelling in Britain had already become largely a charade.

Footbinding, practised for a thousand years in China mainly by the elite, inflicted horrific deformities on the women subjected to it, often causing infection and putrefaction. Men displayed their wives' freedom from work by removing their capacity to perform any, and housebound immobility helped guarantee the chastity of marriageable daughters.

In 1883 Kang Youwei began to build an anti-footbinding movement. Impressed by British efficiency after visiting Hong Kong and Shanghai, he studied Western philosophy, and advocated a Fourier-style utopian socialism, including equality for women and replacing marriage with renewable contracts.

The young Guangxu Emperor implemented some of Kang's reforms in 1898, resulting in a coup by the Empress Dowager Cixi, during which Kang fled to Japan. Weakened after the 1900 Boxer Rebellion, Cixi reluctantly continued to implement reforms until her and Guangxu's deaths in 1908, including the Anti-Footbinding Edict of 1902.

What is clear is that the late Qing reforms were not acts of a benevolent dynasty convinced by argument or motivated by shame, but attempts by an embattled, laggard autocracy to cling to power by implementing reform from above.

Disappointingly, Appiah nowhere mentions by name any of the Chinese women who also campaigned against footbinding.

His explanation of the end of footbinding is patronising: "once enough men among the literati required unbound wives, there was inevitably a cascade downwards of unbinding". So, bound women were no longer the objects of demand. It had nothing to do with the increased education of women themselves.

The chapter on slavery favours the position that ending slavery constituted a form of "economic suicide" forced upon Britain by mass mobilisations, which began with Quaker-organised petitions and boycotts. Reintroducing Hegel, Appiah argues that working class people rallied to abolitionism because the dignity of the labour of slaves was necessarily connected with their own fight for recognition. I have no problem with this.

When Appiah argues that we should convince those involved in honour killings to redefine their actions as dishonourable, he is focusing on the conscience of the oppressors. Similarly Wilberforce's moralism concentrated on the parliamentarians who allowed slavery to continue; the role revolts in the Caribbean played in making slavery unworkable receives no mention from Appiah. In 1791 Haitian slaves killed their masters and burned down their mansions: the role played by fear in ending slavery is not explored. And their leader Toussaint Louverture appealed primarily to the French Revolution's values of liberty and equality, not to the plantation owners' sense of shame.

Appiah's argument relies on the examples he has chosen: duelling and footbinding were eradicated because the aristocracy that had instituted them was being replaced by a rising capitalist class whose power was dictated by the marketplace. Such activities were both obsolete and an affront to their newly acquired dominance. Similarly, slavery has uses in an economy based on low-skilled agriculture, but eventually becomes an obstacle to accumulation with the risk of revolt and uneducated workforce it implies.

As Marx and Engels wrote in *The German Ideology*, each new ruling class tends to present its own values as universal, and has to promote values more capable of being universal than those of its predecessor. Thus "during the time that the aristocracy was dominant, the concepts honour, loyalty, etc were dominant, during the dominance of the bourgeoisie the concepts freedom, equality, etc". Why should the more backward-looking notion of "honour" succeed where the concepts of freedom and equality have failed? Honour cannot be recruited for the fight for a better world for the simple reason that honour is today only used to attempt to justify practices that cannot be justified otherwise.

Put simply, these "moral revolutions" happened because, at the same time, social revolutions happened. This is how we can explain how Kang could start a movement that resulted in footbinding being outlawed whereas the Manchus and the Taiping Rebellion failed. As an engaging meander through the history of ideas of honour, shame and respect, this book has some merit. The section on footbinding, with its history of the fall of the Qing dynasty, is particularly fascinating, despite Appiah's pop-philosophical musings. All four sections cover interesting debates but Appiah's own contribution in attempting to weave a thread between them through the theme of honour comes across as a rather forced conceit, and as a guide to how to improve the world, it is palpably a non-starter.

# Globalising Gramsci

*Adrian Budd*

*Alison J Ayers (ed),* **Gramsci, Political Economy and International Relations Theory** *(Palgrave Macmillan, 2008), £55*

It says a good deal about the nature of the academy that despite Marxism's internationalist perspective it was until recently at best marginalised and at worst ignored in the discipline of international relations (IR). This began to change in the 1980s in large part due to the pioneering work of Robert W Cox and those who subsequently developed his insights in what has come to be called the neo-Gramscian current in IR.

In the early-1980s Cox wrote two important essays on IR theory that challenged the mainstream emphasis on state power, usually conceived in narrow military terms, as the key determinant of world order change. Cox insisted that state power must be analysed in the context of the contending social forces formed at the level of production. He thereby introduced class relations and struggle into IR and argued that the key entities in the world system are not states but "state-society complexes". Of perhaps greater significance for subsequent Marxist international relations analysis was his use of Gramsci's *Prison Notebooks,* and the concept of hegemony in particular, to explain international phenomena. He argued that where a global hegemon is able to exercise "moral and intellectual leadership" and impose broadly accepted rules on subordinate powers, a world order, such as the 19th-century *Pax Britannica* and the post-1945 *Pax Americana*, can be relatively stable and peaceful. But, he argued, contradictions within even hegemonic world order structures contain the seeds of their transformation.

Cox, however, was explicitly not a Marxist and, while many neo-Gramscians consider themselves as such, the neo-Gramscian perspective has been subject to a number of Marxist critiques in the last decade or so. Ayers's book is a contribution to that critique. Unusually in an academic book, Ayers' introduction refers to revolutionary theory and the need to avoid the failures that can arise from an absent or mistaken theory in order that the aspiration that "another world is possible" may be realised. To that end part one is devoted to methodological and theoretical critiques of the neo-Gramscians, while part two challenges what critics have argued is their focus on dominant social forces and states to the exclusion of the resistance of the marginalised and subaltern. It includes chapters on Africa (Siba Grovogui and Lori Leonard, and Branwen Gruffydd Jones) and on gender (Jill Steans and Daniela Tepe). Although, as is usually the case with edited volumes, the quality of the chapters is variable, most contain insights into key weaknesses of neo-Gramscian theory.

Julian Saurin argues that Gramsci's Marxism, forged in struggle, has been largely purged from neo-Gramscian analysis that is produced in the seminar room. The purpose of Gramsci's study of the nature of ruling-class power in his notebooks was to understand the defeat of the revolutionary wave unleashed by the 1917 Bolshevik Revolution and prepare the workers' movement for future struggles. He recognised that there was a consensual aspect of ruling class power, but this primarily concerned relations with classes whose interests were closest to those of the capitalist class. In relations with the working class, on the other hand, domination and force were paramount. For Gramsci, then, bourgeois hegemony represented a combination of coercion and consent. For the neo-Gramscians, by contrast (as well as for many other interpreters of Gramsci in fields other than IR), the coercive aspect of hegemony is largely overlooked and their emphasis is on consensus formation and the forces that have made revolution impossible. Saurin argues that, as far as the international system is concerned, the neo-Gramscians have shifted their focus from world order transformation to the conditions of reproduction of any given order. This is rather an exaggeration and reveals the problems, repeated elsewhere in the book, of treating the neo-Gramscians as a unified school.

For Hannes Lacher the major problems of neo-Gramscian analysis flow from Cox's rejection of a key Marxist concept, namely the mode of production. Cox objects that the use of this concept tends to produce ahistorical and abstract arguments that allow only a minor role to social and political struggle in historical change. He focuses instead on specific conjunctures of social forces and processes—what he calls historical structures, constituted by interactions between material capabilities, institutions, and ideas. There is some merit in Cox's approach, and an appreciation of the conjunctural balance of class forces is essential for an engaged Marxist politics. But, as Lacher points out, Cox's argument that we must choose between analysis of capitalism *per se* and of concrete historical structures of particular phases of its development is "sterile".

Marxists ought not attempt to explain concrete developments—in the international or domestic spheres—solely by reference to capitalism's constitutive social relations. As capitalism's dynamism constantly throws up novel forms and new contradictions, theory must be historicised. Nevertheless, the social relations of exploitation and competitive accumulation at the core of the capitalist mode of production underpin, albeit in historically determinate ways, the concrete phenomena of particular conjunctures. Without an appreciation of this, those con-

junctures (Cox's historical structures) seem to float above capitalism, which is taken for granted and therefore effectively disappears from Cox's analysis. Thus, major epochal transformations, such as between feudalism and capitalism, are reduced to just one more transformation between historical structures, akin to that between, for example, the era of British global dominance and the period of inter-imperialist rivalry at the end of the 19th century. As Lacher puts it, the neo-Gramscian method of historical structures "all but severs the link between the succession of historic blocs and some concept of epochal unity that the 'mode of production' served to designate"

The neo-Gramscians have produced richly textured studies of the international system that expand the range of causal factors beyond the state power that is central to traditional IR. But, without appropriately historicised Marxist concepts that flow from a mode of production analysis which provides a coherent thread that links these factors, the neo-Gramscians often produce merely pluralist descriptions of the events they study. Furthermore, as Pinar Bedirhanoglu argues, despite Cox's own insistence on the importance of state-society complexes, the absence of a coherent theory of the interdependence of states and societies means that these different spheres of human activity come to be seen as autonomous. This, Bedirhanoglu argues, has serious political consequences, for if states are autonomous of underlying social relations then the solution to the problems faced by subordinate classes is not to transform society but to change governments. It also leads to indeterminacy about the role of the state, which in Coxian analysis undergoes a mysterious transformation from being a bulwark against world order pressures to being a "transmission belt" from global neo-liberalism into national economies.

Many of the chapters provide predominantly

theoretical critiques of the neo-Gramscians. The chapter by Alfredo Saad-Filho and Alison Ayers is an exception and demonstrates the superiority of Marxist analysis by offering a more convincing explanation of an important world order shift analysed by Cox. Echoing arguments mentioned above, Saad-Filho and Ayers contend that Cox's analysis of the transition from Keynesianism to neo-liberalism relies not on the way that the contradictions of the long boom and Keynesianism undermined capital accumulation, but on an eclectic and ultimately descriptive account that relies on the machinations of an "autonomous" state, which appears as a *deus ex machina* . Certainly, other factors are noted to give a superficial comprehensiveness to Cox's explanation, but the capitalist logic linking these factors is not explained such that Cox offers a "description of conflicts around (the process of) accumulation, but not about (the nature of) capitalist accumulation".

Saad-Filho and Ayers' example of concretising their critique of Cox could be usefully followed by the authors of some of the other chapters. Jonathan Joseph, for example, offers a convincing critique of the neo-Gramscian understanding of hegemony as the inter-subjective diffusion of ideas and argues for a rooting of hegemony in capitalism's structural underpinnings. This is a reasonable argument and an antidote to the ideologism that infects much neo-Gramscianism. Yet, he makes too little of the class contradictions at the heart of the capitalist structure and so is unable to explore the degree to which ruling class intellectual leadership shapes the world views of subordinate classes. He therefore produces a different, more structurally grounded, version of the somewhat troublesome dominant ideology thesis and, like most analysts of Gramsci's concept of hegemony, ignores Gramsci's arguments about working class contradictory consciousness.

Furthermore, like the neo-Gramscians themselves, he makes no mention of the area where ruling class ideas are most influential. For, while workers' direct experiences lead, even in periods of low levels of struggle, to a resigned acceptance rather than enthusiastic embrace of ruling-class ideas on the market, entrepreneurship, private property, etc. there is more widespread acceptance of the idea of a national community standing against external "others". This is a major challenge to the neo-Gramscian argument that the contemporary world order is characterised by transnational integration and, in a book on the neo-Gramscians and IR, ought to have received a more sustained treatment than a few paragraphs in Bedirhanoglu's chapter.

Marxists do not always have to write about the contemporary world to say something useful and interesting, and many of the chapters here are indeed interesting. But, if Marxist theory is to maintain its relevance as a force that can make another world possible it must always take as its reference point, engage with and test itself against the historical or current realities of the world. With one or two exceptions, too often the chapters in this book engage only with neo-Gramscian theory. More disappointingly, important subjects such as US power and war (one of the great gaps in Cox's work) are not subject to extended discussion—indeed they are barely mentioned and do not appear in the index. The index shows, meanwhile, seven references to Althusser and twelve to poststructuralism. I am not making an anti-theory or sectarian point here. I merely suggest that, in a book by Marxists on IR, I would have liked rather more analysis of the contemporary dynamics of the international system. This is the sort of thing that some neo-Gramscians, however theoretically renegade, can be rather good at.

# Intellectual weapons

*Alex Callinicos*

Ha-Joon Chang, **23 Things They Don't Tell You About Capitalism**, (Allen Lane, 2010), £20.00

Ha-Joon Chang is an economist based at Cambridge who has made a reputation as a critic of the free-market orthodoxy in development economics. Thus in *Kicking Away the Ladder* he showed how the leading Western capitalist states demand that developing economies abjure all the protectionist methods that they themselves had used to industrialise in the first place.

In *23 Things They Don't Tell You About Capitalism* Chang widens his fire to neo-liberalism more generally. The book is a pleasure to read, and not just because of Chang's very clear, conversational style. In a series of brief chapters (or "Things") with titles like "Capital has a nationality", "We do not live in a post-industrial age", and "Despite the fall of communism, we are still living in planned economies", Chang demolishes various sacred cows of the Washington consensus, using a highly effective combination of argument, evidence, and humour.

My favourite chapter is the one where he argues: "The washing machine has changed the world more than the Internet has". Chang shows that the telegraph speeded up communication by 2,500 times, whereas the Internet is only 100 times faster than the fax, and argues that, by making it easier for women to participate in the labour market, the washing machine has had far more revolutionary consequences.

This doesn't mean the book is perfect. There is a dreadful chapter where Chang argues that it is only immigration controls that keep wages in the North higher than those in the South—even though he concedes in passing the role played by differences in labour productivity.

Moreover, Chang is anxious to make clear that his beef isn't with capitalism itself. Rather he wants to rehabilitate the kind of state-directed coordinated capitalism that industrialised his native South Korea in a generation. It is a sign of the suffocating orthodoxy that has made mainstream neoclassical economics an intellectual disgrace that books like Chang's—and an earlier, somewhat similar work by the great economic historian Paul Bairoch, *Economics and World History*—seem so radical. But genuine anti-capitalists can mine *23 Things They Don't Tell You About Capitalism* for weapons to turn against the system itself.

# Pick of the quarter

The latest issue of *New Left Review* (II/65, September/October 2010) starts with a superb article by Robert Wade and Silla Sigurgeirsdottir on the crisis in Iceland. In a piece that combines careful analysis with the pace and tension of a thriller by Henning Mankel or Stieg Larson, Wade and Sigurgeirsdottir show how a tiny, incestuous political and economic elite dominating a country of 300,000 people engineered a financial bubble that saw three banks build up assets eight times national income and penetrate much bigger European economies—all the time with the collusion of an "international community" that until 2009 still rated Iceland the least corrupt state in the world!

The same issue of *NLR* carries an interesting exchange on the relationship between market, state and capitalism in contemporary China—a critique by Joel Andreas of Yasheng Huang's influential book *Capitalism with Chinese Characteristics*, and a reply by Huang himself.

In a fascinating piece in December's *Monthly Review*, John Bellamy Foster, Brett Clark, and Richard York explore the paradox first outlined by the Victorian economist WS Jevons that improving energy efficiency leads to higher energy consumption. The authors argue that this result, a powerful challenge to mainstream attempts at a "technological fix" for climate change, is not, as Jevons thought, a "natural law", but rather a consequences of capitalism being driven by competitive accumulation.*

Two articles stood out in the October issue of *Monthly Review*. First, a piece by David Bacon on organising and unionising immigrants in the US. Bacon argues that the unionisation of immigrants is not simply a case of looking out for the downtrodden but rather a vital task for the rebuilding of working class power in the US.† The same issue contains an interesting overview of the influential Chinese author Qiu Xiaolong by Jonah Raskin, whose seminal *The Mythology of Imperialism* was reviewed by Gareth Jenkins in *International Socialism 127*.‡

The 2011 edition of the *Socialist Register* is now available. This year's theme is "The Crisis this Time". We will be carrying a full review in a forthcoming issue.

Finally, October's *Rethinking Marxism* contains a wonderful essay by Mark Osteen on the links between jazz improvisation and gift giving. "Both", he argues, "are complex rituals that may, at their most powerful, attain the status of secular religious ceremonies. So let us play."

*AC and JJ*

---

\* www.monthlyreview.org/101101foster-clark-york.php
† www.monthlyreview.org/101001bacon.php
‡ www.monthlyreview.org/101001raskin.php